Natural Relations

V

Natural Relations

Ecology, Animal Rights and
Social Justice

———————◆———————

TED BENTON

VERSO
London · New York

First Published by Verso 1993
© Verso 1993
All rights reserved

Verso
UK: 6 Meard Street, London W1V 3HR
USA: 29 West 35th Street, New York, NY 10001–2291

Verso is the imprint of New Left Books

ISBN 0 86091 393 7
ISBN 0 86091 590 5 (pbk)

ISBN 13: 978-0-86091-590-4

British Library Cataloguing in Publication Data
A catalogue record for this book is available from the British Library

Library of Congress Cataloging-in-Publication Data
A catalogue record for this book is available from the Library of Congress

Typeset in Garamond by Ewan Smith at 48 Shacklewell Lane, London
Printed and bound in Great Britain by Biddles Ltd,
Guildford and King's Lynn

Contents

To the memory of my mother and father,
who gave me both life and the enthusiasm to enjoy it.
Above all, they gave me two wonderful
examples of how to live well.

Preface

The arguments presented in various parts of this book have been developing in an uneven way over many years. It would be impossible for me to acknowledge adequately all of the very many people (and other animals!) who have influenced my thinking. First, I must mention Jay and Rowan, who were *always* themselves, and confirmed my growing suspicion that 'social constructionism' did not have all the answers. Shelley, Jay and Rowan also deserve my grateful thanks for their tolerance of my preoccupation when this book was going well, and bad-tempered grumpiness when it wasn't. Their presence in my life is, of course, indispensable to me.

Several cohorts of students at the University of Essex, especially those who chose to take the options I taught on these topics, have greatly influenced my thinking. Many colleagues, too, including David Lee, Onora O'Neill, Sheldon Leader, Pauline Lane, Jean Duncombe, Joan Busfield, Richard Wilson, Mary Walsh, Olga Ojeda, Hugh Ward, Debbie Fitzmaurice, David Rose, Sharmala Naidoo, Dave Samways, Karen O'Reilly, Mary Girling, Brenda Corti, Steve Horigan and numerous others deserve my thanks. In particular, teaching on these topics with Oriel Sullivan and Nick Bunnin has been both a delight and a source of illumination. I also want to thank Diane Streeting for coping brilliantly with my technological backwardness. It is hard to imagine that anyone could find a more supportive or stimulating environment in any other British University.

Beyond my immediate working environment, special mention should be made of Roy Bhaskar (who, I notice, is not mentioned by name elsewhere in this book, but who has been a great inspiration to me), Sue Clegg, Andrew Collier, Gerry Webster, Lynda Birke, Anne Witz, Russell Keat and many other participants in the series of conferences on 'Realism and the Human Sciences'. Likewise my fellow members of the editorial group of *Radical Philosophy*. Their convivial comradeship, as well as specific comments and criticisms have been essential (see specifically the notes to chapter 2). More recently, participation in the Red/Green Study Group, Red/Green Network, and the US Center for Ecological Socialism has helped me to feel that there is some hope that something like the vision sketched here may be more widely shared. I particularly want to thank Steven Rose, Steven Lukes, Andrew McCulloch, Peter Dickens and Tim Hayward for their personal and/or political and intellectual support and encouragement. Lucy Morton, Robin Blackburn and Verso's anonymous reader have been exemplary in their various ways.

Of the non-human contributors to this book, I would like to give special mention to the big, ragged ginger cat who sits on our conservatory roof (nearly) every day, the squirrels in Castle Park, the rabbits of Wivenhoe Park, a dog and a kitten who risked all by irrepressibly joining in one of our Sunday walks, the silver spotted skipper, the scarce emerald damselfly, a grasshopper sunning itself one autumn day on Mersea Island, the Alps and the Pyrenees, Mount Chelmos, Mount Falacron, the North Downs near Dorking, Bernwood Forest, the Purbecks, Thursley Bog, High Woods, the Essex Marshes, the Hexagon Restaurant, the 'Next' Coffee-bar, and W. & G.'s cafe.

The structure of this book is unusual, and might be confusing. It could be described as spiral rather than linear. The first circuit of the progressively widening spiral is completed in the introductory chapter, whilst the final one occupies the whole of chapters 5 to 7.

January 1993

Let the slave, grinding at the mill, run out into the field,
Let him look up into the heavens & laugh in the bright air;
Let the inchained soul, shut up in darkness & in sighing,
Whose face has never seen a smile in thirty weary years,
Rise & look out – his chains are loose, his dungeon doors are open;
And let his wife and children return from the oppressor's scourge.
They look behind at every step & believe it is a dream,
Singing:

>The Sun has left his blackness, & has found a fresher morning,
>And the fair Moon rejoices in the clear & cloudless night;
>For Empire is no more, and now the Lion & Wolf shall cease.
>For everything that lives is Holy.

William Blake

Vixen. Look, Sisters – what kind of leader is this?
He wants you for his own whims,
and gets paid by the humans into the bargain!
Comrades, sisters!
Down with the old regime!
Create a new world
where you'll have equal shares
of pleasure and happiness!
Hens. With no Cock around?
No Cock?
Vixen. What do you want him for?
He snaps up the best grain for himself,
and if there's something he doesn't want to do
he calls you in to do it!
Cock. Greedy guts!
She's promising to get rid of the humans
only so she can gobble us up herself!

Janáček, The Cunning Little Vixen

1

Introduction

This book began as an attempt to address what seems to me a paradox. Politically, the paradox consists in the mutual suspicion, hostility or, at best, indifference which has pervaded the relations between radical social movements (primarily socialist in orientation) and those which campaign for radical changes in our relations to non-human nature, despite evident complementarities or outright convergences in values and policies. Intellectually, the paradox consists in the surprising underdevelopment, even theoretical blindness, of the most influential socialist tradition of thought — Marxism — about precisely these problematic aspects of our relation to non-human nature. This underdevelopment of socialist theory I found surprising in view of the classical Marxian claim to represent a distinctively 'materialist', 'naturalist' and 'scientific' philosophical current within the workers' movement. Why should Marxists come so belatedly and reluctantly to a recognition of the political importance of ecology?

I have had things to say on this topic elsewhere, and will not repeat them here. As to the political paradox, there is no special reason to expect friendliness between political movements to increase with the similarity of their values and policies: precisely the reverse often happens. Similarly, shared philosophical sources are no guarantee of shared political conclusions. Nevertheless, the prize of bringing together a broad spectrum of radical movements for common action wherever it can be achieved is too valuable to be simply written off. Perhaps a critical analysis of their intellectual heritage — both what they share and what separates them — might deepen political understanding, and create intellectual possibilities for mutual cooperation not formerly recognized?

Initially it seemed to me that there were close parallels between this intellectual–political project and the examination of other long-running divergencies between interrelated practical struggles or intellectual inquiries on the left: for example, the ever-promising but deeply problematic relationship between the labour movement and the women's movement. Formally speaking, the available positions do run in close parallel: mutual antagonism ('feminism is a middle-class diversion' versus 'working-class movements are as much about excluding and oppressing women as they are about fighting the employers'); mutual indifference ('we fight for workers' rights – whether they are men or women is irrelevant' versus 'women are oppressed as women in ways which transcend the differences of class') and co-option ('the emancipation of the workers entails universal human emancipation' – no feminist inversion of this?).

However, it soon became clear to me that it was mistaken to lump together all movements calling for change in our relation to non-human nature. While ecological politics and radical concern about human treatment of non-human animals, for example, often shared common sentimental sources, the philosophical sources and political aims of these movements were quite distinct. Thinking about the relationships between ecology and socialism was one, and a large enough task in itself. A consideration of the moral status of non-human animals in its relationship to socialism was another. For one thing, the most fully articulated defences of the idea of human moral responsibility for animals have presented it as an extension of the 'circle' of moral concern by claiming that (at least some) animals are so like humans that it would be irrational not to do so. So, while radical positions on the moral status of animals reject what is sometimes called 'human exceptionalism'[1] or 'speciesism', they remain, in at least one sense of the term, 'anthropocentric'. They acknowledge that human dispositions, capacities and liabilities make us paradigms for the applicability of moral concepts, and include members of other species only to the extent that they share these dispositions, capacities and liabilities. This cuts against the widespread rejection of anthropocentrism at the more radical end of ecological politics, in favour of 'biocentrism' or 'ecocentrism' (variously defined).

Second, the most influential statements of moral concern for non-human animals have (often for strong reasons) adopted established and widely held moral theories – utilitarianism and especially liberal rights-theory,[2] especially – and then gone on to show that such theories cannot be consistently confined within the species-boundary. This is a good *ad hominem* strategy if it can be assumed that the opponents of the 'extended circle' are already persuaded by the established moral theories in their paradigm application to the human case. The weakness of the strategy is that it cuts off the advocates of animal rights (for example) from constructive dialogue with radical critics of the dominant moral discourses. This is in marked contrast with the situation of ecological politics, which, in its more radical manifestations, at any rate, proclaims a qualitatively new moral standpoint. Socialists and ecologists share

2

a commitment to a radical transformation of the moral order, and this puts them into a direct, if often acrimonious, dialogue with one another.

Third, and relatedly, the philosophies of animal rights and liberation, as extensions of a predominantly individualist, human-centred moral discourse, tend to put the primary focus of their source-traditions upon the moral status, duties, rights and so on of individuals. Though institutional criticism is by no means excluded, these advocated forms of moral calculation do tend to focus on the question of how individual deliberating moral agents should treat the individuals of other species which they encounter (or 'have moral dealings with'). By contrast, both ecological and socialist politics emphasize the necessity to individual well-being of being located in a favourable, nurturative community or environment. Holistic or relational modes of thought tend to prevail among both socialists and radical ecologists, but tend to be actively opposed by the advocates of animal rights. Tom Regan, for example, goes so far as to compare concern with ecosystems as against individual organisms with fascism.[3] These differences tend to lead both socialists and political ecologists to envisage a necessity for large-scale social and economic transformations, as against the tendency of the animal rights perspective to favour an extension of individual moral sensibility with associated changes of lifestyle.

For all these reasons it became clear to me that the terms and conditions for a dialogue between socialism and animal rights were quite radically different from those at work in the already up-and-running red–green dialogue. A first approximation to what this book is about, then, is to say that it is an attempt to fill what seemed to me a serious gap in the existing literature: a sustained encounter between the moral perspectives and social analysis of the socialist traditions and the literature and practice of 'animal rights'. In fact, the book is both wider and narrower than this suggests. It is wider for several reasons. The first is that the philosophical case for animal rights upon which I focus most attention – the work of Tom Regan – draws upon what I call a 'liberal-individualist' view of rights which has itself been the subject of a long tradition of radical criticism. Many of the authors of that long critical tradition have, indeed, been socialists, and some particular criticisms have a strong logical link with socialist theory. However, the tradition is much too broad and diverse simply to be labelled 'socialist'.

Feminist thinkers, especially, have played a key role in developing and enriching the critical literature on rights,[4] as have advocates of other emancipatory movements. The approach I have adopted here is informed by and draws upon these diverse contributions and I have tried to signal this by referring indifferently to the critique of rights upon which I draw as 'socialist' and 'radical'. In some cases I attempt to draw attention to ways in which particular arguments have a specific bearing on the social situation or emancipatory requirements of women, or other groups who face oppression, exploitation or social exclusion, but I have not attempted to develop as a separate theme the question of the relation between the movements for women's or black people's rights and the cause of animal 'liberation' or welfare. To have done this would have been to make an already complex argument impossibly so. It could also be argued that these lines of inquiry would be better served by an author differently socially situated. Nevertheless, the present text is hopeful of productive dialogue with each of these emancipatory aspirations and is intended to be in solidarity with them.

Returning to the critique of rights, the situation is rendered less intractable than it otherwise might be by the fact that the diverse political perspectives from which the critique has been mounted have drawn upon a remarkably constant pattern of argumentation. A substantial core of the arguments used by feminists, anarchists, black rights and gay rights activists, 'disablement' campaigners and others rely on the contrast between formal possession of rights and substantive enjoyment of them. This contrast in turn rests on an established body of objective analysis of social, economic and political systems and practices.

This word 'objective' is, of course, quite a hostage to fortune these days. Many of my readers will, I am sure, give up at this stage. But there is no necessity, yet, to enter the thickets of epistemology. If you prefer to bracket the word 'objective', then my point can be made another way. It is that many, though not all, of the criticisms of the moral theory and practice of liberal rights which I will address stand or fall on the truth or falsity of some substantive claims about the effects of occupying this or that social position in this or that kind of society for the ability to do certain things one might wish to do, or for vulnerability to kinds of harm to which one might otherwise not be susceptible. Questions of this sort are asked by sociologists, political scientists, anthropologists, policy-analysts, geographers, economists and others. The evidence they give for or against their preferred answers does not logically imply any particular stand on liberal rights. It is, however, pertinent to the adoption of such a stand, and this evidence is a common source for a wide range of critical positions, including, but not confined to, socialism.

But the book is broader than the phrase 'encounter between socialism and animal rights' might suggest for another reason. I have felt required by the present state of the dialogue between socialist and ecological politics to complicate matters by including in my discussion of both socialist and animal rights perspectives some critical considerations offered by ecological politics: the text is, in effect, an attempt at a discussion between socialism, ecology and animal rights, in which each position may function at different moments as a provisional standpoint from which to enrich critically or correct the others.

4

This does not make for clearly structured arguments, in which premisses are clearly stated and defended, and inferences rationally drawn. Moral argument rarely, if ever, takes this form. I hope, none the less, that much of what I have to say will be found rationally persuasive.

The book is also narrower than my first approximation may have suggested in two ways. The first is that I have not considered the full range of philosophical defences of a positive moral status for animals. I have focused on the work of Tom Regan, partly because I find its rigour and level of articulation particularly challenging, and partly because I find Regan's criticism of his main utilitarian rivals broadly persuasive. Moreover, I have not made a critical investigation of the utilitarian case for extending the circle of moral concern to other species as I feel it would be less productive of critical insights for the socialist and ecological partners to the dialogue. In particular, the richer, more complex view of what it is to be a moral patient or a moral agent in the rights perspective has more to offer the critic than that offered by either hedonistic- or preference-utilitarianism. This hunch may, of course, be wrong, and the lack of an extended treatment of utilitarian and other moral arguments for moral concern for animals is undoubtedly a weakness of the book.

The second source of narrowness in the book is my tendency to take a loosely Marxian view as paradigmatic of socialism. I am well aware of the richness and diversity of the non-Marxian traditions of socialist thought, practice and aspiration. My focus on the Marxian tradition is partly rooted in my greater familiarity with it, as a primary formative influence on my own thinking. But I would defend this focus in terms of quite distinctive philosophical strengths of the Marxian tradition which are currently in danger of being drastically undervalued or even entirely lost in the intellectual culture of the left. However, there are lines of argument common to both Marxian and non-Marxian traditions of critical thought. I have done my best to give voice to a 'broad-spectrum' socialist standpoint, while simultaneously offering detailed critical assessments of the Marxian legacy where this seems to me appropriate.

I make no pretence, of course, that this is the first 'encounter' of its kind. The outlines of a more directly politicized encounter between (some) socialists and advocates of animal rights are already discernible, and, indeed, the combination of socialism with a vegetarianism based on concern for animals has a history going back to the early sources of modern socialism. Some time after the earlier chapters of this book were written there occurred a particularly acrimonious exchange in the pages of the British weekly *New Statesman and Society*,[5] between Steven Rose and Jolyon Jenkins. Despite their brevity, these two contributions clearly focused the principal issues at stake between what we might call 'unreconstructed' animal rights and socialist moral perspectives. But the hostile rhetoric ('cant', 'absolutism', 'sanctimonious hypocrisy') and polemical exaggeration bouncing between the two authors also served to hide a very substantial measure of common ground.

Under the provocative title 'Proud to be Speciesist', Rose advanced five basic arguments against the animal rights position. First, the boundary problem. Where is the cut-off between those animals enough like us to be considered bearers of rights, and the rest (slugs?, ants?, mosquitoes?)? Second, only humans can decide who has rights and who does not (and this seems in Rose's text to be run together with a claim about the conventionality, or 'arbitrariness' of rights-attributions). Third, despite continuities between humans and other 'large-brained animals', humans are unique in that only they can claim rights for themselves and only they are what Rose calls 'subjects of history'. Presumably, for Rose, these attributes are necessary conditions for any being to be properly regarded as a bearer of rights. Fourth, Rose appeals to what he takes to be shared moral intuitions according to which we would, for example, if faced with a choice between saving the life of a human child and that of a much-loved pet, choose the former. The principle here is that duties to animals are overridden by duties to humans and it is rooted in what. Rose takes to be a general sentiment of 'species loyalty'. Finally, Rose finds it 'offensive' that the attribution of rights to animals, and the use of the term 'speciesism' are attempts to put the animal rights movement on a par with struggles for women's rights, black people's rights and for civil liberties generally. I include this as a separate objection, though it clearly follows, for Rose, from his third and fourth arguments. I do so because Rose's objection that protests against the ill-treatment of animals might devalue, or divert energy and attention from struggles against oppression and injustice within the human world is a characteristic response from the left to the animal rights case. This is worth noting in its own terms, independently of the particular grounds upon which it is held.

Jenkins declines to speak for the animal rights movement, but does provide a robust reply to Rose; there are responses to each of Rose's main points. First, the boundary problem: lack of a clear, non-arbitrary boundary-line between the extensions of two concepts does not imply that they mark no distinction (for example, day and night). Second, it is admitted that only humans can have or assign moral rights and duties – but it does not follow that they cannot be assigned to non-human animals (Stephen Clark lampoons this argument particularly succinctly: 'We are absolutely better than the animals because we are able to give their interests some consideration: so we won't'[6]). Third, human uniqueness as self-ascribers of rights. Jenkins argues (*ad hominem*) that Rose would surely hold that women and black people had rights quite independently of whether they actually claimed them. Why should the situation be any different with animals? Fourth is the argument from the widespread moral sentiment in favour of species-loyalty and Jenkins's response here is more complex. He distinguishes between causing suffering and killing. With respect to suffering, it seems that Jenkins does operate with a notion of human/animal moral equivalence ('an animal's pain is as real to it as a human's pain is to him or her'). But Jenkins's intuitions about life-saving coincide with those of Rose. However, his grounds would be different. Jenkins's rhetoric implies that he views 'species loyalty' on a par with 'race-loyalty', and he challenges Rose, a committed anti-racist, to justify the first without justifying the second.

Jenkins's grounds for preferentially saving the life of a human are based on what humans 'happen to be like', rather than with their common species-membership. This might appear to be a rather fine distinction. After all, individual members of the same species are, generally, very much alike.[7] That is commonly how they are recognized as such. But Jenkins strengthens the case by conjecturing choices not between members of other species and 'normal' adult humans, but terminally ill, orphaned, or brain-dead infants. Would the choice be so clear? Presumably for a cross-species egalitarian it would not, but a species-loyalist would still have no hesitation. Finally, on the matter of trivializing liberation struggles among humans by comparing them with the rights and wrongs of human treatment of animals, Jenkins appears equivocal. On the one hand he is prepared to make a jibe about 'race-loyalty', but elsewhere he says 'no one is comparing women and blacks with animals'.

All of these arguments, as they appear on both sides of this particular confrontation, will appear and re-appear throughout the rest of this book. I hope that what follows will take us at least further along a route to a better understanding of the issues at stake, if not to any final resolution.

At this stage, however, I want to make a few preliminary observations about the confrontation in its present form. First, despite the intensity of the rhetoric, the two positions have a great deal in common. Jenkins concludes by returning Rose's accusation of romanticism: it is the scientists not the animal rights movement who are the romantics, 'still in the spell of a fantastic delusion that they have been granted dominion'. But Rose quite explicitly distances himself from what he refers to as this 'arrogant claim to the domination of nature'. Rose is also clear that he is metaphysically committed to a view of the continuity between humans and other animals, and in particular to the sentience of other 'large-brained animals'. He also says, 'And I am sure that we do have ... duties, to behave kindly to other animals, with the minimum of violence and cruelty, not to damage or take their lives in so far as it can be avoided, just as we have duties to the planet's ecology in general.' In the broad setting of the dominant Western traditions (Christian and secular) of moral and metaphysical thinking, this puts Rose and Jenkins on the same side against most of the real heavyweights – Aristotle, Aquinas, Descartes and Kant – all of whom denied what both Rose and Jenkins assert: that we have moral duties towards animals.

Rose and Jenkins agree that animals are proper objects of moral concern, but they differ, first, on whether one part of our moral vocabulary – the concept of 'rights' – can be extended to them, and, second, on whether some principle of cross-species egalitarianism can be sustained. On both these questions the exchange is, to my mind, quite inconclusive. Rose is surely correct to argue that it makes a very significant difference to the sense and content of a rights-claim if it can be asserted or accepted by its subject. Neither militant black activists nor feminists have been content to allow whites or men to define or advocate their rights on their behalf. They have, of course, been right about this.

But Jenkins is also correct to argue that rights are frequently assigned to individuals who do not themselves claim them, or who are not in a position to do so. While we may not all agree that young infants, profoundly psychologically disabled adults, and even foetuses have rights, the claim that they do is not obviously without sense. Rose's point about the assigning of rights as a specifically human activity is pertinent here. The situation may be one in which we are not logically required by established, consensual uses of the term 'right' either to confine it to human moral agents (or to members of the human species whatever their powers), or to extend it to non-human animals with morally relevant similarities to normal humans. But neither is the decision about where to draw the dividing line an 'arbitrary' one. There may be strong reasons, moral, pragmatic or conceptual in character, for going in either direction. Some extended moral deliberation will be required to become clear what these reasons are and how to weigh them.

The second issue which divides Rose and Jenkins is just as recalcitrant. This is the matter of cross-species egalitarianism. Jenkins's position appears to be that where beings, irrespective of species membership, are similar in their vulnerabilities to suffering, then justice requires us to assign equal importance to this suffering. Where it is a matter of killing, or of saving life, however, a sense of self, place in a social network, or the capacity to make plans or projects are features which distinguish normal humans from other animals. This is why we are justified, other things being equal, in saving a human life in preference to that of an animal. Jenkins explicitly refers to the work of Peter Singer here, defending the idea that equality of consideration does not imply sameness of treatment. Indeed, equality of consideration will require difference of treatment where there are differences of need or interest. Singer puts the point like this:

> The extension of the basic principle of equality from one group to another does not imply that we must treat both groups in exactly the same way, or grant exactly the same rights to both groups. Whether we should do so will depend on the nature of the members of the two groups. The basic principle of equality, I shall argue, is equality of consideration; and equal consideration for different beings may lead to different treatment and different rights.[8]

One difficulty with positions like Singer's and Jenkins's is that they do not settle differences of view about what the differences between groups are, and what moral significance should be assigned to them. Neither racism nor sexism have been commonly based on the simple assertion of mere group-belonging as a criterion for discriminatory treatment. Supposed differences in intelligence between the races, women's lack of rational powers, or physical frailty, for example, are among the many differences adduced to justify inequality of treatment. Though Singer's principle of equal consideration is designed to put moral theory above such empirical considerations, it cannot make any practical difference to the question of how we should treat animals unless these factual matters are addressed at some point. If we decide that there are, after all, profound qualitative differences between humans and animals, and that these differences are of the utmost moral significance, then equality of consideration may imply massively discriminatory treatment. In such an eventuality, is the principle of equality of consideration doing any real work other than, perhaps, offering a gloss of moral legitimacy?

We might take these considerations as suggesting that the species-boundary does after all have a moral significance. Where individuals have as much in common as do the members of a single species, there can be reasonably well-grounded rules about which individual differences to take into account in applying the principle of equal consideration. Across the species-boundary, differences of anatomy and physiology, of emotional constitution, psychological powers and modes of life begin to make the question, 'What counts as equal consideration?' undecidable. For moral theories such as utilitarianism, which tie moral deliberation to a single dimension of subjective experience, this problem appears far less serious. The point, here, is not to decide the issue against the animal rights position, but to emphasize the extent to which arguments one way or the other will depend on substantive evidence about what both humans and other animals are actually like.

For Singer and Jenkins, humans and other animals are sufficiently alike in morally significant respects for it not to appear wrong or absurd to argue for better treatment of animals in the same terms as are employed by human liberation groups (though, as we have noted, Jenkins does say 'no one is comparing women and blacks with animals'). Singer's argument is quite explicitly designed to show that there is no good justification for equality between human groups which does not also entail equality between humans and non-human animals: any rational feminist or anti-racist must also favour equality of consideration for animals.

This, I think, is at the core of the acrimony between Rose and Jenkins. Rose says:

> Put like this, the spurious nature of the term speciesism becomes apparent. It was coined to make the claim that the issue of animal rights is on a par with the struggles for women's rights or black people's rights, or civil rights. ... Non-human animals cannot conceive or make such a claim, and to insist the terms are parallel is profoundly offensive, the lazy thinking of a privileged group. (See note 5)

Rose's insistence upon the political and moral priority of the struggles of oppressed or exploited groups of humans is what puts him into polemical opposition to the animal rights cause, despite the sharing of a wide area of common ground.

The same is true of a more extended treatment of the issue by Leslie Pickering Francis and Richard Norman. Like Rose, Francis and Norman oppose the extension of rights to non-human animals from a clearly articulated position on the political left. Like Rose, they reject the equation of animal rights and human liberation struggles:

> The emphasis of this paper has been mainly negative – perhaps excessively so. ... Why then has our emphasis been predominantly negative? The phrase 'animal liberation' says it all. By equating the cause of animal welfare with genuine liberation movements such as black liberation, women's liberation or gay liberation, Singer on the one hand presents in an implausible guise the quite valid concern to prevent cruelty to animals. At the same time the equation has the effect of trivializing those real liberation movements, putting them on a level with what cannot but appear as a bizarre exaggeration. Liberation movements have a character and a degree of moral importance which cannot be possessed by a movement to prevent cruelty to animals.[9]

In the first part of their paper, Francis and Norman provide what are by now fairly familiar criticisms of the animal rights case. The second part of the paper, which they concede is more contentious, is also more challenging and original. They argue that Singer and others who consider the moral relevance of characteristics which differentiate humans and animals base their case on non-relational features – rationality, sentience and so on. Francis and Norman focus, instead, on a consideration of the moral significance of the various kinds of social relationship which prevail both among humans, and between humans and animals. They conclude:

> that human beings may justifiably attach more weight to human interests than to animal interests of a similar intensity, not in virtue of the supposed differentiating properties, but because human beings have certain relations to other human beings which they do not have to animals.[10]

This focus on social relations is commendable, and there is much in common between the approach adopted in this pioneering paper and the one which informs this book. However, it does not seem to me that their argument for moral privileging of humans is effective. They do, indeed, argue persuasively that humans share a range of social relationships which they rarely or never have with animals (nor animals with one another), and that humans achieve a degree of sophistication in those relations rarely or never achieved by animals. Francis and Norman distinguish four such kinds of relationship: communicative, economic, political and familial. They acknowledge that animals communicate with one another, and also that some humans communicate with some animals, but that human communication involves self-consciousness and understanding. The degree of sophistication achieved in human communication involves mutual recognition, and identification with the other. What follows from this? 'That beings may assign more weight to the interests of those with which they share such relationships as communication, than to the interests of those with which they do not.'[11]

In economic life, the relationships of exchange and co-operative production are paradigms of relationships in which the participants reciprocally recognize one another as independent beings in their own right. Cheating and exploitation do, of course, occur, but for Francis and Norman it makes sense to criticize certain relations in these terms only by contrast with the morally proper forms of reciprocal relation. Since animals are incapable of rising to the paradigmatic reciprocal economic relations, it makes no sense to speak of their being 'exploited', for example. In an interesting parenthesis Francis and Norman qualify this point – they are not denying that there may be 'flaws' in our economic relations with animals, but they are questioning the use of the term 'exploitation' to characterize such flaws as there are. Francis and Norman repeat that factory farming and laboratory experimentation often involve morally unacceptable treatments of animals, but they offer nothing by way of an alternative language for characterizing this moral unacceptability.

Humans, unlike animals, jointly enter into institutions which protect them and regulate their activities – political institutions. Francis and Norman point out that it is in the context of economic and political relations, and so of human communities, that principles such as liberty and equality have meaning. This meaning, or purpose, is to give an 'authentically co-operative character' to human economic and political groups. Not being members of human communities, and not being capable, in any case, of 'authentically co-operative' activity animals are presumably excluded from the concepts of liberty and equality. Finally, in Francis and Norman's account, there are familial relations, especially relations between parents and children, which are not merely 'custodial' but also educative, in which the child becomes increasingly capable of reciprocity. The moral character of this relation, again, is different in kind both from the relation of pet-keeper to pet, and from the relation between other animal species and their offspring (although Francis and Norman seem less clear on this).

It seems to me that one problem with this line of argument against Singer is the familiar one of the passage from 'is' to 'ought'. Let us suppose that it is true (and I am inclined to believe it is) that such relationships to other humans as Francis and Norman describe do make us more likely to 'attach greater weight' to the interests of those other humans. Why does this justify our doing so? This part of the argument, in so far as it figures at all, does so by way of an appeal to widespread moral intuitions. For example, Francis and Norman rightly point out that 'a parent who can save one child but not two might well not be morally censured for preferring his/her own'.[12] Parents do, indeed, have 'special permissions and duties with respect to their children'.

This case is very interesting, but I submit that our reluctance to blame a parent who, under such constraints, chooses to save the life of her or his own child does not imply any withdrawal from such principles as equality, justice, or equal rights to life. We may, in other words, remain committed to these principles, while not expecting parents to abide by them in such special circumstances.

There are, I think, two sources or grounds for this expectation. In this case they are mutually supporting, but they need not always be. The first ground is that what we know about the special feelings parents have for their own children (I am, incidentally, here following the practice of Francis and Norman in speaking of 'parents' not in a narrowly biological way, but in terms of their social role) tells us that such feelings are liable to make them act preferentially towards their own children in such extreme circumstances. In such situations, in other words, moral appeals are relatively very weak motivators and parental feelings very powerful ones. We know that it would be pointless, in the face of this, to morally censure parents who acted out of parental concern rather than in accordance with principles of justice and, moreover, our capacity for imaginative identification tells us that to do so would be to make unreasonable demands on our fellow humans.

Now, it seems to me this is quite a good analogue of the general case Francis and Norman make in favour of the privileging of human interests. We respond to our fellow humans in distress by saving them rather than animals out of a fellow feeling which emerges from precisely the framework of social relations which Francis and Norman describe. But, just as in the parental case, nothing follows from this about the justice of our behaving in this way. Nothing in this shows that the human and the animal do not have equal rights to life. The situation is simply that humans will in such circumstances (very understandably) save the being with whom they most closely identify, quite independently of issues of rights and justice.

But we are now on very thin ice. What if we shift from humans and animals, parents and children, to adults of different races, or of different cultures? Perhaps here, again, social relational, communicative, cultural and other bonds may lead a person to identify with a person of her own race more than one of another race, and so to attach a 'greater weight' to the interests of the one rather than the other. Though Francis and Norman might admit that such preferential dispositions are, indeed, widespread, they certainly would be prepared to censure them on moral grounds. But would this be consistent with their preparedness to justify the analogous dispositions and sentiments in relation to animals? The shift from non-relational to relational differences between humans and animals does not, it seems, allow of any ready way of opening up the required gap between racism and speciesism.

But I mentioned above, that in the case of parental sentiments there is a second ground for our reluctance to censure. This is, in fact, one suggested by Francis and Norman themselves: the special moral duties and 'permissions' involved in the relation of parenthood. But these special duties apply only obliquely in the situation we have been considering. It is not a parental duty (or, even, I think, a 'right') to choose to save one's own child rather than another. Rather, the situation is one in which assigning special responsibilities for the care and upbringing of *particular* children to *particular* adults is the normative framework within which, in most societies, the problems of human infantile dependency and the requirements of socialization are met. To accept the moral rightness of such an arrangement is also to accept that among its consequences will be those we have just encountered: that parents will develop powerful feelings towards their children which will lead them on occasion to disregard the principles of justice and equality. We accept such consequences, if we do, because we believe that the harms which would proceed from abandoning the normative framework of parenthood would be far greater.

Comparison of these cases suggests, then, that the disposition to privilege the interests of those we are intimately socially related to is a widespread and familiar feature of our lives. This is not, however, nor should it be, universally morally tolerated. Where it is condoned, it is not, as Francis and Norman suggest, accepted as 'fair'. It is condoned despite unfairness, either because we recognize the force of the emotions involved, or because we bring countervailing moral considerations to bear, or both. In such cases as, for example, racism, all parties to the present debate agree that socially engendered feelings of preference and dispositions to privilege are not morally tolerable. Lacking any countervailing moral considerations, considerations such as rights, justice and fairness are binding. But what is the practical force of this? Apart from the moral justification of the relationships which generate racist sentiments and practices (assuming indeed that we have an understanding of what they are), we may still be confronted with a situation in which the force of the sentiments involved is overwhelming and, as in the parental case, countervailing considerations of justice are weak motivators (as I write, our news bulletins are dominated by images of inter-ethnic violence between Serbs and Croats, and the re-surfacing of ethnic tensions and hatreds across the disintegrating Soviet Union).

There are two characteristic responses to this. One is to agree that justice and rights must become stronger motivators – that is, to back up moral appeals with legal authority and sanctions. The other, not incompatible, but often thought to be, is to work to understand and then change the pattern of relationships which produces the offending sentiments. Now, it is a great strength of Francis and Norman's paper that it brings the moral argument for animal rights up against such facts of social life and the psychological forces associated with them. However these facts are pertinent not, as Francis and Norman suggest, primarily because they affect the moral case for animal rights, but because they constitute the contextual conditions which obstruct or facilitate our hearing the moral case, or acting in accord with it.

As it stands, the argument offered by Francis and Norman is very vulnerable to the response that if our social relationships produce a morally justifiable preference for the interests of humans, why should not similarly produced racial sentiments be likewise justified? They are vulnerable to this rejoinder because for the most part their case rests on what purports to be a description of how such human relationships are rather than how they should or could be: actual primacy of human-to-human relations actually generates human privileging of human interests, and this is justified. A case for racialism could easily be made on the same grounds.

Quite explicitly to avoid this, Francis and Norman introduce the idea of a universal human community – a world-order of economically and politically interconnected local communities. It is only by appeal to such a universal community that, in their terms, legitimation of racism (or other restrictions of principles of equality and justice to sub-groups *within* the species) can be avoided. But what is this universal human community? Sometimes they speak as though it actually exists, implicitly, perhaps, in networks of trading links, intergovernmental agreements and so on. However, the world order as it exists is quite evidently not one in which universal rights and principles of justice are actually operative, either within local or national communities, or between them. Relations of exploitation, oppression and the like among humans are the rule rather than the exception. The notion of a universal human community, the necessary anchor for species-wide principles of equality, liberty and so on, must therefore be some form of regulative ideal: we should behave towards other humans as though such a community existed and, perhaps, work practically to bring this community into existence.

This view of universal human community has a powerful appeal to many radical thinkers.[13] It was, as we shall see, very much at work in Marx's thinking about human emancipation. It was, for example, at the core of his key concept of humanity as a 'species being'. But can we really conceive of a 'community' on that scale? What would 'mutual recognitions of autonomy' and 'reciprocal identifications' amount to spread across a polity and an economic division of labour global in scope? And what if some members of the species chose to exercise their autonomy by ceasing communicative interaction and economic co-operation with the rest (as seems not improbable)? Can we conceive of individuals as bearers of rights and as entitled to equality of consideration independently of the plausibility of such a notion of universal human community? If not, then so much the worse for the concept of universal human rights. If so, then why should the imagined non-membership of animals in the imagined universal human community be a bar on their possession of rights?

This brings us, finally, to the question of the relation of animals to human communities. Francis and Norman take the social relations into which humans enter with one another as a new basis upon which to resurrect an increasingly beleaguered metaphysic of human/animal opposition. The mark of humanity is, now, not sentience, rationality, language, or tool-use but sociality of a certain complex and sophisticated sort. But, as they agree, animals are often social beings, and many species are capable of social relations with humans. This is why mere 'sociality' will not do as the mark of distinction. When we push this further, we find that what is peculiar to human sociability, what grounds our justifiable preference for our fellow humans, are certain very specific dimensions of sociability: self-conscious intention in communication, recognition of mutual autonomy in economic activity, the growth of reciprocity in parent–child relations, and so on. I want to draw attention to two things here. First, to morally privilege these features of human social relations is a disguised way of reasserting the moral priority

15

of the non-relational human capacities (autonomy of the will, rationality, self-consciousness and so on) which grounded the older metaphysic of human/animal opposition. The opening up of a new field for exploration of common ground between the human and the animal which was promised by the introduction into the picture of social relations is at one stroke retracted.

My second point is that (supposedly) distinctive features of inter-human sociality are by no means realized in all human social relations, and even where they are realized, they do not cover all there is to say about such relations, nor all that is morally important in them. To take the case of economic relations, Francis and Norman identify relations of exchange and co-operative production as embodying reciprocity and mutual recognition of independence of an order not (generally) possible for non-human animals. Clearly there are human economic arrangements (some would say the capitalist firm, most would agree the slave plantation as examples) in which such mutuality and reciprocity are not, or not fully, realized. Such institutions can be regarded as exploitative or oppressive precisely because they deny reciprocity and autonomy to beings capable of standing in those relations. But if these really are the only forms of deprivation to which moral importance is attached, then we have no basis for morally objecting to any economic arrangements which incorporate non-human animals. Yet Francis and Norman do wish to object morally to many such arrangements.

Francis and Norman place their consideration of the moral status of animals within the context of human social relations. This is, I think, a major advance. However, they pull back from the radical implications of their own achievement by reinstating, within the social-relational approach, a traditional human/animal opposition. By contrast, the broad framework of thought which informs my approach in this book is one which shares this emphasis on the significance of social relations, but which at the same time takes seriously the 'human/animal continuism' which is presupposed in the animal rights literature. The point is, as Mary Midgley famously argued, that humans are not just *like* animals, but *are* animals.[14] There are good, if not overwhelming, arguments to be drawn from modern biology to the effect that we share a common ancestry, more or less close or distant, with the other species with which we now interact – we are, in other words, more or less distant kin. It is this kinship which grounds a wide field of commonality which we share as 'natural beings'. We, like other species of animals, have needs which require us to interact with our environment (living and non-living), and with one another if we are to survive and reproduce. Many of our capacities for interpreting our environment and adapting our responses to it, for interacting with others of our own species, and for developing complex social bonds and relations are also shared with many, though of course not all, other animal species.

These are among the considerations which tell in favour of 'human/animal continuism'. Of course, nothing in this should give us doubts about whether we can reliably tell the difference between members of our own and other species when we encounter them![15] Nor, indeed, is it at all suggested that there are not deep and far-reaching differences between humans and other species. Humans are, in my view, bearers of 'emergent powers' which require us to consider them as a very special case, quite independently of our vested interests in the prospects of our own kind, of our 'anthropocentrism'. To be against the human/animal opposition is, rather, to be against a certain way of conceptually ordering these acknowledged human/animal differences. What the standpoint of human/animal continuism objects to are those ways of thinking about relations between humans and animals which:

1. conflate differences among beings on either side of the boundary but especially on the 'animal' side, for the sake of representing them as more-or-less homogeneous 'kinds';
2. efface the plurality of species-specific differences which might sustain illuminating inter-specific comparisons between humans and other particular species or groups of species;
3. respond to the discovery of boundary-threatening abilities in non-human animals by continuous re-conceptualization of human-definitive powers (such as language) so as to keep the boundary in place;[16]
4. ontologically and morally foreground human-definitive powers over against needs, powers, and liabilities of humans which they share with many other species.

Human/animal continuism, then, rejects these ways of thinking about the relation between humans and animals, but I need to say more about why, in particular, (4) above is rejected. A broader way of characterizing the philosophical grounding for human/animal continuism itself would be to think of it as a consequence of 'naturalism'. According to this view, humans are to be thought of as a species of natural being, as part of the order of nature, rather than as ontologically privileged beings, set apart from, or even against, the rest of nature. A naturalistic approach to understanding the relation between humans and other animals gives centre stage to what humans share with animals in its account of the nature and well-being of humans themselves. More specifically it focuses on organic embodiment, in all its consequences and requirements, as basic to any such account. Health, physical security, nutrition, shelter are all as indispensable to human well-being as to the well-being of any other animal species. But to recognize this is also to see that in these aspects of their lives it is true not just that humans and other animals have much in common, but also that they are materially interdependent. We are bound together not just by bonds of kinship and similarity of predicament, but also by relations of mutual dependence. Any consistently naturalistic view of human well-being will necessarily have implications for the ability of non-human animals to secure conditions for *their* well-being.

What I am suggesting is that a naturalistic (but not reductionist) view of human nature, and the human/animal continuism which goes with it will complement the social-relational approach of Francis and Norman with an attention to the moral significance of embodiment and to ecological interdependence. It will do so in the way it considers both the question of the moral status of animals and the matter of how humans themselves should live. Further, introducing the body and ecology will influence how we understand social relations themselves. To return to the economic paradigm of Francis and Norman, for example, it is, on a naturalistic view, possible to recognize the distortion and suppression of normal behaviour, exposure to disease and suffering, or destruction of habitat imposed by human economic activities upon non-human animals as morally significant. This is so quite independently of whether we suppose the animals affected to be capable of fully reciprocal mutual recognition, or of personal autonomy in the same sense as humans are capable of it. In the same way, the naturalistic view enables us to see that many of the economic relations between humans themselves are morally unacceptable for reasons other than, or which go beyond, their coerciveness and denial of recognition. This is not, of course, to deny the moral importance of recognition and coercion in human relations. It is, rather, to say both that other things can go wrong in human social relations and that a consideration of some of those 'other things' will go a long way to showing just why coercion and denial of recognition are such grave harms.

One aspect of human embodiment – our requirement for food – engages us in social relations and practices which inescapably include animals: as partners in human labour, as objects of labour, and of consumption, as well as competitors for habitats and common sources of food. There are numerous other respects in which, if we adopt a broader (and, I would argue, richer) view of what social relationships are, animals figure not just marginally but quite centrally within the domain of human social life. Even where they do not figure directly as 'terms' in human social relations, other animal populations are profoundly affected by the ecological outcomes of our social practices in ways which clearly call for moral reflection.

This provisional framework is the one which informs the rest of this book. But before I press on to a further elaboration and exploration of its implications it will be worth one final reflection on the historical ancestry of the project. My experience of writing the book was one of an intellectual struggle to make intellectually convincing links between positions I felt intuitively

already had close affinities. Yet the most influential contemporary voices seem
to tell us the opposite: that the aspirations of socialists, feminists and others
are of really quite a different order from the demand for a moral status for
animals. The two movements do, indeed, appear to be set in hostile
antagonism to one another and to draw upon quite distinct intellectual
sources. But this is, I think, only appearance, a function of the way we draw
selectively upon our historical sources in the light of our contemporary
priorities. A significant figure among radical and progressive political circles
in Britain, around the turn of the century, was Henry Salt. Salt is frequently
referred to in contemporary animal rights literature as a much-admired
predecessor, with barely a mention of his other activities and concerns.
Meanwhile, he also appears as an associate of the well-known socialists and
feminists of his time in histories of the left, but with barely a mention of his
concern with the moral status of animals. In fact, Salt saw a seamless web
connecting each of these concerns, as is made clear in the more balanced (if
unsympathetic) account given in a recent sociological study of animal rights
by Keith Tester.[17] This quotation from Salt's autobiographical writing makes
the point:

> Humanity and science between them have exploded the time-honoured idea of a
> hard-and-fast line between white man and black man, rich man and poor man,
> educated man and uneducated man, good man and bad man; equally impossible
> to maintain, in the light of newer knowledge, is the idea that there is any difference
> in kind, and not in degree only, between human and non-human intelligence. The
> emancipation of men from cruelty and injustice will bring with it in due course the
> emancipation of animals also. The two reforms are inseparably connected, and
> neither can be fully realized alone.[18]

PART I

Humans and Other Animals

===2 ===

Marx on Humans and Animals:
Humanism or Naturalism

In this chapter,[1] I focus attention on one of the most important and influential texts in modern socialist thought: Marx's *Economic and Philosophical Manuscripts* of 1844 (the 'Paris Manuscripts' as they are sometimes called). Few commentators on this text have taken seriously the fact that its central organizing concepts – species-being and estrangement – are developed by Marx in terms of a fundamental opposition between human and animal nature. This opposition is so fundamental to Marx's thinking in the *Manuscripts* that his whole moral case against the regime of private property and advocacy of a communist future turns upon it. In effect, capitalist private property stands condemned for its tendency to reduce humans to the condition of animals.

The notion that animals themselves might be vulnerable to moral abuse seems hard to reconcile with this 'humanist' dimension of Marx's early philosophical thought. On the other hand, as I shall also try to show, Marx's text is committed against philosophical idealism in ways which favour a naturalistic (though not reductionist) view of human nature. Humans are both contrasted with animals and also theorized together with them as 'active natural beings'. Though Marx thought of his text as a synthesis of humanism and naturalism, I shall suggest that the discourses of humanism and naturalism co-exist in unresolved tension with one another. My purpose in this chapter is to excavate and defend the relatively neglected naturalistic side of Marx's thinking in this early text. This naturalistic view of human nature will, suitably qualified and elaborated, form the basis for much of the argument in subsequent chapters in the book.

The standpoints of political ecology and animal rights have in common an insistence upon the moral significance of non-human beings. In some versions, but not all, these perspectives insist upon that moral importance quite independently of any claim as to the importance of other species, natural conditions or ecosystems to human well-being. Nevertheless both positions

23

generally do involve a view of humans as both sharing a common nature and conditions of life with other species, and as joined with them in bonds of ecological interdependence. Humans are to be understood as a part of the wider order of nature, rather than as set apart from or against nature.

Initially, at least, it seems there is much in common between both of these perspectives and that adopted by the Marx of the early *Manuscripts*. Consider, for example, Marx's striking metaphor for nature as man's 'inorganic body':

> Nature is man's *inorganic body* – nature, that is in so far as it is not itself human body. Man *lives* on nature – means that nature is his *body*, with which he must remain in continuous interchange if he is not to die. That man's physical and spiritual life is linked to nature means simply that nature is linked to itself, for man is a part of nature.[2]

And Marx is by no means stating merely a shallow-ecological, enlightened self-interest of the species. The view of communism which informs the whole of the *Manuscripts* gives a central place to a proper ethical, aesthetic and cognitive relationship to nature as inseparable from true human fulfilment.

In his later works it sometimes seems as if Marx has retreated into a view of the overcoming of the opposition between humanity and nature as merely the main historical means by which humans are enabled to achieve fulfilment. This is very much the kind of picture of Marx's argument presented in Gerry Cohen's very influential defence of Marx's theory of history.[3] But the Marx of the *Manuscripts* is by contrast clear in the recognition that a transformation of our relation to nature is a key aspect and content of the process of human emancipation itself.

This, indeed, is something I would like to hold onto as a fundamental insight which Marx reached in the *Manuscripts*. But – and this is the topic of the rest of this chapter – it also seems to me that there are fundamental ambiguities and tensions in the overall philosophical position adopted by the early Marx as it bears on this range of problems. These ambiguities and tensions threaten to undermine what is of value in Marx's achievement and have sustained readings of Marx which have been deeply inimical to environmental values. A serious effort of critical re-structuring and revaluation of the most basic philosophical ideas and arguments of the early Marx is necessary if their 'rational kernel' is to be extracted.

There are two elements in the argument of the *Manuscripts* which seem to me to sit very uncomfortably alongside the naturalism of the passage quoted above and its possible 'deep-ecological' reading. These elements are, first, the use of the human/animal contrast as Marx's central device in the ethical critique of the estrangement of labour under regimes of private property and, second, the specific content Marx gives to his vision of human emancipation as involving the 'humanization of nature'. I shall say most about the first of these elements, leaving what I have to say about the second rather under-developed.[4]

With regard to the human/animal opposition the argument is, very roughly, as follows. The estrangement of labour is supposed by Marx to have disastrous effects on human beings, their relations to one another, and their relationships to their external, material world. These disastrous effects can be summed up by saying that the estrangement of labour reduces human life to the condition appropriate to non-human animals and, within human life, inverts the relation between the human and the animal. The overcoming of estrangement means restoring to human beings their properly human status, and relationships to one another and to the rest of nature.

But what is the rest of nature? Does it include other animals? Marx's use of the metaphor 'inorganic body' suggests not. On the other hand, nothing Marx says in connection with that metaphor can be sustained unless animals are included. A human life dependent upon the forces and mechanisms of inorganic nature, unmediated by other forms of life is impossible. There is no reason to think Marx actually thought it possible. And, notwithstanding the arguments of some that the possibility now exists of a satisfactory human life which does not rely on the consumption or exploitation of other animals, the phrase 'man lives on nature', written in 1844, must have included within its reference a whole range of uses of animals as a source of energy in agricultural and industrial labour processes, as well as for food, entertainment and companionship.

If, for Marx, human emancipation involves a qualitative transformation of our relationship to the rest of nature, a 'humanization' of nature, and if nature includes other species of animal, then human emancipation must involve a transformation in our relations to other animals. But what could this transformation be? A literal 'humanization' of them in the sense of 'rendering them human' by selective breeding (or, for us, genetic engineering?)? Or, as with the rest of nature, a deliberate alteration of their character so that they better fulfil human purposes (that is, a continuation of those breeding and 'husbandry' practices whereby farm animals have been rendered more productive and docile, pets more 'domesticated', companionable, child-like in appearance, and so on)? If either of these were intended by Marx, his critique of the estrangement of humanity from nature would lose all its force: the 'humanization' of animals (as part of nature) in either of these senses would be a continuation and augmentation, not a transcendence of the treatment of animals under capitalism and, indeed, in pre-capitalist societies too.

Moreover, Marx draws on an absolute and universal, not a provisional and historically transcendable opposition between the human and the animal in grounding his ethical critique of the capitalist mode of life. If what is wrong with these societies is that humans are reduced to the condition of animals, then the transcendence of capitalism, in restoring humanity to the human, simultaneously restores the differentiation between the human and the animal. If what is wrong with capitalism is, essentially, that it does not differentiate the human and the animal, then the antidote to capitalism must offer to restore the proper differential. But this is precisely what the notion of 'humanization' seems to deny. The ontological basis of the ethical critique of capitalism (embedded in the notion of estrangement) appears to be inconsistent with the coherent formulation of its transcendence (in particular, the notion of 'humanization' in relation to animals as part of nature). As I shall suggest later, this dilemma can be resolved by a revision of the ontology of the *Manuscripts* which nevertheless leaves intact a good deal of the ethical critique of capitalist society. However, before I move on to that task it is worth spending some time investigating in rather more depth the sources of the dilemma, and, in particular, looking at some of the implications of the way Marx draws his contrasts between the human and the animal.

Humanity as Species-being

Central to Marx's account of human nature is the claim that man is a species-being. The term is derived from Feuerbach, but Marx gives it a new and richer philosophical meaning:

> Man is a species-being, not only because in practice and in theory he adopts the species (his own as well as those of other things) as his object, but – and this is only another way of expressing it – also because he treats himself as the actual, living species; because he treats himself as a *universal* and therefore a free being.[5]

This 'universality' of human theoretical and practical activity distinguishes humans from (other) animals. The sensory, cognitive and transformative powers of other animals are exercised 'under the dominion of immediate physical need'. They produce 'in accordance with the standard and the need' of their species. Humans, by contrast, know how to produce in accordance with the standard of every species, only truly produce in freedom from immediate physical need, and take the whole world of nature as the object of their practical, aesthetic and cognitive powers.

Whereas animals produce to meet the needs of themselves, or their young, the activity of individual human beings is, at least potentially, a part of the activity of the species as a whole. Not only, then, is human activity 'universal' in the sense that it takes the whole world of nature as its object, but it is also universal in the sense that it is a species-wide activity. The activity of each individual is not a mere instance of its type, but a living part of an interconnected whole – the activity, or 'life', of the species.

In his exposition of the concept of the estrangement of labour, Marx lays great emphasis on this aspect:

> In estranging from man (1) nature, and (2) himself, his own active functions, his life activity, estranged labour estranges the *species* from man. It changes for him the *life of the species* into a means of individual life. First, it estranges the life of the species and individual life, and secondly it makes individual life in its abstract form the purpose of the life of the species, likewise in its abstract and estranged form.[6]

In separating individual life from the life of the species, and inverting their proper relationship to one another, the estrangement of labour imposes upon humanity a mode of existence in which its distinctive species attributes cannot be manifested. Human potential remains unactualized, development is stunted, and human powers are exercised in a distorted or inverted way.

The character of 'man' as a species-being is not a manifest, empirically detectable feature in contemporary societies. It is, rather, an unachieved potential. The achievement of this potential is the work of the human historical process. So, implicit in the idea of humanity as a species-being is also the idea of humanity as a historical being. And by this is meant, not simply a being whose activities and forms of association change through time, as these changes of manifest activity and forms of association have a cumulative and directional character, an overlying pattern in terms of which we can make sense of each successive phase or period. To say that the human species is historical in this sense is to say that the species as a whole undergoes, in the historical process, something analogous to the development undergone by both individual human beings and other animals in their transition from embryo through infancy to adulthood. Only in the adult are the potentials of the infant fully actualized. The development of the individual is the process of its self-realization. So, in the case of the human species, communist society is the form under which what was mere potential in earlier historical phases becomes actual. The historical process is the 'developmental' process of humankind, through which its species-powers are fully developed, its distinctive species-character is realized.

The analysis of the estrangement of labour shows that there is no necessary or universal connection between the 'developmental' process of the species and the developmental process of the individual. Where labour is estranged, the 'development' of the species occurs at the cost of individual development:

> It is true that labour produces wonderful things for the rich – but for the worker it produces privation. It produces palaces – but for the worker, hovels. It produces

beauty – but for the worker, deformity. ... It produces intelligence – but for the worker, stupidity, cretinism.[7]

On the other hand, the historical 'development' of the species is a precondition for the development of the distinctively human powers of individuals:

Only through the objectively unfolded richness of man's essential being is the richness of subjective *human* sensibility (a musical ear, an eye for beauty of form – in short, *senses* capable of human gratification, senses affirming themselves as essential powers of *man*) either cultivated or brought into being. The *forming* of the five senses is a labour of the entire history of the World down to the present.[8]

Humans are different from other animals in that they undergo 'development' at the level of the species (historical development) as well as at the level of the individual. In the human species, the 'development' of the species may take place at the cost of stunting or distorting the development of individuals but, in the long run, full development of the individual with respect to the most distinctively human characteristics is only possible on the basis of a high level of 'development' of the species. None of these considerations apply to other animals, which for Marx have a fixed, species-characteristic relationship between need, instinct and transformative powers, each producing 'in accordance with the standard and need of the species to which it belongs'.[9]

What makes possible this supra-individual 'development' in the human case is the distinctive character of human activity as 'free, conscious activity':

Yet the productive life is the life of the species. It is life-engendering life. The whole character of a species – its species-character – is contained in the character of its life activity; and free, conscious activity is man's species-character.[10]

A being who freely and consciously engages in a practice is able to reflect critically upon that practice, to change it in line with its existing, or newly formulated purposes. Free, self-conscious transformative practice has within it a potential for change and development which the direct and instinctual need-meeting activity of (other) animals does not have. And since this 'productive life' is the life of the species, to characterize its 'development' – the development of human productive powers – is to characterize what is essential to the formative process of humanity itself:

It is just in his work upon the objective world, therefore, that man really proves himself to be a species-being. This production is his active *species-life*. Through this production, nature appears as his work and his reality. The object of labour is, therefore, the *objectification of man's species-life*: for he duplicates himself not only, as in consciousness, intellectually, but also actively, in reality, and therefore he sees himself in a world that he has created.[11]

And, again:

> But since for the socialist man the *entire so-called history of the world* is nothing but
> the creation of man through human labour, nothing but the emergence of nature
> for man, so he has the visible, irrefutable proof of his *birth* through himself, of his
> *genesis*.[12]

Of course, this self-creation through labour, through the augmentation of
human transformative powers, should not be confused with self-creation
through mere economic or industrial activity – an 'economistic' view of
history. Certainly Marx recognizes in industrial production 'the *exoteric*
revelation of man's *essential powers*',[13] but full human historical 'development'
will involve a transcendence of the prevailing fragmentation of human
activities:

> The positive transcendence of *private property*, as the appropriation of *human* life,
> is therefore the positive transcendence of all estrangement – that is to say, the return
> of man from religion, family, state, etc., to his *human*, i.e. *social*, existence.[14]

The historical 'developmental' process, then, is to be understood as a multi-
faceted and progressive augmentation of human transformative powers vis-
à-vis nature. This process can be understood as one of human self-creation,
or self-realization, in that the bearer of these powers is transformed along with
the object of their exercise (nature). In particular, human cognitive powers
('science') underlie the development of productive powers, and are themselves developed through reflection upon the outcomes of productive activity.
Human sensory powers are likewise (see above quotation, p. 28) developed
along with the transformation of the objects of human perception: the power
to create beautiful objects and the growth of aesthetic sensibility in the human
subject are internally related to one another. And, finally, the *purpose* of
transformative activity is itself historically transformed as humans acquire
new needs in the course of their historical self-development:

> We have seen what significance, given socialism, the *wealth* of human needs
> acquires, and what significance, therefore, both a *new mode of production* and a new
> object of production obtain: a new manifestation of the forces of *human* nature and
> a new enrichment of human nature.[15]

Central to Marx's notion of this historical transformation of need is the
idea that self-realization comes itself to be the object of need:

> It will be seen how in place of the wealth and property of political economy come
> the rich human being and the rich human need. The rich human being is
> simultaneously the human being in need of a totality of human manifestations of
> life – the man in whom his own realization exists as an inner necessity, as need.[16]

The historical self-creation of humanity is a process in which human transformative, sensory, aesthetic and cognitive powers and liabilities are transformed and augmented, along with a transformation of the structure of human need itself. But this process is not one which takes place *in vacuo*, so to speak. It would make no sense to speak of these powers, liabilities and needs without some notion of their object: 'nature' (including human nature).

History and the 'Humanization of Nature'

The species-wide and communal project through which humanity creates itself is summed up by Marx as the 'humanization of nature'. Nature as an external, threatening and constraining power is to be overcome in the course of a long-drawn-out historical process of collective transformation. The world thoroughly transformed by human activity will be a world upon which human identity itself has been impressed, and so no longer a world which is experienced as external or estranged:

> On the one hand, therefore, it is only when the objective world becomes everywhere for man in society the world of man's essential powers – human reality and for that reason the reality of his *own* essential powers – that all *objects* become for him the *objectification* of himself, become objects which confirm and realize his individuality, become *his* objects.[17]

And this applies not merely to the objects of human practical, transformative powers, but also to the world as object of human sensory and cognitive powers:

> The *manner* in which they become *his* depends on the *nature of the objects* and on the nature of the essential power corresponding to *it*; for it is precisely the *determinate nature* of this relationship which shapes the particular, real mode of affirmation. To the *eye* an object comes to be other than it is to the *ear*, and the object of the eye *is* another object than the object of the *ear*. ... Thus man is affirmed in the objective world not only in the act of thinking, but with *all* his senses.[18]

These quotations, and others like them, suggest a certain view of the transformation wrought by human history in the relationship between human beings and their natural environment. An external, limiting, conditioned relation between the two is transformed in favour of an internal, unlimited, unconditioned (that is, 'universal') relation which amounts to a fusion of identities. The 'conflict' between humans and nature is overcome in favour of an incorporation of the natural into the domain of the human without residue. Only when the *whole* world is appropriated cognitively, aesthetically and practically can humanity itself be fully realized:

This communism, as fully developed naturalism, equals humanism, and as fully developed humanism equals naturalism; it is the *genuine* resolution of the conflict between man and nature and between man and man – the true resolution of the strife between existence and essence, between objectification and self-confirmation, between freedom and necessity, between the individual and the species. Communism is the riddle of history solved, and it knows itself to be this solution.[19]

This historical vision is clearly incompatible with the content of Marx's metaphor, elsewhere in the same text, of nature as 'man's inorganic body', the insistence upon the permanent necessity of the 'metabolism' between humans and their natural environment as a condition of survival: the reality of nature as a complex causal order, independent of human activity, forever setting the conditions and limits within which human beings, as natural beings, may shape and direct their activities. These materialist theses about the relationship of humanity to nature, which are elsewhere, and more especially in later works, also assented to by Marx, are absent from this utopian and idealist vision of human emancipation.

The important value-content of this early view of history is also put at risk by its residual idealism. Marx insists that the proper relation between the human species and its natural environment is not reducible to instrumental, need-meeting activity (important though this of course is). A properly human relationship with nature is a many-faceted relationship in which aesthetic, cognitive, practical and identity-forming aspects are communally realized. This multi-faceted, properly human relationship to nature is one which not only meets need, but has itself *become* the prime human need.

These ideas are powerful, persuasive and very much in line with modern environmentalism. But when we turn to Marx's specification of the kind of relationship to nature which would realize these values their critical potential is vitiated. If we can be at home in the world, be properly, humanly connected with the world only on the basis of a thorough-going transformation of it in line with our intentions, then what space is left for a valuing of nature in virtue of its intrinsic qualities? If we can 'see ourselves' only in a world which *we* have created, then what is left of our status as part of nature? Nature, it seems, is an acceptable partner for humanity only in so far as it has been divested of all that constitutes its otherness, in so far, in other words, as it has become, itself, human. This view of a properly human relation to nature is comparable to the eighteenth-century practice of landscape-gardening, but extended to the global environment. It is a vision which certainly differs profoundly from any merely utilitarian-exploitative view of nature as a vast 'storehouse' of potential means and resources for human material 'progress'. Not only are aesthetic and spiritual moments or aspects of our relation to nature given their place alongside the meeting of organic need, but also Marx grasps in a deep way the links between human identity and our relationship to our environment. Nevertheless, Marx's vision of a 'humanization' of nature is no less anthropocentric than the more characteristically modernist utilitarian view of the domination of nature. It is, indeed, a quite fantastic species-narcissism.

The Opposition between the Human and the Animal

I shall leave aside the question of how far the acceptable part of the value-content of Marx's view of a fully human relationship to nature as a whole can be supported on the basis of a critical revision of his ontology. Instead, I shall return to the rather narrower question of the human/animal contrast. We have seen that for the Marx of the 1844 *Manuscripts*, (other) animals are characterized by a certain fixity in their mode of life. In so far as they are able to act transformatively upon external nature they do so in accordance with a definite 'standard' characteristic of their species, and their activity is oriented to the meeting of their individual needs (also fixed, and characteristic for each species) and those of their offspring. By contrast, human beings act upon the external world in a way which is free, self-conscious and socially co-ordinated. Because of these distinctive features of human life-activity, their forms of association and modes of practical engagement with the world are subject to directional historical transformations. Only an account of the human mode of life which took into account the place of any specific phase of activity in the overall historical 'development' would be capable of adequately specifying what was, in the full sense, 'human'. What distinguishes humans from animals, in other words, is something which only becomes manifest in the course of human history itself. As we saw, this historical-developmental process, peculiar to the human species, consists in an augmentation of our transformative powers *vis-à-vis* nature, amounting to a residueless 'humanization' of nature; an associated augmentation of our knowledge both of ourselves and of nature (towards a synthesis of the two); a transformation of our sensory powers, equivalent to the 'humanization of the senses'; and a transformation in the structure of need.

The contrast between the human and the animal is, then, a contrast both between humans and other animals, and between fully developed humanity and undeveloped humanity: 'History itself is a real part of natural history – of nature developing into man.'[20] The process of historical development is a movement from animal-like origins to a fully human realization, and this is so with respect not only to our powers and liabilities, but also with respect to need. Even when human transformative powers are well-developed but the estrangement of labour has not been overcome, truly human needs are not manifested. The worker experiences need, and is constrained to meet need in a manner which belies his true human potential, resembling, rather, the animal mode of experiencing and satisfying need.

Underlying both Marx's concept of historical development and his critique of estrangement is a contrast between what he variously calls 'crude', 'physical' or 'animal' need, on the one hand, and 'human' need, on the other:

> It [the animal] produces only under the dominion of immediate physical need, while man produces even when he is free from physical need and only truly produces in freedom therefrom.[21]

And again:

> The *sense* caught up in crude practical need has only a *restricted* sense. For the starving man, it is not the human form of food that exists, but only its abstract existence as food. It could just as well be there in its crudest form, and it would be impossible to say wherein this feeding activity differs from that of animals.[22]

Speaking of estranged labour, Marx says: 'It is therefore not the satisfaction of a need; it is merely a means to satisfy needs external to it.'[23] Needs, in this sense, determine the worker's share of the product of labour: 'as much, only, as is necessary for his existence, not as a human being, but as a worker, and for the propagation, not of humanity, but of the slave class of workers'.[24]

Marx's attempt, in passages such as these, to provide an account of human nature in terms of a thorough-going opposition between the human and the animal is very much in line with the mainstream of modern Western philosophy and such more recent disciplines as cultural anthropology and sociology. The conceptual oppositions nature/culture; animal/human; body/mind play a foundational, structuring role in the theoretical traditions which dominate these disciplines.

For each of these disciplinary matrices, an opposition between the animal and the human implies also an opposition within the human between what is animal (-like) and what is 'truly' human. In the paradigm dualist philosophy of Descartes, for example, the contrast between persons and animals implies a contrast within the person between a spatially extended bodily mechanism and a self-conscious 'thinking' substance. What is distinctive and valued in human nature is emphasized and its unsullied autonomy preserved, but at the cost of rendering unintelligible the connections both between humans and the rest of nature and, within persons, between those aspects which are and those which are not distinctively human.

Now, Marx's utopian vision of an eventual reunification of humanity with itself and with nature seems, at first encounter, to promise a way out of the dilemmas posed by such dualist ways of thinking. However, the systematic use of human/animal contrasts in his early work tells against this. These contrasts are not presented as historically transcendable. On the contrary, the human potential for historical transcendence is precisely what differentiates us from animals. Whatever changes take place in our human relationship to nature, animals are, and will remain, mere animals.

Many of my readers, of course, will now be saying 'well, so much the better for Marx'. The main historical alternatives to philosophical dualism – materialist and idealist 'monisms' – are the object of well-rehearsed and seemingly decisive objections. Idealisms have great difficulty in sustaining plausible or even coherent accounts of those aspects of our experience in which the mind-independent reality of our world is manifested. Materialisms have a symmetrical difficulty in accounting coherently or plausibly for the existence and nature of human consciousness and experience itself. Materialisms have, more often than not, begun with the aim of explaining some supposedly distinctive and highly valued human characteristic or potential, and ended with explaining it away. In our day, biological reductionist accounts of human nature are the best-known culprits.[25]

If these were, indeed, the only available options, then the case for dualism could be made to appear relatively strong. But they are not the only available options. The philosophical and ethical difficulties of the dualist aspects of Marx's early writings are quite formidable, not only in their own right, but also in terms of other aspects of Marx's overall intellectual and practical project.

Against Marx's Human/Animal Dualism

I'll deal first of all with his dualism as it manifests itself 'externally', so to speak, in the opposition between humans and animals (as distinct from 'internally', in the opposition between the bodily, or animal, and the mental, or distinctively human, within the person). My criticisms of the way Marx counterposes animal and human nature draw upon ways of thinking about non-human animals which have become generally available only in the latter part of the twentieth century, but my aim is not simply to show that Marx has been superseded by the science of ethology. Rather, my view is that a naturalistic account of human nature remains to be 'excavated' from the *Manuscripts*, and that the philosophical core of this naturalistic account is quite compatible with and, indeed, sustains the human/animal continuism implicit in the subsequent development of Darwinian evolutionary theory, ecology and ethology. It is this naturalistic account of human nature which also forms the underlying philosophical thread of much of the rest of this book. However, the difficulty presented by the *Manuscripts* is precisely that this emerging naturalistic standpoint remains entangled with dualist and idealist philosophical patterns of thought which have, indeed, predominated in the most influential readings of Marx's early works.

So, my aim is not so much to use twentieth-century ethology against the early Marx, as to use some aspects of Marx's thinking against others, acknowledging as I do so that Marx's texts are riven by internal contradictions. Though it would take me too far from my present focus of concern, a sustained analysis of historical shifts in Marx's position on these questions would be revealing. In his 1839 notebooks on Epicurean philosophy Marx says: 'If a philosopher does not find it outrageous to consider man as an animal, he cannot be made to understand anything.'[26] This extreme and unequivocal human/animal dualism contrasts markedly with the virtually contemporaneously written (and, likewise, unpublished) notebooks on 'Man, Mind and Materialism' by Charles Darwin. These were written in 1838 and 1839 and are studded with observations and speculations on intelligence, emotional expression and sociability in other animals, and also with remarks on the striking analogies between humans and other animals in these respects. For example:

> Plato says in *Phaedo* that our 'imaginary ideas' arise from the pre-existence of the soul, are not derivable from experience – read monkeys for pre-existence. 1. The young orang in Zoological Gardens pouts. Partly out [of] displeasure ... When pouting protrudes its lips into point. Man, though he does not pout, pushes out both lips in contempt, disgust and defiance.[27]

By 1860 Marx's view had shifted so far from his position in the late 1830s that he was able to recognize in Darwin's recently published *Origin of Species* the 'foundation in natural history for our whole outlook'.[28] In view of this fundamental about-turn in Marx's thinking over the intervening twenty years, it should not surprise us to find in the 1844 *Manuscripts* such an unstable and evidently transitional discourse.

I'll return, now, to the text of the *Manuscripts*, critically considering each of the characteristics in terms of which Marx sustain his opposition between the human and the animal.

1. *Animals are mere 'instances' of their species, whereas humans relate also as 'part to whole' to theirs.* This is Marx's reference to the open-ended capacity of humans for social co-operation. For Marx this is potentially, though not yet actually, a species-wide co-operation in a common species-specific project. But the very cultural diversity which Marx's notion of 'free creativity' also recognizes must render implausible his historical projection. What grounds are there for expecting a spontaneous merging of geographically discrete and culturally diverse lines of historical development and visions of the future? What reasons are there for supposing that humans have the potential to evolve non-coercive forms of social co-ordination on the gigantic

scale required? (There are obvious parallels here with the idea discussed in chapter 1 of a global 'community'.)

On the animal side of Marx's contrast, subsequent ethological study has revealed a wealth and complexity of social life in other species. In the case of such animals as dogs, cats, and herd animals such as sheep and cattle, their very sociability was a necessary initial requirement for their distinctive human uses. So also was a degree of malleability, and 'openness' in their forms of sociability. If we leave aside, then, what is merely speculative in Marx's contrast – his as yet unfulfilled historical projection – the picture is one of highly differentiated and species-specific capacities for forms of sociability between animal species. The extent and form of human sociability are, indeed, distinctive, but the other social species are also social in ways which are distinctive and peculiar to them. The capacity for and disposition to social co-ordination of activity as such is not a distinctive feature of our species.

2. *Humans take the whole world as the object of their activity, whereas animals appropriate the world only partially, and according to the fixed standard of their species.* Again, the human side of this opposition is misleading. Certainly it is a plausible extrapolation from the expansion of the geographical scope of human activity to suppose that one day the whole surface of the globe may bear the imprint of human intentional activity – the last of the rainforests and wildwoods destroyed or cultivated, the poles populated and industrialized, the oceans farmed or rendered sterile by accumulation of toxic wastes, and so on. But what is now supposed to be true of the large-scale, immensely complex, interacting cycles of chemical and physical energy transfer in the ecosphere suggests that our species would destroy itself (and many others) by the unintended consequences of its own activity long before such a 'utopian' possibility were actualized. All transformative activity presupposes a distinction between those attributes of its objects which undergo alteration and other attributes of the objects, conditions and agents of the activity whose persistence, unaltered throughout the process, is indispensable to it. Because of this, even if we suppose a limitless increase in human technical powers in any imaginable direction, the notion of a residueless subordination of the world intensively or extensively to human purposes is incoherent.

On the animal side of this contrast ethological studies reveal great diversity among other animal species with respect to the extent, nature and intra-species variability of their interaction with their environments. As Marx notes, birds build nests which are to a considerable extent species-specific in the materials used, site chosen and 'design'. Nevertheless many species show considerable adaptability in all respects, especially if confronted with non-standard environmental conditions. Inventing, making, using, and inter-generational teaching of the use of tools are now well recognized as powers of non-human primates, notably chimpanzees.[29] That there are profound differences in these capacities between humans and other species is clear, but it remains true that such profound differences also separate non-human animal species from one another. For his intellectual purposes, Marx exaggerates both the fixity and limitedness of scope in the activity of other animals, and the flexibility and universality of scope of human activity upon the environment. At the same time he abstracts from diversity among non-human animal species, and obscures human ecological diversity by way of a global historical extrapolation. Each of these 'intellectual tactics' contributes to the formation of a dualistic categorial opposition instead of a recognition of complex patterns of species-specific diversity.

3. *Humans possess historical potential, whereas animals exhibit fixed standardized modes of activity, from generation to generation.* This contrast presupposes the first two, but goes beyond them in important respects. To become clear how the contrast works, and to see the difficulties in the way of sustaining it in this form it is first necessary to examine the notion of 'historical potential' and that of 'historical development' with which it is closely connected in Marx. First, it is important to distinguish between powers, or capacities, on the one hand, and potentials on the other. To attribute a power or a capacity to, say, an organism is to say that it is able to do something (even though it may not be in fact doing it – it may never have done it). To attribute a potential is to say it has the ability to acquire some future capacity or power which it presently does not have. We may distinguish different kinds of potential on the basis of the nature of the processes through which they are progressively acquired, on the basis of the nature of the external conditions which enable their acquisition, or on the basis of the nature of the bearer of the capacities concerned.

In its infancy an animal, human or non-human, can be said to have capacities, or powers, specific to its stage of development. A child of one year old may be able to crawl but not stand, a little later to stand but not walk, and so on. The infants of most mammal species are less helpless when born than the human infant, and they tend to acquire the species-specific capacities of adults more quickly, but basically the same considerations apply. If we know what capacities are characteristic of adults of the species then we can say of normal infants which have not yet developed these capacities that they have the potential to do so. The nature of the organism is such that given satisfaction of minimal external conditions it will undergo development resulting in the acquisition of the characteristic capacities of adults of its species. Such potentials of infants may be termed 'developmental potentials'.

At any stage in its development, an organism may be said to lack certain capacities – 'skills' are the paradigm here – not because it lacks the necessary organic constitution, nor because it is insufficiently mature, but because it has lacked appropriate learning experience. Of such an organism we can say it lacks a particular capacity (to, for example, catch its own prey, fly long distances, understand long words, do simple arithmetic, depending on the species), but has the potential to acquire it. Such a potential might be termed a 'learning potential'.

Both developmental and learning potentials are potentials of individual organisms. Within the whole range of potentials of individuals we may distinguish between those potentials the fulfilment of which constitutes a species-wide characteristic, and those potentials which are fulfilled only in virtue of the exposure of (a sub-population of) the organisms to a distinctive set of environmental conditions. The former I shall call 'individual species-potentials', the latter 'individual context-potentials'. In the human case, the potential (in small infants) for language-acquisition is an individual species-potential, whereas the potential to acquire the French language would be an individual context-potential for infants reared in French-speaking cultural environments. Pet dogs can learn to respond to human commands; captive chimps can acquire a degree of competence at learning sign-language.[30] The potentials to do this in the animals acquired for the appropriate training are, in my sense, individual context-potentials.

But Marx's notion of a historical potential includes at least the idea of potentials as possessed by associated groups of individual organisms. Humans characteristically produce means of subsistence, for example, through some form of more-or-less stable pattern of combination of the activities of more-or-less numerous individuals. The productive powers of the group are certainly different in degree, and might indeed be argued to be different in kind from those possessed by individuals. This distinction between individual and group-capacities can also be sustained for other social species of animals. Social bees and wasps, beavers, predators such as lions, hyaenas and others are all species in which sub-populations form more-or-less stable groupings which possess capacities not possessed by individuals independently of their grouping.

But can we speak of group-potentials as distinct from mere group-capacities? Are there, for groups, analogues of the processes of development and learning at the level of individuals which might serve as the foundation for a cumulative acquisition of powers through time? Do groups augment their powers of co-ordination of their own activity, or of transforming their environments? To the extent to which they do we may speak of 'collective potentials'. In fact, collective potentials are probably possessed in any significant degree only in some mammalian social animals, and to a high degree only in the human case.

Where the acquired capacities (the fulfilled potentials) of groups can be transmitted from generation to generation in such a way as to enable a continued augmentation of powers of the associated group which is independent of preservation of the identities of the members of the group I shall speak of collective historical potentials. The acquisition of a written language, for example, can retrospectively be recognized to have been a collective historical potential of some pre-literate civilizations. Literacy, like the wheel, does not have to be re-invented in each generation but, unlike spoken language, it is not a collective possession in all cultures, or in all historical periods. I think that the notion of collective historical potentials is required if we are adequately to understand historical processes, but I also recognize that there are serious difficulties in the way of coherently specifying the concept. Not the least of these is the problem of establishing identity of reference to the 'bearers' or possessors of such potentials. In the case of simple collective potentials this may be relatively unproblematic – as long as the group stays together, and continues to interact, it can be identified and re-identified as 'the same' group. Identifying and re-identifying 'the same' collectivity of human beings through prolonged expanses of historical time is another matter.

However, for (the early) Marx, the problem is compounded, since he attributes to the human species alone yet another type of collective potential: the potential for species-wide co-ordination of activity. The potential is not, here, attributable to any empirically delimitable socially combined *population* of human beings, but to the species as a whole. For Marx, then, over and above simple collective potentials, and collective historical potentials, there are also what we might call 'species historical potentials'.

Finally, for any species capable of historical potentials of either of the two kinds so far distinguished ('collective' or 'species') the conditions exist for a further kind of individual potential to be distinguished. To the extent that collective (or species) historical potentials are fulfilled, the environmental context in which individuals realize their individual developmental and/or learning potentials is transformed. In other words, for species susceptible of collective historical 'development' (cumulative acquisition of collective powers across generations) we can distinguish within the category of individual context-potentials a sub-class of individual historical potentials. Individual historical potentials are capacities which individuals are able to acquire in virtue of their membership of a collective in which cognate collective historical potentials have been fulfilled. The individual potential for reading or writing, for example, is an individual historical potential in this sense. It is a potential which can be realized only by individuals who belong to a culture which possesses the institution of a written language. The idea of collective historical potentials is necessary if we are to understand the extent to which · the possibilities for individual development and fulfilment are dependent upon the historical achievements of the culture in which they find themselves.

Clearly, a good deal more needs to be said by way of defining these distinctions. But enough has been said to enable me at least to state my case against Marx's use of the concept of historical potential in sustaining his opposition between humans and animals. On the human side of the opposition, it seems to me that the attribution of *species* historical potentials to humans is, to say the least, highly speculative. Certainly this is so if we try to follow Marx in saying which potentials these are (humanization of nature, and so on). Further, the normative connotation which the notion of potential generally carries in Marx does not seem obviously to apply to historical potentials, whether individual or collective. The individual historical potential to deliver 'megadeaths' at the press of a button is dependent upon the realization of the collective historical potential to construct hi-tech weaponry. But how do we value this historical achievement? Do we recognize in it just one aspect of the historical unfolding of human nature, a dimension of human fulfilment, along with our increased capacities for curing the sick, making the deserts bloom and so on? If we take this option, then it entails recognizing that humans have, as part of their nature, a potential for destructiveness, for evil. In this event, human well-being, the pursuit of happiness, may require us to find ways of suppressing or blocking off some of our potentials. Well-being, the 'good life', cannot be identified straightforwardly with the fulfilment of our human potential.

The alternative option would be to keep the positive value-connotations of the notion of 'potential', refusing to recognize as potentials those historical possibilities whose realization would be undesirable – evil, destructive, and, ultimately, self-destructive. This option strikes me as a particularly indefensible form of 'speciesist' special-pleading. The temptation towards utopian blindness to the causal importance of those individual and collective historical possibilities denied the status of 'potentials' is both strong and dangerous. As Mary Midgley has eloquently shown, the human/animal opposition has served as a convenient symbolic device whereby we have attributed to animals the dispositions we have not been able to contemplate in ourselves.[31] The point of these considerations is to suggest that if Marx was right in supposing that only humans have historical potentials, it does not follow directly from this that any great gulf stands between the animal and the human with respect to their moral status.

The significance of this point becomes clearer if we look at Marx's contrast from the animal side of the divide. As we have seen, many animal species display a complexity, diversity and adaptability in their behaviour which is denied in Marx's view of them as rigidly stereotypical in their species-characteristic modes of life. For many non-human animal species it is possible to speak defensibly of developmental and learning potentials, of simple collective powers, and even to a limited extent of collective potentials. Some evidence exists of cultural transmission of learned skills in the cases of some species of primate but not (as yet, at least) of any generation-by-generation cumulative direction in these collective skills.[32] This does seem to be a distinctive feature of humans by contrast with all other animal species currently inhabiting the earth. It is, however, worth noting that this is a purely contingent matter. There is no *a priori* reason for supposing that some other species might not evolve these potentials in the future, and there are good empirical grounds for thinking that our planet has previously been inhabited by other hominid species which did have historical potentials.

Now, the moral contrast which Marx draws between the historical potential of humanity and its estranged, distorted, stunted, merely animal mode of existence under the dominion of estranged labour is only effective on two conditions. First, it is necessary to equate the fulfilment of human historical potential with the well-being, the flourishing, of humans in their forms of association with one another and their material environment. I have just suggested that this equation is not justified.[33] Second, it is necessary to attribute to human beings the capacity to exist in two contrasting states: as merely existing, or surviving, as beings whose 'crude, physical' or 'merely animal' needs are met (as mere bearers of the capacity to work and to physically reproduce that capacity), or, by contrast, as flourishing, as fulfilled, as 'fully human'.

But the place of the reference to 'animal needs', here, and the associated use of the human/animal contrast to sustain the ethical critique of human estrangement, requires a denial of this capacity in the animal case. Animals, we must suppose, merely exist. As animals they have merely animal needs and the satisfaction of these needs is both necessary and sufficient for the existence and reproduction of the life of the individual and its species. But if, as we have seen, (some) animals also have developmental, learning, species, context, and collective capacities and potentials, then for these as well it must be possible to distinguish between mere existence, on the one hand, and thriving, well-being and the fulfilment of diverse potentials, on the other. The mere fact of distinctively human historical potentials does not obliterate either the ethical distinction between flourishing and merely existing for other animals, or its ontological presuppositions.

41

The point here is not just that Marx was simply wrong about animals. It is rather that he was wrong in ways which undermine his own view of the desirability of a changed relationship between humanity and nature in the future communist society. Connectedly, he is also wrong about animals in ways which cut him off from a powerful extension and deepening of his own ethical critique of prevailing (capitalist) modes of appropriation of nature.

Let us adopt a 'weak' interpretation of 'humanization of nature' and allow that it may include not the literal 'humanization' of animals but, rather, an alteration of our relationship to animals – perhaps a rendering of that relationship more consistent with our 'humanity', a more humane relationship. This is the very least that would be required to make Marx's notion consistent with his own professed naturalism. Now, whatever content is given to 'a more humane relationship', it presupposes that 'crude, physical need' and the needs of animals are not equivalent. Only if there is a difference between mere existence of animals at a level which minimally satisfies human-utility, on the one hand, and flourishing or well-being, on the other, can we distinguish between 'inhumane' and 'humane' ways of treating those animals whose conditions of life are dependent upon the exercise of our powers.

Moreover, the pathological distortions from the properly human mode of life which Marx attempts to capture in his concept of 'estrangement', or 'alienation', are in important respects paralleled in the modes of life imposed upon animals by precisely the same structures of social action. The treatment of animals as mere means to external purposes, the forcible fragmentation of their life-activity, and the dissolution of their social bonds with one another are, for example, features of commercial agriculture which have become progressively intensified since Marx's day with each technical reorganization of agricultural production. As I will try to show later in chapter 5, the ethical critique of such practices should not be seen as an alternative to a Marxian critique of modern capitalist forms of labour-discipline, but rather as an extension and a deepening of it. But Marx's contrast between the human and the animal cuts away the ontological basis for such a critical analysis of forms of suffering shared by both animals and humans who are caught up in a common causal network.

Marx's attribution to animals of a fixed and standardized mode of activity in relation to nature, and his apparent failure to recognize in any significant way the social life of non-human animals are both at work in his use of the phrases 'physical need' and 'animal need' as if they were equivalent. This suggests a denial of the complexity and diversity of the emotional, psychological and social lives of other animals. Such a denial renders merely rhetorical Marx's characterization of history as 'nature developing into man', and cuts off two significant sources of insight into human nature and history. The first, which would require giving serious theoretical content to the idea of 'nature developing into man', would be an inquiry into the prehistorical origins of the human species, and the processes of our differentiation from other primate lineages.

The second, in part dependent for its rational justification on the first (that is, a recognition of the kinship of humans and other animals), would be a comparative psychology and ethology in which what is genuinely distinctive about human beings could be viewed in the light of what is shared between human and non-human animals. That these lines of inquiry have a long post-Darwinian history of politically tendentious and methodologically suspect misuses[34] is not a sufficient reason for a wholesale abandonment of the enterprise. While there is certainly plenty of room for legitimate controversy within modern evolutionary theory it is no longer reasonable to deny the main claims of the evolutionary perspective in relation to human ancestry in some primate stock, and our kinship with contemporary primates. Unless social scientists wish to stand with the flat earthers, the Inquisitors and the bible-belt creationists they have no choice but to engage with the questions posed by our animal origins and nature. As we have noted, Marx and Engels themselves enthusiastically embraced this perspective after 1859.[35]

Against Marx's Dualist View of Human Nature

Perhaps, however, the most telling arguments against the dualist aspects of Marx's early work relate to the dualism within human nature which follows from the external dualism of the animal and the human. It is characteristic of dualist approaches, baulking at the prospect of a comprehensively idealist view of our nature, to recognize an animal component, layer, or aspect, within the human. The human is an animal, but an animal with a special 'something' extra which makes all the difference – soul, mind, will, self, reason, and so on.

Marx's early writings, as we have seen, still fall within this tradition. In so far as humans work only to meet their subsistence needs, and do not experience their work as a need in itself, their activity is mere animal activity. In so far as their leisure activities, their eating and drinking, their 'dressing up' and so on are ends in themselves, segregated from the wider species-project, they are mere 'animal functions'. When the starving man is fed 'it would be impossible to say wherein this feeding activity differs from that of animals'.[36] This reproduction of the animal/human opposition within the domain of the human involves a sequestering of certain of our needs, powers, functions and activities as animal, or animal-like, from others (generally more highly valued and assigned a more fundamental ontological status) which are designated 'human'.

The main objections to this broad strategy for understanding what humans are can be usefully placed into three groups:

1. Those powers, needs, activities, functions (etc.) which fall on the human side of the divide, are represented as a self-sufficient, *sui generis*, autonomous complex which is thus rendered unintelligible in relation to the rest (the animal side) of human life. But what sense could be made of, for example, human powers of reasoning in abstraction from the bodily needs and activities in which they are exercised? In Marx's own case, the ethical ideal for humanity is a mode of being which integrates the diverse activities of persons within a coherent communal project. This notion of integral self-realization remains incompatible with the residual dualism of the *Manuscripts*.

2. Those powers, activities, needs, functions (etc.) which fall on the 'animal' side of the division are correspondingly profaned as, perhaps, rather shameful residual features. Their continued, uncomfortably insistent presence, eruptions and interruptions are demeaning and rob us of the full sense of self-respect to which we feel entitled. A combined dread and contempt for bodily existence and function is barely disguised in much philosophical dualism. It provides grounding and sustenance for the valuation of mental over manual labour, of masculinity ('cultured') over femininity ('natural'), of reason over sentiment, of mind over matter, and of the 'civilized' over the 'savage'. It makes for a culture that is guilt-ridden, fearful and confused over such fundamental features of the shared human and animal condition as sexuality and death.

3. The dualist philosophical heritage is at work in many of our most problematic contemporary institutional forms and practices. The development of modern 'health-care' as a form of organized, hi-tech 'body mechanics', (at its best) detecting, diagnosing and correcting defects in the bodily machine has an unmistakable Cartesian legacy about it. The pertinence of the psychological, emotional, cultural and socio-economic aspects and contexts of the person to both the causation of and recovery from disease has been widely understood only in recent years.[37] It has yet to gain the central place it deserves in policy disputes and health-care reform. In other areas of public policy, too, a segregation of 'basic' (physical) needs from 'higher' (emotional, cultural, self-realizing) needs underlies priorities of welfare state provision in such areas as housing, the setting of nutritional standards and even education.[38] A great deal of overseas aid policy, too, neglects the cultural, socio-economic and environmental contexts within which such 'basic' needs as food and shelter are met. The sequestering of kinds of need from one another, often well-intended, equally often is disastrous in its consequences. Needs

which are inseparably interconnected both in the way they are experienced and in the interweaving of the causal conditions of their satisfaction are all too often abstractly 'targeted' in single-priority interventions which bring extended chains of unintended consequences in their wake. The environmental and social cost of the export of so-called 'green revolution' technologies to large parts of Asia and Latin America is a case in point.[39]

I have tried to show that much of Marx's thinking in the early *Manuscripts* is governed by two closely related dualistic oppositions: between humans and animals, and between the human and the animal *within* the human. I have advanced some considerations which I believe tell against these dualisms, both as they appear in Marx, and as they are present more widely as a constitutive dimension of Western cultures. I have also suggested that human/animal dualisms are incompatible with key features of Marx's own intellectual and practical project. But if this is so, then it follows that there are other elements or aspects of Marx's thinking, even in his pre-Darwinian days, which cut against the dualist aspects upon which my proffered reading has so far been based.

Naturalism without Reductionism or Speciesism?

In what remains of this chapter, I shall offer a sketch for an alternative reading and re-construction of Marx's early *Manuscripts*, centred on those elements which tell against both philosophical dualism and idealism, and which favour a naturalistic, but still not reductionist view of human nature. A view, that is, which gives due place to the specificity and distinctiveness of the human species, but does so without compromising what remains defensible in Marx's assertion that 'man is part of nature'.

Some of the most promising textual materials for this alternative approach are to be found, not surprisingly, perhaps, in the manuscript entitled 'Critique of the Hegelian Dialectic and Philosophy as a Whole'.

> *Man* is directly a *natural being*. As a natural being and as a living natural being he is on the one hand endowed with *natural powers, vital powers* – he is an *active* natural being. These forces exist in him as tendencies and abilities – as *instincts*. On the other hand, as a natural, corporeal, sensuous, objective being he is a *suffering*, conditioned and limited creature, like animals and plants. That is to say, the *objects* of his instincts exist outside him, *objects* independent of him; yet these *objects* are objects that he *needs* – essential objects, indispensable to the manifestation and confirmation of his essential powers. ... *Hunger* is a natural *need*; it therefore needs a *nature* outside itself, an *object* outside itself, in order to satisfy itself, to be stilled.[40]

In this passage, Marx is asserting the status of humans as 'natural beings', a status they share with (other) animals and with plants. As natural beings there are three interconnected features which humans share with other living beings. First, they have natural needs whose objects lie outside themselves, independent of them. All living things, for example, have nutritional needs. The objects of these needs – foodstuffs – exist independently of them. Second, all living beings have natural powers which enable them to satisfy these needs, and natural tendencies ('instincts') to exercise them. Third, this need-satisfying activity in relation to external objects is essential to the 'confirmation' or 'manifestation' of the essential powers of the species.

In other words, interaction with external nature is necessary for the survival of all natural beings. Each species of natural being has its own distinctive mode or pattern of interaction with nature – its own 'species-life'. And finally, (a member of) each species only fully manifests its essential nature – only becomes what it has the potential to be – in virtue of its participation in this distinctive species-life.

'But', Marx goes on to say, 'Man is not merely a natural being: he is a human natural being. That is to say, he is a being for himself.'[41] Having begun to speak of human nature in a thoroughly naturalistic way, Marx appears, again, to pull back and re-establish a dualistic opposition, this time between the 'human' and the 'natural'. However, there is no necessity for such a reading. The 'human' here can be understood as a qualification, a specification or subdivision within the natural, rather than its opposite. This remains a form of naturalism, in that what humans share with other 'natural beings' is regarded as ontologically fundamental, and is accordingly given priority for purposes of understanding and explaining what humans are and how they act. But it is not a reductionist naturalism in the sense that it allows for a full recognition of the specificity and distinctiveness of humans, their forms of sociability and their potentials within the order of nature. Whereas dualist and idealist accounts of human nature fix upon features which are held to distinguish us from (other) animals and elaborate their views of human nature upon that basis, a naturalistic approach begins with the common predicament of natural beings and moves from that basis to render intelligible their specific differences in constitution, structure and modes of life.

In Marx's account all living beings have needs, the objects of which are external and independent. The satisfaction of need, therefore, requires interaction with and appropriation of the environment of the organism. The particular content of need, the mechanisms which mediate between needs and forms of activity, and the nature of need-meeting activities themselves are, of course, almost unimaginably diverse – from the chemistry of photosynthesis through the hunting of the tiger to the 'biting' of the mosquito. The point, however, is that the common framework of analysis enables us to recognize the significance of all these detailed specificities of biochemical, neuro-physiological, anatomical, ethological and ecological facts and processes within the overall 'mode of life' of the species concerned.

Each species has its own characteristic species-life. Organisms can 'confirm' or 'manifest' their essential powers only within the context of their species-life, and so can be said to flourish only when the conditions for living the mode of life characteristic of their species are met. For each species we can distinguish conditions for mere organic survival – the meeting of minimal nutritional requirements, protection from predators, and so on – from conditions for flourishing, for the living of the species-life. But how this distinction is made, the specific survival conditions and flourishing conditions which are identified, will vary from species to species. The empirical determination of such conditions is at least part of the content of the sciences of ethology and ecology.

So far, then, my alternative, non-dualistic reading of Marx's early *Manuscripts* has yielded a significant shift in the conceptual means for dealing with Marx's central theme in this text: the estrangement of labour. Under regimes of private property, conditions which enable the survival of workers are provided but the conditions for them to confirm their powers and potentials in the living of their characteristic 'species-life' are denied to them. A distorted and pathological mode of life is the consequence. This theme can be further specified and elaborated with little if any loss of the ethical power of Marx's critique, but with the double gain that precisely the same framework of analysis can be applied in the critique of the mode of life imposed upon many of the other living species caught up in this distorted mode of human life, and that Marx's highly speculative notion of a distinctively human 'species historical' potential is rendered redundant.

I will conclude this chapter with some brief and preliminary indications as to how the form of naturalism I am advocating might offer a preferable way of understanding the relation between the 'human' and the 'animal' within the human, how it might, in other words, displace dualism without falling into reductionism. A naturalistic specification of 'human nature', I have suggested, would be a matter of differentiating and then elaborating our specific features from an initial recognition of the common core of 'natural being' which we share with other living creatures. But this process of differentiation, of saying what is specifically human, can all too easily fall into a dualist mode. If it becomes centred on a specification of those powers, potentials and requirements possessed by humans 'over and above' those they share with animals, the approach falls short of naturalism. This is not to deny that there are things (reading, writing, talking,[42] composing symphonies, inventing weapons of mass destruction, and so on) which humans and only humans can do. Rather, it is to say that those things which only humans can do are generally to be understood as rooted in the specifically human ways of doing things which other animals also do. It is this feature that I want to emphasize as the hallmark of a naturalistic approach.

What this approach might mean in practice can, perhaps, be illustrated by way of a study of Marx's treatment of the concept of 'need' in the *Manuscripts*. As we have seen, Marx speaks variously of 'crude', 'physical' or 'animal' needs, contrasting them with 'human needs'. In some passages it seems as though the human needs constitute a separate, *sui generis* class of needs, set over and above our 'animal', subsistence needs, and peculiar to us as humans. We may distinguish two broad types of human need in this sense. First, what might be called 'self-realization' needs:

> The *rich* human being is simultaneously the human being in need of a totality of human manifestations of life – a man in whom his own realization exists as an inner necessity, as *need*.[43]

Marx seems to suggest that such inner needs for self-realization, for the fulfilment of potential, are possible only for self-conscious beings, and even then are only fully acquired on the basis of an extended process of historical 'development'.

The second class of distinctively human needs is similarly linked with our status as self-conscious beings, but not necessarily with our historicity. Marx speaks of the elements of our external environment ('plants, animals, stones, air, light, etc.')[44] as constituting 'spiritual nourishment' in so far as they are objects of human science and art. Over and above the need (which they share with other animals) to appropriate nature physically, humans have spiritual needs to appropriate nature aesthetically and cognitively. This reading is strongly suggested by such passages as this:

> It [the animal] produces only under the dominion of immediate physical need, while man produces even when he is free from physical need and only truly produces in freedom therefrom.[45]

There are, it seems, two possible kinds of human practice in relation to nature: one, physical-need satisfaction, which we share with animals, the other, spiritual (aesthetic, cognitive) need-satisfaction, which is special to us, and constitutes production in the 'true' sense. This distinction reappears in the later works as a distinction between the realms of 'necessity' and of 'freedom'.

However, an alternative, naturalistic reading of the passage is also possible. To qualify as properly human, it is necessary not that production have no relation to the satisfaction of physical need, but rather that it should not be performed under the dominion of immediate physical need. Leaving aside

Marx's apparent equation of the animal with the 'not-properly-human', Marx can plausibly be read as making a distinction not so much between practices which satisfy different needs, as between different modes of satisfaction of common needs. The satisfaction of aesthetic and cognitive needs does not require the performance of further practices, over and above the practices through which physical needs are met. In a fully human, or 'true' practice of production physical needs would be met in a way that was aesthetically and cognitively satisfying. For at least this sub-class of 'human' needs, then, we can say that they are not a *sui generis* complex of requirements, over and above the physical needs, but that they are, rather, requirements which bear on the manner of experiencing, identifying and satisfying the physical needs.

Let's take the physical need for nutrition as an example. This need is common to both humans and other animals. Some non-human animals, but not all, have sufficient psychological and behavioural similarity to ourselves for us to speak non-metaphorically and unequivocally of them as experiencing hunger, searching for, and consuming food. For all such animals the objects and substances which can count as 'food' are a sub-set only of the total range of objects and substances which would satisfy their nutritional requirements. Moreover, only some modes of acquiring and consuming these objects and substances are characteristic of the 'mode of life' of the species concerned, or are activities in which their specific powers and potentials are exercised or fulfilled. The feeding activities actually engaged in by such animals are the overdetermined outcome of inherited predispositions, learning and environmental opportunity-structures.

All of this is true of humans and many other species of animals, especially mammals and birds. So, in the passage quoted above (p. 33) Marx's parallel between the feeding activity of the 'starving man' and that of animals is undermined. Neither for humans nor for other species can we simply equate the mere satisfaction of nutritional requirements with the feeding activity characteristic of the species. The distorted, or pathological relation to food induced by starvation in humans is not an animal or animal-like relation to food, but a specific distortion or pathology of *human* feeding activity. But, despite this mistaken equation of the pathologically human with the animal, Marx's comment is susceptible to an illuminating and naturalistic interpretation. What makes the relation of the starving man to food a pathological one is that the object of hunger exists merely as food, its sole significance is that its consumption will satisfy the hunger. Such feeding activity is performed under the 'domination' of 'immediate' need, to quote what Marx says elsewhere. This feeding activity is means/ends activity, not activity with its own intrinsic satisfaction. It is also activity in which the aesthetic, cognitive, and 'spiritual' dimensions of human activity are missing.

49

On this naturalistic reading, what makes the difference between a 'fully', or 'properly' human way of satisfying hunger and a less than human, or pathological way of satisfying the same need is the presence or absence of intrinsic cognitive and aesthetic satisfactions in the activity through which the need is satisfied. We can now get closer to answering the question, what are the enabling conditions for the satisfaction of hunger to take a properly human form? In addition to the availability of nutritional items in the environment and the technical powers on the part of persons to appropriate them, these enabling conditions must also include appropriate aesthetic and cognitive rules and resources.

But we can ask the further question, under what conditions can these aesthetic and cognitive rules and resources exist? The short answer is: within the context of a human culture. That this reading is in line with Marx's thinking is indicated by his use of the word 'immediate' to specify the non-human relation to physical need-satisfaction. Properly human feeding-activity is symbolically, culturally mediated need-satisfaction. All cultures contain classifications which define (well within the range of all possible means of meeting nutritional requirements) what are and what are not to be counted as food, often with severely sanctioned taboos against the consumption of some items. Similarly normative regulations govern the mode of appropriation of culturally recognized foodstuffs, their preparation for consumption, their distribution within the community, the order in which they are consumed and so on.[46]

Now, there are two questions which might reasonably be raised at this point. First, in exemplifying the ways in which a naturalistic approach such as I am advocating may still recognize human distinctiveness, I have focused on the need for food, a physical, or organic, need. It may be that in attempting to deal with other classes of need, my approach will revert to dualism for want of any non-human comparators. So, it is crucial to investigate whether this approach can be made to work for other classes of need, or other aspects of human nature which are held in common with (at least some) other animals. A second question about my proposed approach pulls rather in the opposite direction. In seeming to suggest that all 'human' needs can be analysed as distinctive modes of satisfaction of generic needs which are shared with other species, doesn't my programme revert to a form of reductionism, after all? Can I consistently acknowledge any class of needs, powers or activities which is genuinely peculiar to our species?[47]

My response to the first question is to recall the earlier criticism of Marx's representation of animals as subjects of such organic needs as food, shelter and reproduction, and as 'active' beings, disposed to satisfy those needs by way of inflexible, unreflective and stereotypical patterns of individual behaviour.

Drawing upon contemporary work in ethology and animal ecology, we must now recognize among animal species both diversity and complexity of need. Each species has its own distinctive pattern of need, and a mode of life appropriate to the meeting of that pattern of need. Furthermore, for at least some species this distinctive pattern of need includes a complex articulation of psychological, social and organic needs and dimensions of need. 'Animal needs' cannot be reduced to 'organic' needs. So, a naturalistic, a human/animal continuist approach to human nature or need is in no way limited to the analysis of 'organic' or 'physical' needs (such as nutrition) alone.

However, it is clearly insufficient merely to state this. To meet even the minimal requirements of plausibility for such a programmatic claim I should be able to offer a framework for identifying and classifying needs which is applicable across both cultural and species boundaries, while at the same time enabling explanatory differentiations to be made between species and particular cultures. This is, of course, an extremely tall order. Much of the rest of this book will consist of a prolonged exploration of the implications of different ways of doing this. What I can offer at this stage is, first, to point out in a preliminary way the sources of evidence or rational grounding which might tell for or against such a framework. Second, I can provide, albeit in a sketchy and provisional form, the general outline of what such a framework might look like. I stress, again, this is intended as a provisional point of orientation, both for this book and for subsequent research. It is in no sense offered as a definitive account of human nature or need.

First the question of sources of evidence and argument. Several interrelated disciplines – animal ecology and ethology, palaeo-anthropology, evolutionary theory itself, and others – have obvious and direct pertinence as sources of both substantive evidence and argumentative themes. Of course, there are no uncontroversial inferences to be made here: these disciplines are themselves characterized by conflicting schools of thought, and interpreting their relevance to our understanding of human nature and need is also not a matter of applying 'given' principles, but is a creative intellectual challenge.

Two further sources of grounding for our proposed naturalistic view of human nature and need are conventionally grouped among the human social sciences. I want to draw attention to them because they are generally taken to provide the most powerful arguments against the kind of naturalistic project I'm advocating. The first of these sources is cultural anthropology. This is the disciplinary basis for some of the strongest arguments against the idea of universals in human nature (let alone the idea of universals which cross the species divide itself). For cultural anthropologists, the nature and meaning of any human activity is given by its place in the symbolic and normative order provided by the 'local' cultural context of activity. Any 'invented' classificatory scheme imposed by the social scientists in their generalizing project must necessarily do violence to the self-understandings of diverse cultures and so misrepresent the activities under study. Arguments like this point in the direction of some form of cognitive cultural relativism, but in their efforts to demonstrate these consequences, cultural relativists face a paradox. They have to provide convincing accounts of 'alien' beliefs and practices and, at the same time, show that these beliefs and practices are unintelligible in terms of 'our' culture. To the extent that the anthropologist succeeds in making us understand the 'alien' practice, she fails in showing that it is unintelligible to 'us'. Arguably, cultural anthropology is itself either a wholly worthless and incoherent enterprise, or cross-cultural understanding is, after all, possible (though, often, difficult). This suggests a way of making cultural anthropology relevant to our task of investigating human universals: if cultural understanding is possible, in virtue of what is it possible? What are the cross-cultural bridgeheads through which quite different human cultures can achieve mutual communication and comprehension?[48]

A second line of argument often employed against the idea of human universals has a range of disciplinary sources – historical, anthropological, sociological, psychological. The emphasis in this line of argument is upon human adaptability and malleability: our capacity (and need) to be socially 'constructed' or 'formed'. Individual 'identities', 'subjectivities' (even 'the subject' itself) are held to be constituted and transformed by locally variable relations and practices as human individuals become social beings.[49] However, set against this, as no less evident a feature of the sociological, historical and psychological record, is the pervasiveness of resistance, estrangement and discontent in the relations between individuals and the requirements of their local cultural contexts. Significantly, these features are often present to the extent of psychological breakdown, physical illness and suicide. They are one source of evidence about the limits to human adaptability and malleability. An analysis of the pathological consequences of some of the demands placed upon individuals by their socio-cultural conditions of life, particularly if pursued with an eye to cross-cultural patterns, can offer important insights for the inquiry into human universals. Further, taking human adaptability and malleability as our datum, it may be illuminating to ask what must be true of humans for them to possess these capacities, what part do they play in the distinctively human 'mode of life'?[50]

Of course, there is no advance guarantee that these distinct sources of insight will all yield answers that are conformable to one another in some general theory of human nature. More seriously for my position here, neither is there any guarantee that if such a general theory were supported by these different lines of inquiry, it would confirm my commitment to naturalism and human/animal continuism. There is no reason *a priori* to suppose that this inquiry would not result in an anti-naturalistic view, confirming human/animal dualism. However, the indications are that the pursuit of these lines of inquiry would converge on a definite pattern of inter-related features which together constitute a distinctively human mode of life, but yet which provide sufficient points of contact with the modes of life proper to non-human animal species to ground illuminating comparisons. In summary, these interrelated features are:

1. *An organically limited life-span: birth and death.* These are shared features of the human and animal condition, but in the human case they are distinctively problematic because of the requirement for socio-cultural continuity across generations, and the consequent metaphysical and moral significance assigned to these organic processes in human cultures, and because of the requirement to normatively regulate reproductive activity and affective dimensions of loss.

2. *Temporal phasing of organic growth, development and decline in individual life-spans.* Again, these are shared features of the lives of humans and other animals. Many non-human social species also share with humans patterns of social life in which shifts of social position, relations and patterns of activity are associated with these organic transitions. Humans are, however, distinctive in the length of infantile dependence relative to the total life-span. This is associated with the requirement for acquisition of complex and sophisticated socio-cultural skills and capacities, and, in turn, presupposes prolonged interpersonal relations to sustain socializing and parenting.

3. *Sexuality.* Sexual reproduction and social regulation of sexual activity are common to humans and many other non-human animals, though humans are physiologically distinctive, especially in the lack of external signs of oestrus in the menstrual cycle.[51] This is linked with continuous sexual receptivity, and suggests an evolutionarily significant role for sexual activity in human social life to some extent dissociated from the immediate requirements of reproduction. Humans are distinctive in the complexity of socio-cultural and psychological dimensions of the organization of sexual difference, and in the use of sexual activity to consolidate long-term affective bonds between pairs. It seems reasonable to suppose that these differences are linked both to their physiological distinctiveness and also to features (1) and (2) above.

4. *Social co-operation in the meeting of organic needs.* All animals as 'active natural beings' must engage in some activity upon their environments to sustain life. Social animals may co-ordinate the activity of more or less

numerous individuals in hunting prey, in territorial defence, and so on, presumably increasing their chances for success in these tasks, but at the same time imposing further requirements for social co-ordination: ways of regulating distribution of the catch between individual members of the co-operating group, development of sophisticated means of communication to facilitate co-ordination, and so on. Conventionally established symbolic modes of regulation of social interaction and co-ordination, though present in other species, for humans are developed to a unique extent. Though all humans must act socially upon the material environment to meet their needs, the conventional character of the means of co-ordination which enable them to do this facilitates an indefinitely varied range of possible ways of socially appropriating nature.

5. *Stability of social order, and the integration of social groups.* The development of strong affective bonds (and not solely with close kin), of regular associations of groups of individuals, and of distinctive patterns of social interaction (for example, hierarchies of dominance, divisions of labour and of consumption) are features of the social life of many non-human species, especially primates. For humans, such features as prolonged infantile dependency, pair-bonding and conventional symbolic and normative regulation of organic need-meeting activity all presuppose a mode of social life marked by long-run integrity and stability. It is to be expected that all cultures will possess institutional mechanisms to secure this requirement, at least at the level of localized 'face-to-face' social groupings.

All of this does, of course, require much more argumentation and elaboration. Nevertheless, I hope enough has been said to indicate at least the initial plausibility of an approach to human nature which is naturalistic in its acknowledgement of a continuity and commonality between humans and other animal species, but which remains able to identify and illuminate human specificity. The starting-point for the analysis is the recognition of an attribute or requirement which is common to both humans and many non-human animals. The specification of the distinctively human then proceeds not by identifying some further, *sui generis* class of attributes or needs possessed only by humans, but, rather, by identifying the species-specific ways in which humans exhibit attributes or meet needs which they share with other species. This leaves open the possibility of making further comparisons between humans and other species and it avoids the effacement of the manifold differences among non-human animals in their modes of social life.

This sketch for a naturalistic view of the human has been an attempted answer to the charge that the approach I have advocated is 'dualism at one remove'. I have tried to show that using our commonality as 'active natural beings' with other animal species as a framework within which to articulate a view of human distinctiveness does not require us either to suppose that what we have in common with other animals is merely our organic being or to conceptualize our distinctiveness in terms solely of culture or consciousness. Humans have many anatomical and physiological peculiarities, but also share much with other animal species in their social and mental life.

However, as we saw above, it may still be objected that this approach is a form of reductionism – albeit a potentially relatively sophisticated one. By way of response to this it may be worthwhile to distinguish my approach from two other well-established (but widely criticized) rival naturalisms. The first of these is sociobiology. This is not the place for an elaborate discussion of this discipline,[52] but I hope enough can be said in a short space to distinguish my approach. At least in its classic formulations, sociobiology works with a rather small repertoire of hypothesized evolutionary mechanisms (kin selection, reciprocal altruism, sexual selection) to explain animal social behaviours in so far as they are genetically regulated. Its key problem is the presence of 'altruistic' behaviour or, more generally, of patterns of social activity which appear not to maximize individual chances of survival and reproduction. Taking the molecular gene as the ultimate unit upon which selective pressures bear, sociobiologists attempt to reconcile some observed 'altruistic' behaviour with their particular conception of the evolutionary process. There remains an important residue of social behaviour, particularly in the human case, which has to be either explained away or excluded as learned behaviour beyond the scope of sociobiological explanation. My approach is non-reductionist in the sense that it takes as 'given' the level of ethological and ecological description[53] of the modes of life of animal species. Instead of the *a priori* requirement that this level of description be made conformable to some particular vision of evolutionary theory, the inverse possibility, that evolutionary theory be made adequate to the explanatory challenge of ethological and ecological discovery, is held open.

The second 'rival' naturalism is a certain version of historical materialism which takes the mode of social production of material goods as the basis of its explanatory accounts of other human social activity. This approach may be, but need not be, reductionist in character, but the above considerations suggest a different defect: its 'one-sidedness'. My sketch for a view of human nature does, indeed, recognize (under section 4) the pertinence of socially co-ordinated appropriation of nature as a necessary element in any adequate naturalistic account.[54] However, the systematic use of human/animal comparison which, I suggest, must be an implication of any thorough-going naturalism yields other explanatorily significant dimensions of human nature (such as sexuality, reproduction, birth and death, and so on) which are commonly (but not universally) under-theorized in the historical materialist tradition. Some recent feminist writers have made major advances in correcting, or compensating for this imbalance in the historical materialist view.[55]

But, finally, it may still be insisted that my view is reductionist in its attempt to represent all human distinctiveness as distinctiveness in our mode of expression of, or way of doing, things which other animals also do. What, for example, of those needs – self-realization needs – which appear to be peculiar to self-conscious and historical beings? My response to this is, first, to reiterate that once the relative sophistication and complexity of the mental and social life of many other animal species is fully acknowledged, the formula 'distinctive way of meeting common need' will be seen to give insight into a great deal of human social life: much more than would at first thought be imagined.

But, of course, it is not required by the form of naturalism which I advocate that the reality of such supervenient needs, powers or attributes should be denied. Rather, the commitment is to viewing them as in some sense consequential upon those needs which are common to natural beings, or upon the species-specific ways in which those common needs are met. Explanatory strategies in relation to such supervenient needs would be to make them intelligible in terms of the (ontologically) more fundamental common needs.

It would be difficult for me to claim any more than that this is a very open-ended promissory note, and I acknowledge that many readers will understandably find it unsatisfactory in its present state. For the moment it will have to suffice for me to suggest that the broad naturalistic but non-reductionist approach advocated above would provide the beginnings of a methodological defence for some already-existing explanatory strategies (not, of course, grounds for accepting as true any specific social-scientific explanation). Marx's attempt to explain the fragmentations and distortions of human personal and social life under capitalism as the (direct or mediated) consequences of a pathological relationship to nature is clearly one such strategy that would be defended. An interesting and provocative comparison here would be with the genre of explicitly ethologically-rooted social pathologies, of which Desmond Morris's *Human Zoo*[56] is perhaps the best-known example.

Such sociological/anthropological strategies might usefully be compared and complemented by psychoanalytical approaches which operate at the level of the human individual. What Freud does with the concept of 'sublimation' is a clear case of an attempt to explain in a non-reductionist way the rootedness of some distinctively human activities (aesthetic and scientific, for example) in needs and propensities (sexuality and affectivity) which we share with other species. Finally, at the level of phylogenetic explanation, S.J. Gould[57] and others have shown how the concept of natural selection can be used in the explanation of human origins (as with other species) without in any way denying the specificity and distinctiveness of human powers and potentials. The notion that biological modifications which are adaptive may bring in their wake a train of consequences which are non-adaptive in evolutionary terms is an important concept for this strategy.

3

The Social Life of Animals and the Philosophy of Animal Rights

I have tried to show that the synthesis of 'naturalism' and 'humanism' proclaimed by Marx in his early writings was, in reality, an unstable combination of two quite incompatible discourses. Taking contemporary concern for the moral status of animals, together with its ontological commitment to human/animal continuity, as my provisional philosophical standpoint, I have tried to show that Marx's moral critique of estranged labour relies upon a human/animal dualism. Not only is this dualism indefensible in its own terms, but it contradicts the naturalistic view of human nature and prospects which Marx requires for his critique of idealist philosophies of history. I have begun to say something about how the naturalistic side of Marx's thinking might be elaborated in ways which would avoid both animal/human dualism and biological reductionism. My hope is that such a naturalistic view might be further developed in ways which would sustain both a positive view of the moral status of non-human animals and an intellectual justification for the deeper end of ecological politics.

So far, however, I have addressed primarily the ontological, rather than the directly moral or normative and evaluative aspects of these questions. I have suggested that Marx's human/animal dualism took a form which limited the critical force of the concept of estrangement. If, under regimes of private property, humans live a merely animal existence, what space is left for a critique of the condition of animals themselves under regimes of private property?

> Factory methods and equipment vary from species to species, but the principles are the same: to keep costs down and to manipulate animals' productivity upward. These principles ensure that factory animals are crowded, restricted, stressed, frustrated, held in barren environments and maintained on additive-laced, unnatural diets. ... Veal factories are perhaps the harshest of all the confinement systems. Newly born calves are taken from their mothers and turned into anaemic neurotic animals to provide the luxury-grade 'milk-fed' veal preferred by gourmet

cooks and fancy restaurants. The young calves, stressed by separation from their mothers, are placed in narrow wooden stalls, lined up row on row in the confinement buildings. For between fourteen and sixteen weeks each calf is confined to a space scarcely larger than its own body and is often tied at the neck to restrict movement further. The calf is fed only 'milk replacer', a liquid mixture of dried milk products, starch, fats, sugar, antibiotics and other additives. The milk replacer is deficient in iron to induce anaemia – a necessary condition if the producer's calves are to have flesh white enough to fetch the market price for 'prime' veal. No hay or other roughage is permitted, for that too might darken the flesh.[1]

Production regimes such as these impose massive constraints and distortions on the mode of life of species of non-human animals caught up in them. Their lives are sustained solely to serve purposes external to them, conditions and means for the acquisition and exercise of their species-powers are denied to them, and, more specifically, their social needs and capacities are systematically denied and suppressed. In short a good deal of the content of Marx's contrast between a fulfilled or emancipated human life, and a dehumanized, estranged existence can also be applied in an analysis of the conditions imposed by intensive rearing regimes in the case of non-human animals. But the 'humanist' philosophical framing of Marx's concept of estrangement renders extension of that analysis beyond the human case literally unthinkable. This form of 'humanism' conceptualizes the needs of animals as instinctual and fixed in a way which simply leaves no room for a morally significant difference to emerge between mere existence and thriving, or living well. No space is allowed for concepts of harm, suffering, stress, enjoyment or benefit sufficiently rich to render applicable to animals the range of moral considerations paradigmatically employed within the sphere of human social relationships.

What I have yet to show is how, suitably elaborated, a naturalistic view of both humans and non-human animals and their conditions of life might sustain both the critical moral standpoint inherent in Marx's denunciation of human self-estrangement and its appropriate extension to non-human beings who, through their 'incorporation' into forms of human social life, are subjected to directly comparable forms of impoverishment, fragmentation and distortion in their modes of life. The starting point for my attempt at a response to this challenge will be to address, more directly than I have so far done, the prevailing non-Marxian ways of considering the moral status of non-human animals. I shall try to show that the ontological naturalism – the human/animal continuism – presupposed in such arguments can yield insights, and help to resolve deep ambiguities in socialist moral theory. Symmetrically, I shall try to show, the Marxian insistence upon the causal importance and moral significance of specific and historically transformable structures of social relationships exposes important limitations in the form of naturalistic thinking presupposed in the non-Marxist literature, and can offer its own distinctive positive insights into the moral status of animals and how it might be changed. My claim is, in other words, that both socialist moral thinking and the concern for the well-being of non-human animals can benefit significantly by being put into critical relationship with one another.

The relatively recent emergence of a radical politics centred on opposition to maltreatment of non-human animals can be understood as one response to an increasingly sharp cultural contradiction of urban-industrial capitalism. The associated emergence of an academic philosophical literature concerned with the moral status of animals is also stimulated by, but does not always adequately address this cultural contradiction. To set the politics and philosophy of the animal liberation, rights and welfare movements in their cultural and socio-economic contexts, it will be necessary to offer an account of the part played by non-human animals in the various forms of human social life. The account I will offer is brief, but it is intended to illustrate several features of our relationship to non-human animal species that will play a significant part in the later stages of my argument.

Animals in Society

There is strong evidence of the domestication of a number of wild animal species by human communities in the Americas, the Middle East and South East Asia from as early as 7,500 to 12,000 years ago. The archaeological evidence from the Middle East has been most prolific and the most commented on. The discovery of animal bones in the vicinity of human remains is, of course, no evidence of domestication, though it is reasonable to conjecture that the evolutionary histories of humans and some wild species such as wolves, cats, mice, pigs and sheep may have been intertwined long before domestication in the full sense of the word. Domestication in the sense of deliberate segregation of sub-populations of a wild species, associated with human regulation of their social life, food supply, territorial organization, and, most significantly, reproductive activity,[2] seems first to have been achieved in the Middle East some 12,000 years ago. The evidence for this is the discovery of canine skeletal remains which differ in ways characteristic of domestication from the ancestral wolf populations.

The evidence from excavations at Jericho and elsewhere in the Middle East suggests an increasing scale of human settlements (involving 2,000 or more people), combined with the first evidence of cereal cultivation around 10,000 years ago. Over the next thousand years or so, an increasingly arid climate (combined, possibly, with over-hunting) led to a decline in populations of wild game animals. This was associated, over the same time-span, with a consolidation of cereal agriculture and the first clear evidence of domestication of sheep and goats, and then cattle and pigs. In other parts of the world, and probably somewhat later, other species, such as members of the camel family (camel, dromedary, llama, alpaca), the yak and the water buffalo were also brought into domestication.

It is significant, however, that only relatively few species of non-human animals have been successfully domesticated. Clutton-Brock sets out six conditions which must be met for full domestication to be possible, among which the most significant are 'hardiness' (or adaptability to the artificial conditions of their new environment), a social structure which enables the animals to be brought under human leadership or dominance, and that they should be capable of breeding freely under conditions of captivity.[3] In view of this, it is perhaps less surprising that so few species have been subject to domestication. However, for those species which have, it is worth noting the extent to which either *similarities* to humans with respect to sociality, behavioural adaptability, and forms of communication, or interdependence with human populations with respect to ecological conditions of existence (or both) are preconditions of domestication – not simply consequences of it.

Clutton-Brock[4] emphasizes the 'primary function' of captive animals as 'itinerant larders', but she also mentions the common practice of hand-rearing the young of wild animals among contemporary hunting-and-gathering peoples, and there is widespread evidence of the non-utilitarian presence of animals in ancient civilizations. Most famously, of course, the cat was considered a sacred animal in Ancient Egypt. It was forbidden to kill cats, but when they died they were embalmed and buried. Clutton-Brock tells us that so many of these mummified remains were excavated at the beginning of this century that they were shipped back to England to be ground up for agricultural fertilizer.[5] The somewhat extreme fluctuation in human cultural valuations of the domestic cat is confirmed by the intensely debated sixteenth-century Parisian practice of cat-burning.[6] In the Pope-burning processions during the reign of Charles II, Keith Thomas tells us 'it was the practice to stuff the burning effigies with live cats so that their screams might add dramatic effect'.[7]

This suggests that any attempt to review the relations between human societies and non-human animals which focused on the mere fact of convenient meat-eating would be grossly reductive. So, as a preliminary way of contextualizing my discussion of the conditions of emergence of contemporary concern with the moral status of animals, I offer a provisional classification of the parts that may be played by animals in human social life. The emphasis is on the range of human needs or wants which animals may meet, or be used to meet (I have refrained from asking the interesting and potentially very instructive reverse question as to the parts humans play in the lives – including the social lives – of other animal species). I distinguish nine broad, and to some extent overlapping, categories of human/animal relationships:

1. The use of animals to replace or augment human labour. The primary characteristics of animals which render them useful as a source of labour include muscular strength, stamina, obedience and psychological reliability. Various uses of such animals as horses and donkeys, camels and oxen to pull heavy objects, to carry heavy weights over long distances, to drive lifting or pumping machinery and so on will serve as typical examples. But animals are also trained to work for humans in other, more complex and sophisticated ways. Guide-dogs and sheep-dogs illustrate this. In cases like these, the non-human animals involved have to learn to co-ordinate their activities with those of humans by means of the interpretation of behavioural and linguistic cues, but also are required to act relatively autonomously within an overall purposive framework which they must comprehend to some considerable degree.

2. The use of animals to meet human bodily, or organic needs. The most obvious case here is the use of animals as a direct source of food. This may, as usually with meat-consumption, require that the animal be killed. Alternatively, as with the use of milk, milk-products or eggs, animals may be kept alive for these purposes. Clothing and shelter are further bodily needs which are, in many cultures, met by using materials drawn from animals. Animal skins and furs are the most obvious such materials and, again, these uses may or may not (as, for example, in the case of sheep's wool) involve killing the animal. Some cultures use animal materials – especially bones – for tools, weapons and vessels. Animal products are also used as ancillary materials in food production – as fertilizer or animal-feed, for example. Finally, there is the widespread and deeply controversial practice of using animals in bio-medical experimentation – in testing drugs or studying the aetiology of human diseases.

3. The use of animals as a source of entertainment. A large range of activities (with widely differing moral and social significance) fall within this category. Some, such as badger-baiting, bull-fighting and dog-fighting, it is fairly uncontroversial to say, involve extreme cruelty. Hunting of deer, foxes, hares and other wild or semi-wild animals, together with activities such as fishing, are conducted in some cultures as a means of meeting bodily needs, but also feature in modern agricultural/industrial societies as sporting activities,

engaged in for pleasure rather than for food. Animals are, of course, often used to assist the hunt, as well as being the quarry. Horse- and dog-racing, like circuses, involve the use of animals for entertainment, but they do not, or do not generally, require the killing of the animal involved, and the degree of cruelty or harm inflicted upon the animals used is a matter of controversy. Zoos, nature reserves and wildlife books, films and programmes also come into this category, but in these cases, animals are simply observed and enjoyed.

4. A closely related set of uses, which might be called 'edificatory', to some extent overlap with the above. As well as being entertained by wildlife films, or zoos we may – and the current trend is to emphasize this aspect – learn from them. The growth of the sciences of animal ethology and ecology since the second World War has involved extensive field-observation of non-human animal communities in natural or semi-natural habitats. Verbal description has to a significant extent been displaced or complemented by visual representation on film in ways which have provided researchers in these specialisms with a direct mass audience for their research which is perhaps unparalleled in any other field of science. Of course, questions can and should be raised about the conceptualization and editing of these studies, and the ideological connotations inherent in their popular presentation in the communications media. Frequently the 'message' of these presentations is the drawing of generally tendentious parallels between human cultural practices and the behaviour patterns of the species represented.[8] Despite all this, however, there can be no doubt that today's mass viewing public in the West has regular access to sources of understanding of principles of ecology and an appreciation of the social and psychological complexity of non-human animals which does have a genuine cognitive and educative content. The keeping of animals as pets, at home and at school, arguably, also has a significant educative role for children who learn to recognize and acknowledge a responsibility for the needs and well-being of other sentient beings.

5. Many of the animal-involving human activities listed in the above categories may also, in societies dominated by the institutions of private property and market exchange, take the form of a commercial exploitation of non-human animals. Animals as sources of work, food, entertainment and edification may also be animals as sources of profit. This is worth inclusion as a category of uses in its own right since, as the earlier brief mention of 'factory' farming makes clear, the superimposition of commercial requirements upon activities involving the use of animals may have very significant material effects on the form taken by those practices. There are, too, specific uses of animals which arise as a direct consequence of commercial relations and pressures. The experimental use of captive animals in the safety-testing

of new commodity lines such as cosmetics, novelty food products and, indeed, in many categories of health products where these are subject to commercial considerations are important and sharply controversial examples.

6. In many societies, and clearly associated with institutions of private property and state power, animals are used in the coercive maintenance of social order, and in the physical protection of both domestic and commercial property: 'sniffer' dogs, police dogs and horses, guard-dogs and so on serve as examples here. In several of these examples, the capacity of non-human animals to physically harm or terrorize humans is crucial to their use, while in all cases these uses of animals presuppose antagonistic human social relations.

7. Though species of non-human animals such as dogs and cats have a very long history as commensals of human communities, it is arguable that their specific status as domestic pets is much more historically and culturally localized. Keith Thomas, for example, lays considerable emphasis on the historical emergence and establishment of domestic pet-keeping in Britain in the sixteenth and seventeenth centuries as 'a normal feature of the middle class household, especially in the towns, where animals were less likely to be functional necessities and where an increasing number of people could afford to support creatures lacking any productive value'.[9] Thomas may well be right in identifying the historical emergence of a distinctive cultural practice of what he calls 'obsessive pet-keeping', but there is, equally, considerable evidence of non-utilitarian human associations with animals, which have much of the affective character of modern Western pet-keeping, both in ancient civilizations and among contemporary non-Western peoples.[10] However, in the paradigm of modern Western pet-keeping the utility of domestic pets – for personal or property protection, as elements in status-displays, as scavengers or 'mousers', and so on – is of marginal significance. Much more central is their place as members of a household, as partners in quasi-personal or familial relationships. Pets are named, assigned identities, acknowledged to have a range of bodily and affective needs, and to be capable of reciprocity in affective bonds and in communicative interaction.

Their well-being is acknowledged to be an object of direct moral obligation on the part of human members of the household and may, indeed, be acknowledged in the form of legal requirements by the wider society. The association between children and pets is an important one, both in the part played by pet animals in the moral and affective development of children themselves, and in the part arguably played by animals as child-surrogates in the lives of many adults. That non-human animals can play these significant parts in the personal lives of humans serves to draw attention to the quality and sophistication attainable in non-verbal communication between species, and also (from a human point of view) the high degree of satisfaction of the need for emotional support and companionship to be found in relationships with non-human animals.

8. Although I have not emphasized it, there is no doubt a symbolic place occupied by domestic pets in the household: they may be valued for what they represent as well as for what they are. This is an instance of the universal cultural practice of using animals as a means of thought, as symbols.[11] Forces of good and evil, the emotions, types of human character, natural forces and processes, objects of worship and structural units of human societies may all be defined in terms of, and represented in, the forms of non-human animal species. These forms of representation are arguably more central to the cultures of many non-Western, 'traditional' societies but, as Mary Midgley has eloquently shown, animal metaphors continue to play a significant part in our thinking about ourselves in modern Western societies.[12] Indeed, the intense interest in, and mass popularity of, films and programmes about animal behaviour has much, as I suggested above, to do with their use as resources for thinking about the human character and social relations.[13] The ubiquitous presence of animal characters in children's literature, the popularity of cartoon animations, and the use of animals in advertising are all so many testimonies to the continuing symbolic importance of animals in our culture.

It is, however, important to keep our feet on the ground. A fusion of the interpretive methods of cultural anthropology with recent 'discourse' or language-centred approaches to the social sciences takes some writers to the point of reducing all social relations to their symbolic aspect. Keith Tester, for example, explicitly advocates a 'blank paper' view of animals, according to which all our relations with them must be interpreted as expressions of our own historically formed symbolic practices, and all our thinking about them as displaced or concealed modes of thought about ourselves:

> Mary Midgley believed that a fish is always a fish but she was wrong. A fish is only a fish if it is socially classified as one, and that classification is only concerned with fish to the extent that scaly things living in the sea help society define itself. After all, the very word 'fish' is a product of the imposition of socially produced categories on nature. Writers like Lorenz, Wilson, and Midgley are wrong; animals are indeed a blank paper which can be inscribed with any message, and symbolic meaning, that the social wishes.[14]

I am tempted, here, to parody Marx's comments about the man who, believing gravity to be a product of human consciousness, felt himself to be sublimely proof against drowning. Perhaps, if we were to impose the socially produced category of fish upon the viper its bite would lose its venom? Of course, views like Tester's, daft as they are, are currently very fashionable among intellectuals. But I do not propose to provide a sustained philosophical analysis of these views here.[15]

9. My final category of human/animal social relationship is one which by definition would seem to be the very denial of any such relationship: this is the category or relation of 'wildness'. In one obvious sense, of course, 'wildness' *is* a social relation. A whole series of symbolic connotations attaches to the description 'wild': a liberty of action and expression, a carefree and dangerous libidinal abandon, unrestrained by the burdens and disciplines of civilized existence, or unaffected by the degeneracy, enfeeblement and dependency of domestication and regulated existence. Some of these themes were, indeed, constitutive of the pioneering ethological work of Konrad Lorenz, in which they bore a close relationship to the Nazi preoccupation with the causes of the rise and decline of civilizations.[16]

But, independently of these symbolic connotations, the existence of populations of animal species in the wild prior to incorporation into human social practices is a precondition for those practices. In most cases, where domesticated animals have a prolonged history of human use, significant genetic alterations, brought about by generations of selective breeding, differentiate them from the wild stock from which they were drawn. In some important cases (for example, the progenitor of domestic cattle, *bos primigenius*) that wild stock has subsequently ceased to exist.[17] But, for the overwhelming majority of animal species (even if we confine ourselves to the extremely narrow meaning implicitly given to the word 'animal', as 'mammal', in much of the animal-rights literature) there exists no such history of direct entwinement of their lives and fate with that of human societies – at most they may figure as potential sources of food for humans, as 'competitors' for common sources of food, or as objects of curiosity or amusement. So, what of the 'wild' animals which are sometimes hunted for fun or food, captured for display in zoos and circuses, filmed in their most intimate moments for vast human audiences, or of the many more which simply live out their lives unrecognizing and unrecognized by their human kin?

Some – the animal liberationists – within the radical politics of animal welfare think of 'the wild' in this sense as the proper place for all non-human animals: the 'liberation' of domesticated and 'captured' populations consists precisely in returning them to 'the wild', evacuating them from the sphere of human social power and domination. One feature of human/animal social relationships which is often overlooked on this perspective is the extent to which non-human animal species have, over long periods of time, become adapted to conditions of life provided by human social activity. This applies both to domesticated species and to non-domesticated species such as rats, mice, house-sparrows, head-lice and so on which are, in a sense, our uninvited guests. This is one aspect of the ecological interdependence between humans and many species of non-human animal species. In this respect 'the wild' is already present in the interstices of human social life itself: from the standpoint of those species whose habitat our social practices have become, we constitute part of the order of nature.

Symmetrically, 'the wild' itself, nature beyond the confines of human social power, the proper repository of 'wild' animals, is by now at most a fragile and marginal presence. This is the outcome of two distinct but intertwined global historical processes. First, the global spread of human populations, and with them the ecological transformations brought by their pastoral, agricultural and urban industrial activities. Wherever life-sustaining physico-chemical conditions exist on the land surface of the globe and in the seas, rivers and lakes, natural habitats have been subjected to transformation by direct human intentional activity, or have been affected to some degree by the unintended consequences (climate changes, changes in the circulation of energy or nutrients, entry of toxic substances into food-chains, and so on) of those intended transformations. Perhaps the only organisms unaffected by these global ecosystem changes are those deep oceanic forms which have persisted largely unaffected by the major environmental fluctuations which have long shaped evolutionary change among terrestrial and more superficial aquatic life-forms.

These processes are not uniform in their impact across the globe or with respect to different biotopes. Huge areas of rain-forest, and patches of temperate 'wild wood' remain relatively unaffected by deliberate human interventions or by their ecological impacts. Is it not reasonable to continue to think of these as 'wild' places? Here we encounter the second global historical process – the appropriation of areas of land-surface or oceanic zones as private property, as territorial acquisition by nation-states, or as objects of contractual agreement for purposes of extraction or appropriation rights between nation-states. In this sense the whole biosphere comes within the scope of human social relations and institutions. To the extent that relatively unaffected natural habitats remain, they are nevertheless either the objects of as-yet-unexercised rights to exploit them or are objects of forms of conventional or juridical protection from such interference. Either way, they are properly considered as within the domain of the social, considered as a normative order of powers, rights and obligations.

In these important respects, then, non-human animal populations in 'the wild' already stand in social relations with human populations and are affected by human social practices, by way of human socially-established powers with respect to, and impacts upon, their environmental conditions of life. To the extent that we may still speak of 'wild' populations of non-human animals the term must refer to populations which are not domesticated, but which nevertheless survive in habitats either maintained deliberately for this purpose (for example, nature reserves, conservation zones), or maintained for other purposes but contingently providing habitat requirements for such populations (for example, much 'semi-natural' farmland and forest), or in habitats not (yet) significantly modified by human uses (for example, terrain not yet technically utilizable, or not yet profitably so).

This brief survey of the diversity of relations between humans and non-human animals illustrates five main considerations which have a significant bearing upon our discussion of the moral status of animals:

1. Humans and animals stand in social relationships to one another. This is so obvious, it might be thought hardly worth saying. But it has consequences of the utmost importance. It implies that non-human animals are in part *constitutive* of human societies – any adequate specification of societies as structures of social relationship or interaction must include reference to non-human animals as occupants of social positions and as terms in social relationships.

2. These social relationships between human and non-human occupants of social positions are very diverse in their character. This is true both with regard to the geographical and historical diversity of instantiated forms of human society and with respect to any specific society.

3. The social relationships which bind humans and animals, and regulate their interactions, are not trivial, or marginal, but quite central in their causal importance (and potentially, therefore, in their moral significance).

4. Humans and animals are *socially* interdependent. Just as the conditions of life and opportunities for development and fulfilment of human individuals are subject to change as a consequence of changes in the patterns of social relations to which they are bound, the same may properly be said of the non-human animals who likewise occupy positions in changeable patterns of human social relations.

5. Humans and non-human animals are *ecologically* interdependent. In part, this point is simply a further elaboration of the previous one. Animals may have their conditions of life altered by changes in human social practices precisely because of the ecological effects of those social changes. But, reciprocally, it is important to recognize the extent to which humans are dependent both for survival and for their well-being upon other species of animals. These other species of animals are, therefore, components in the

ecology of the human species itself. In some respects, and for some non-human animal species, humans and animals share common conditions of life. Some populations of non-human animals are dependent upon non-interference by humans in their habitats, while others (for example, both domesticated and 'wild' inhabitants of semi-natural and 'artificial' habitats) may be dependent on regular and sustained human intervention (habitat maintenance – 'ecoregulation').

Animals and Ethics

As might be expected from the sheer diversity of forms taken by human/animal relationships, the sources, objects and intensities of moral concerns about their well-being are enormously varied. It is also the case, as we shall see, that the moral traditions which give articulation to these concerns are also diverse, and variously adequate to the task. Two groups of practices which arouse the most severe censure are intensive stock rearing ('factory' farming) and animal experimentation. In the case of the first, as we have seen, animals are kept in conditions which impose extreme restrictions on physical movement and severely dislocate and suppress their social and affective requirements. They are fed on unnatural diets, and are subjected to hormone treatments which alter their developmental rhythms. High emotional stress and decreased resistance to disease necessitate further treatments, such as extensive use of antibiotics.

These systematic abuses of animals arouse moral concern in their own right, but it is also worth noting that there are important consequences for human health and well-being. General environmental pollution arises from unresolved problems of waste-disposal from intensive units, and from the stimulation of antibiotic-resistant strains of micro-organisms. Direct risks to human health arising from consumption of meat produced in this way – involuntary consumption of hormones, antibiotics and other chemical additives, and the risk of infectious diseases 'jumping' between species, and so on – are increasingly widely recognized. Less fully recognized are the health implications of human dietary distortions encouraged by the marketing strategies of a politically powerful and highly monopolized meat production, processing and marketing industry.[18]

The second major object of moral concern is the use of animals for experimental purposes.[19] Some experiments involve surgical removal of vital organs, including sections of the brain and central nervous system, systematic administering of electric shocks or toxic chemicals, and so on. Extreme and prolonged physical pain and psychological distress are undoubtedly suffered by very large numbers of animals used as experimental subjects. This suffering itself is enough to evoke moral outrage on the part of animal rights and welfare campaigners. For many of them the imposition of such suffering is a moral wrong, quite independently of the aims of the experimenters or any beneficial consequences which might flow from their work. In the wider public debate, however, the distinction between experiments which might contribute to the cure of life-threatening human diseases and ones used to serve arguably less commendable human purposes, such as safety-testing of new cosmetic products, would be widely held to be morally significant.

There are, of course, other animal-related human activities which evoke moral outrage, political mobilization and direct action. Actions against hunting, and other 'cruel sports', against seal-culling and whaling, against the fur and ivory trades, and also against the use of animals in circuses and zoos, all have dedicated bands of supporters and periodically achieve a high media profile. But here, again, the sources of moral concern are diverse. Sometimes, as in the cases of experimentation and intensive stock-rearing, the emphasis is upon the suffering imposed on the animals. This is often, but not always, complemented by considerations of the relative triviality or outright moral unacceptability of the human desires satisfied or purposes served by the activity. The status as 'luxury' goods of some targeted animal products (fur and ivory, especially) connotes not only relative triviality, but also is often given a class significance. Similarly, in the British context, direct action against fox-hunting, a traditional sport of the landed upper-classes, is widely supported, while action against angling, a predominantly working-class pleasure, is relatively rarely contemplated.[20]

The literature of such campaigning groups frequently pays attention to the motivations of those who inflict suffering on animals. In such sports as dog- or bull-fighting the fact that the humans involved take pleasure in the suffering of non-human animals has a moral significance over and above the mere causing of suffering.[21] Further, in the opposition to zoos and the uses of animals in circuses there emerges a broader concept of harm and well-being in relation to animals, to some extent detached from a mere acknowledge-ment of their capacity for pain and suffering. The degradation and distortion of its natural mode of life imposed on a circus-animal which has been trained to perform 'tricks' for human amusement can be considered a morally unacceptable harm, even if it cannot be shown that the animal suffers psychological or physical pain. Finally, for campaigns such as those against whaling and the fur and ivory trades, a significant part is played in the public debate by considerations as to the relative rarity and vulnerability of the species of animal concerned. The implication here is that the extinction of a species has a moral significance of its own, over and above concern for the pain, suffering or death of individuals of the species.

Those relationships between humans and animals least likely to evoke moral concern on behalf of animals include, paradigmatically, the keeping of animals as domestic pets, but also the deliberate setting aside of habitat for 'wild' species, many educational uses of animals (especially ecological and ethological study of 'wild' populations), and, for some purposes at least, the retention of captive populations of animals in zoos. But here a new set of moral issues arises. The incorporation of animals into these social practices as such may not be found objectionable. Rather, the consequences for animals when things go wrong within these practices may be a matter of widespread moral concern. Pets, for example, may be subjected to deliberate cruelty, but also, and perhaps more commonly, may become victims of mere indifference and neglect. Detached from environmental conditions in which animals are able to act autonomously in meeting their needs and acquiring and exercising their species-powers, they are dependent on humans to provide substitutes for the environmental conditions and/or to directly meet the needs concerned. The well-being and even survival of these animals depend on continuing practical acknowledgement and provision on the part of the humans responsible for them. In these instances, moral concern on behalf of the animals involved takes the form not of a demand that humans be prevented from harming animals but, rather, that they be required or enabled to fulfil positive responsibilities to them.

Where positive action is required to sustain the life or well-being of non-human animals, whether directly as in the case of captive animals or domestic pets, or indirectly as in the case of habitat management or protection for 'wild' species, moral issues arise in relation to the rights and interests of the humans who are required to act in ways they would not otherwise do, to abandon traditional ways of life, or to forgo opportunities for economic development. Much of the opposition to animal rights and to environmentalists draws powerfully on the perception of a conflict of interests between humans and animals, or, sometimes, a conflict of priorities between the defenders of animal interests or rights, and the defence of human interests in 'development', economic growth or standards of living. Sometimes such arguments can reasonably be dismissed as spurious special pleading on behalf of economic and political interests, and often, as I have suggested above, a good case can be made for a community of interests between (some) animal populations and (some) social categories of humans. Nevertheless, it would be absurd to suppose that occasions never arise in which, for those who recognize non-human animals as bearers of interests and rights, those interests and rights directly conflict with human interests and rights. Any serious consideration of the moral status of animals would be required to provide a coherent framework for thinking through such dilemmas.

Modernity and the Moral Status of Animals

Now it is possible to begin to specify the 'cultural contradiction' which I mentioned as an underlying condition of the emergence of our contemporary moral concern about animals. I recently watched a television programme in which peasant farmers in (what was then) the Soviet Union were interviewed about their recollections of the period of Stalin's rule. Apparently incidentally, and as a backdrop to the main theme of the programme, one of the interviewees, an old peasant woman, stood in her farmyard, calling her hens, and feeding them as she did so. Suddenly she reached out and deftly caught one of them. Still talking to it, she carried it out to another part of the yard and slit its throat. 'And that's the end of you', she said, as it died in her hands. Very few of us in urban-industrial societies, whether we eat meat or not, are actually called upon to kill our fellow sentient beings. Without prior 'desensitizing' it is quite likely that many, if not most of us would find it difficult to overcome the powerful inhibitions against doing so. This would be particularly so if we had cared for and nurtured the animal, and recognized it as an individual with its own subjective life (this is graphically illustrated by the old peasant woman's almost compulsive talking to the chicken as she killed it). How many pet-owners could contemplate slitting the throat of Fido to satisfy however desperate a hunger?

Yet, the great majority of the populations of the urban-industrial countries *are* meat-eaters, and massive industrial and commercial businesses meet the demand for animal products through intensive rearing regimes, industrial processing and mass-marketing. Unlike our peasant ancestors, the immense majority of us have no experience remotely comparable to that of the Russian peasant woman. As meat-eaters, we purchase meat as a commodity, processed, cut up, packaged and re-named in ways which set us as consumers at a safe distance from any recognition of our purchase as the carcase of a once-sentient being. Our position in a complex division of labour further sets us apart from any direct involvement in the labour-processes by which these products arrive on the supermarket shelves, and, moreover, those who are involved in these labour-processes have an involvement quite different from that of traditional peasant 'husbandry'. Intensive stock rearing is adopted in part *because* it reduces and de-skills human practical involvement, and the human labour which continues to be required takes forms which specifically exclude the establishment of any quasi-personal, subject-to-subject relationship to the 'processed' animals.

In this central dimension of our relation to non-human animals, they are subjected to an intensified reification, a systematic exclusion from recognition as beings with a subjective life, or sentience, let alone interests or rights.

At the same time, the practice of including domestic pets as members of households, as companions, as partners in reciprocal, if asymmetrical, quasi-personal relationships has also grown to a near-universal cultural ideal. These widespread practical experiences of subject-to-subject relations with non-human animals are reinforced and complemented by the pervasiveness of media representations of animals which emphasize their sociality and, in many cases, psychological complexity. The co-presence, within contemporary Western cultures, of central socio-economic practices which reify animals and of pervasive cultural forms and representations which assign them quasi-personal status forms the basis of an acute cultural contradiction.

This contradiction can be seen as the outcome of a long-run historical process, earlier phases of which are insightfully described by Keith Thomas. Thomas notes that the dominant theological teaching of the medieval and early modern periods maintained a strict separation of 'man' and nature, but that popular attitudes and practices nowhere corresponded to this. Though that earlier period abounded with what would now be recognized as abominable cruelties to non-human animals, there was also an intimacy and interconnection between humans and animals (wild and domesticated) which it is now hard to comprehend. In many parts of Britain humans and animals ate and slept under the same roof, and, according to Thomas, it was not until the sixteenth and seventeenth centuries that the farmhouse became an exclusively human residence, displacing the 'long-house' which combined both house and byre, with only a low wall separating humans and animals. As he puts it, 'In many ways ... domestic beasts were subsidiary members of the human community, bound by mutual self-interest to their owners, who were dependent on their fertility and wellbeing.'[22]

The growth of towns and of industry in the early modern period undermined this familiarity as a part of the common texture of life, but it did not result (as Tester seems to argue) in an unqualified detachment of the urban population from animals. Not only, as Thomas shows, were urban settlements also teeming with animals, but also new and, if anything, more distinctively sympathetic bonds between humans and animals were in formation in the new urban, and especially middle-class, setting. The urban population (or, rather, significant social categories within it) was increasingly detached not from animals as such, but from direct involvement in the utilitarian and exploitative side of our relationship to them. New patterns of residence, patterns of class relations and occupational divisions of labour facilitated the rise and consolidation of primarily affective and non-utilitarian relations with 'unnecessary' animals, most especially in the practice of pet-keeping. This latter practice:

> Encouraged the middle classes to form optimistic conclusions about animal intelligence; it gave rise to innumerable anecdotes about animal sagacity; it stimulated the notion that animals could have character and individual personal-

ity; and it created the psychological foundation for the view that some animals at least were entitled to moral consideration.[23]

There are some inconsistencies in Thomas's account, however. The growth of new sensibilities, and of pressure for legislation in favour of animals in the latter part of the eighteenth century and early nineteenth century may well have been informed by the changed perceptions of animals which were made possible by the widespread practice of pet-keeping. However, as Thomas points out, much of this new concern focused on the treatment of domestic animals which were used for food, transport and other utilitarian purposes. Here, the shift in attitudes may be related to new ways of understanding their economic value as capital or 'stock' which would repay kind and considerate treatment with greater utility.[24] This reservation aside, however, Thomas's characterization of the emerging cultural contradiction which is the condition of possibility for our contemporary concern for the moral status of animals could hardly be bettered:

> The early modern period had thus generated feeling which would make it increasingly hard for men to come to terms with the uncompromising methods by which the dominance of their species had been served. On the one hand they saw an incalculable increase in the comfort and physical well-being or welfare of human beings; on the other they perceived a ruthless exploitation of other forms of animate life. There was thus a growing conflict between the new sensibilities and the material foundations of human society. A mixture of compromise and conceal-ment has so far prevented this conflict from having to be resolved. But the issue cannot be completely evaded and it can be relied upon to recur. It is one of the contradictions upon which modern civilization can be said to rest. About its ultimate consequences we can only speculate.[25]

So far as the prevailing traditions of moral thought are concerned, the pressure to extend moral concern beyond those species currently assigned 'quasi-personal' status to include those species subjected to the most system-atically reifying economic regimes is disruptive, even subversive in its practical implications. But, short of the establishment of some deep ontological gulf between the two groups of species the implications seem hard to evade. The converse strategy, of sustaining moral blindness to the reifying domain, would require us to dismiss two centuries or so of insight into the social and psychological complexity of other species as some form of collective anthro-pomorphic delusion. This is, as we shall see, very close to the position taken by the leading opponents of 'animal liberation'.

It is, I think, illuminating to consider the relatively recent emergence of a radical politics of animal rights and welfare, along with the associated shift of philosophical attention to the question of the moral status of animals, and put it against the background of this cultural contradiction and its various specific expressions. Making the contradiction and the practical dilemmas with which it is associated explicit also provides us with a clearer sense of the practical–political demands which any adequate philosophical view of the moral status of animals would be required to meet.

The Moral Status of Animals: Direct and Indirect Obligations

Modern Western moral philosophy has been almost exclusively centred on the moral character of the actions of human individuals, the moral status of persons, and the ethical legitimacy of human social institutions. On this dominant view, only humans, with their autonomous will, capacity for free action and for rational thought, are capable of acknowledging and acting in accordance with moral principles. Only humans can, on this view, count as moral agents. But this dominant, human-centred approach involves a some-what stronger claim than this. The proper *scope* of moral concerns, too, is to be limited to human moral agents and their acts. Since I want to use the term 'anthropocentric' in a very broad sense to include any moral perspective which takes the human case to be 'central', or paradigmatic, this specific form of anthropocentrism will require its own distinctive label. I hope I will be forgiven the neologism 'anthroposcopism'. Even if the claim that only humans can be moral agents is sustained, it does not follow that only humans can be objects of moral concern. Morality, it may be argued, is not exclusively a matter of how moral agents ought to behave towards each other, but also a matter of how they ought to behave towards the other kinds of being which they encounter in the course of their activities.

We often do acknowledge moral responsibilities with respect to other beings, both living and non-living, natural and artificial (for example, works of art), so that an anthroposcopic moral theory which sought to confine questions of moral obligation to the reciprocal relations between moral agents would appear to be strongly counter-intuitive. There is, however, room for moral obligation with regard to beings which are not moral agents, even within the anthroposcopic perspective. A distinction can be made between direct and indirect obligation. For example, obligations with regard to non-human animals are not direct obligations *to* them, but should be analysed and justified as indirect obligations to moral agents whose interests or rights might be affected by the ways animals are treated. So, I have an obligation not to kick your dog, not because it would be in itself wrong to treat the animal in this way, but because my doing so would be an offence against *your* rights, as owner of the dog (you may claim, as owner, exclusive rights to kick it!).

I will ignore, for the moment, the question of whether we can reasonably be said to have direct obligations with regard to non-living beings, and to non-conscious living beings. I'll follow the American philosopher Tom Regan[26] in concentrating my attention on non-human animal species which possess relatively sophisticated psychological powers and needs. Regan's argument that we do, indeed, have direct duties to at least this class of non-human beings has five main stages. First, Regan points out that not all humans are moral agents. Young children and severely mentally 'enfeebled' humans may be incapable of recognizing moral principles, or of orienting their actions in relation to them, yet they may still have psychological capacities sufficient to ground notions of 'experiential interests' and have the capacity for harm or benefit from the actions of moral agents. Second, he advances, as a valid moral principle, that moral agents have a *prima facie* duty not to harm other individuals, and that this duty is owed to the individuals themselves. Third, since both human moral agents and such beings as young children and the mentally enfeebled are alike in their capacity for harm or benefit from the actions of moral agents, it would be arbitrary, and therefore unjust, to exclude humans who fail to count as moral agents from the scope of the harm principle. Though not themselves moral agents, humans such as young children and the mentally enfeebled are properly regarded as coming within the scope of the moral responsibilities of humans who are. They are, in Tom Regan's terms, 'moral patients'.

The fourth step in the argument is the claim that at least some non-human animals can be harmed or benefited by the actions of human moral agents in ways not different in kind from the ways in which human moral patients and, indeed, human moral agents, themselves, may be harmed or benefited. In connection with the lives of these animals, it must, if this claim is to be sustained, be appropriate to make distinctions between mere survival and living well, suffering and satisfaction:

> To live well is to have a life that is characterised by the harmonious satisfaction of one's desires, purposes and the like, taking account of one's biological, social and psychological interests. More generally, animals (and humans) live well relative to the degree to which (1) they pursue and obtain what they prefer, (2) they take satisfaction in pursuing and obtaining what they prefer, and (3) what they prefer and obtain is in their interests.[27]

There are some difficulties in this characterization of living well, not least the circularity in Regan's definition which is in part in terms of the concept of interests which is itself defined in terms of living well. Nevertheless, there is much to be said in favour of Regan's account, and I shall proceed on the assumption that this logical difficulty is surmountable. Clearly, to be a being capable of living well, or failing to do so, on Regan's account, is also to be a being with a range of complex psychological powers and dispositions. Regan's thesis is that there are at least some non-human animals which both possess these attributes and are able to live well or fail to do so:

> Perception, memory, desire, belief, self-consciousness, intention, a sense of the future – these are among the leading attributes of the mental life of normal mammalian animals aged one or more. Add to this list the not unimportant categories of emotion (e.g. fear and hatred) and sentience, understood as the capacity to experience pleasure and pain, and we begin to approach a fair rendering of the mental life of these animals.[28]

Leaving aside the seeming arbitrariness of Regan's reference to the chronological age of his chosen animal taxon, the questions arise: do we know, and how do we know that animals have these sophisticated psychological attributes? Regan himself offers what he concedes is an inconclusive 'cumulative argument'. Belief that animals have these attributes is, he claims, in accordance with both common sense and ordinary language. But neither fact provides sufficient reason for accepting the belief as true, as Regan recognizes. For Regan, however, the burden of proof is on those who advocate a revision of common sense or ordinary language, to show that it is rationally ill-founded. Attempts at mechanistic or behaviourist re-description of animal activities have, argues Regan, never carried rational conviction: they have yet to give us sound reasons for abandoning common-sense ways of thinking and talking about animals as conscious, purposive beings. These common-sense ways of thinking and talking get further support from evolutionary theory, the explanatory scheme of which makes it unlikely to suppose that consciousness might offer selective advantage to one species, ourselves, but not to any of our evolutionary relatives.

This step in Regan's argument is, of course, quite decisive, and accordingly is at least as widely contested in the critical literature as his more specifically moral arguments. Since my reservations about Regan's position have more to do with the character of his moral theory than with any strong disagreement with his attribution of complex psychological abilities to animals I shall not enter too far into these debates. However, some acknowledgement of the case against non-human animals in this respect is clearly required. An early opponent of the animal-rights case, R.G. Frey,[29] conceded that animals are conscious beings, and that they may properly be said to have needs, but more complex psychological powers may be attributed only to beings capable of using language. Even desires, for example, are peculiar to such beings. Only someone capable of beliefs (for example, that this is a bowl of milk, and that drinking it will satisfy thirst) is capable of desires. Further, for Frey, beliefs are to be analysed as beliefs *that* such and such a sentence is true. Since animals are incapable of language they are incapable of beliefs and, being incapable of beliefs, are incapable of desires.

Regan himself responds to Frey, arguing both that belief is not necessary to desire, and, also, that animals are capable of beliefs. The core of the latter argument is that we frequently attribute beliefs to humans on the basis of pre- or non-verbal behaviour, and do so even in relation to individuals incapable of any language. There is sufficient purchase in the complexity of animals' behavioural responses to the world around them for us to make reliable attributions of beliefs to them, in the absence of their being able to speak.

Frey's position is given a qualified endorsement and is further developed by M.P.T. Leahy.[30] He goes along with the readiness of Frey and others to attribute sentience to animals but is prepared to concede the applicability to them of only a minimal repertoire of psychological concepts. His argument is a complex one, relying primarily (in my opinion excessively) on his reading of the later philosophy of Wittgenstein. Leahy reminds us of Wittgenstein's use of descriptions of 'language games', and their place in 'forms of life' to dispel the erroneous philosophical temptation to think of words like 'desire', 'expect', 'believe', 'hope' as naming, or standing for 'private' inner states of the self, attributable to others only on the basis of some shaky inference from one's own case. We do all kinds of things with words, and using them as names is only one, while words like 'desire', 'expect' and so on refer to capacities to participate in language-games rather than to 'private' mental happenings. As Leahy puts it, later in the argument, 'remorse and hope are linguistic transactions'.[31] Although they 'will occur with accompanying sensations and behaviour' they should not be confused with either.

To oversimplify somewhat, Leahy's case against the attribution of complex psychological powers to non-human animals amounts to this. Such powers are logically bound up with the ability to participate in human-specific linguistic practices. We know from our own case that we often have the characteristic sensations, or may behave as if exercising these powers (believing, hoping, etc.) without actually using language. Confusing the psychological powers with the sensations or non-linguistic behaviours with which they are associated, we are mistakenly tempted to attribute them to non-human animals which are quite incapable of participation in our language-games. Leahy combines this 'Wittgensteinian' argument with support (contra Regan) for behaviouristic and mechanistic re-descriptions of animal behaviour.[32]

Without wishing to endorse what seems to me to be Leahy's rather unquestioning reliance on the authority of Wittgenstein,[33] it is worth questioning Leahy's reading. Regan's argument that non-linguistic belief and understanding are presupposed in the practices whereby young children are able to *acquire* abilities to participate in language-games is, for instance, very much in line with the drift of Wittgenstein's thought, but is rapidly dismissed by Leahy. Similarly, Wittgenstein's concepts of language-game and form of life can plausibly be understood as attempts to draw our attention to the crucial part played by the extra-linguistic context of our uses of language in our ability to make sense of our linguistic transactions themselves. In the concept of 'indexicality' this is, indeed, one of the most pervasive uses of Wittgenstein's later philosophy. Several of the quotations which Leahy carefully assembles from Wittgenstein are at least as plausibly read as asserting, rather than denying, the centrality of non-linguistic behaviour to our capacities for interpreting one another's psychic lives. For example:

> 'Grief' describes a pattern which recurs, with different variations, in the course of our life. If a man's bodily expression of sorrow and of joy alternated, say with the ticking of a clock, here we should not have the characteristic formation of the pattern of sorrow or of the pattern of joy.[34]

Yet, a page later, Leahy is to be found assimilating grief to the 'linguistic transaction' analysis, along with remorse and hope.

Leahy's use of Wittgenstein's notion of language-games is, rather, to promote language-use as a species-specific attribute, cutting off the possibility of any very rich or complex cross-specific understanding. At one point he refers to language as providing 'the context in which we can be said to understand each other'.[35] It would, I think, be closer to the truth (and also closer to Wittgenstein) to say that a shared form of life, a shared natural history, provides the context in which we can use language to understand one another. But to argue, as I am doing, that our non-linguistic expressions, bodily form and physiological requirements form a context without which linguistic understanding would be impossible is not of itself enough to sustain Regan's case for psychological complexity in animals. It is also necessary to show either that enough of that natural history is shared across the species-boundary for comprehension to get a foothold, or that there are sufficient 'bridgeheads' for us to gain a comprehension of the psychic life of species whose behavioural expressions and modes of life are quite different from our own.[36]

Leahy does acknowledge that within definite limits something of the sort is possible. He speaks, symptomatically, of 'pre-linguistic prototypes' for psychological capacities, which in the human case go on to be elaborated and manifested in the full variety of language-games we learn to play. Much of this pre-linguistic heritage is, he considers, shared with other species, to a degree dependent upon our evolutionary relationships. But it does not get us very far in attributing complex psychological abilities to animals. Very elementary states, such as pains, fears and wants can be attributed on the basis of analogies between their natural expression in humans and (some) other animals. But even here, since animals lack the capacity to learn to participate in the more complex human language-games in which these concepts figure in the human case, these uses must be regarded as 'thin', secondary, and parasitic on the paradigmatic uses.[37]

My reply to Leahy's argument here is necessarily abbreviated, but its content may be guessed from what I have said so far in elaboration of the thesis of human/animal continuity. First, it is a mistake to think of non-linguistic expressions as 'pre-linguistic' (as Leahy invariably does), as this suggests that in human communication we can dispense with the non-linguistic once we are elevated to the status of language-user. My rival reading of Wittgenstein, above, was the beginning of an explanation of why this cannot be so. Second, the counterpart to Leahy's over-valuing of language is his under-valuing of the complexity, subtlety and adaptability of non-linguistic communication in both humans and animals. The non-linguistic expressions of other social animals such as dogs and chimpanzees are, like those of humans, not confined to a limited repertoire of 'fixed', 'instinctual', 'natural' patterns (as Leahy suggests) but are taught and learned in the course of infant development, and frequently have a significant conventional element. Unless this were the case, it would be impossible to domesticate social animals in the many ways we do. Third, the use of the word 'prototype', along with Leahy's repeated reference to an evolutionary 'scale', upon which various species are said to be 'higher' or 'lower' suggests that Leahy (interestingly like Regan in this respect) remains implicitly committed to an anachronistic and indefensible version of the 'great chain of being': animal behaviour is 'primitive', 'prototypical' in relation to our more sophisticated step up the scale. This is profoundly misleading in several respects. Most importantly, it cuts Leahy off from the thought that the non-linguistic expressions of other species may play a part in a mode of life which is just different from ours, which may have a complexity and sophistication derived from a divergent evolutionary history and ecological adaptation. This thought is an important one: it may lead us to value the study of animal ethology as a source not just of 'primitive' antecedents of ourselves, but also of resources for extending and enriching our concept of what it is to think, expect, believe, desire or communicate.[38]

Of course, none of this tells against the claim, made by both Leahy and Wittgenstein, that some psychological powers can only be sensibly attributed to beings capable of language. 'There is nothing astonishing about certain concepts only being applicable to a being that e.g. possesses a language.'[39] Animals may coherently be said to have beliefs but not, for example, belief in an omniscient god or the theory of relativity. But neither is this required for the moral case Regan wishes to make. All that is required for this is for some species of non-human animals to have sufficient psychological complexity to allow such distinctions as well-being, suffering, or harm to be applied to them.

Not only is Regan's 'cumulative argument' left intact, but I think the above reflections upon the parts played by animals in human social life allow us to strengthen it. Such activities as the use of animals as working collaborators (sheep-dogs), as companions (domestic pets), as experimental subjects in psychological research presuppose complex and sophisticated psychological abilities and needs on the part of those animals. To participate in such activities (and virtually everyone does, at some point in their lives) while denying that animals are conscious, purposive beings, would commit us to a performative contradiction.

The fifth, and final, step in Regan's attempt to show that human moral agents have direct obligations with regard to non-human animals is his claim that at least some of the latter have the potential to be benefited or harmed by the actions of human moral agents which are not different in kind from those potentials in human moral patients. If the 'harm' principle applies to human moral patients, such as young children and the mentally enfeebled, then we cannot reasonably exclude non-human mammals with the appropriate degree of psychological complexity. Though these animals are not moral agents, and so cannot, for example, be held morally responsible for their actions, they belong, like humans whose agency is as yet undeveloped, or in certain ways impaired, to the category of moral patients.

The Moral Status of Animals: Utility or Rights?

Supposing we are prepared to go this far with Regan (and, with some reservations, I am), we have still not settled some important questions about the moral status of animals. Is the 'species barrier' between ourselves and other species coincident with any morally significant differences (given that not all humans are moral agents)? Just how psychologically complex does an animal have to be to enter the human moral universe by this route? How are conflicts between the interests of animals and humans to be justly resolved? Does an animal's moral status depend in any way on its place in human social practices?

Regan's response to questions such as these is to test out the resources of a range of established moral theories. Most attention is given to two of these – utilitarianism in its various forms, as the main exemplar of consequentialist moral thinking, and 'the rights view' as a deontological perspective, followed by Regan himself. Regan commends utilitarianism for its inclusion of animal well-being within the scope of moral theory, and for its historical record in opposing the abuse of animals. Traditionally, utilitarianism identified the good with pleasure or happiness (hedonistic utilitarianism), but the good may also be equated with the satisfaction of wants (preference utilitarianism).

Since (at least some) non-human animals have wants which may or may not be satisfied, and can experience pleasure and pain, there is no reason, in justice, why their wants, pleasures and pains should be ignored in the calculations undertaken by moral agents in deciding how they should act. Indeed, for utilitarianism, the pleasures and pains of animals count equally with those of humans, right action being defined as that which brings about the maximum aggregate balance of pleasure over pain in the total population (including non-human animals) affected by the (contemplated) action.

A moral theory which apparently allows the interests of animals not only to count, but to count equally with those of humans would appear to offer animals powerful protection from abuse. But Regan's view is that this is not the case and for reasons which also show that utilitarianism cannot offer this even in the human case. The main point is that maximizing the aggregate of pleasures over pains (to consider only hedonistic utilitarianism – the argument works equally well with preference utilitarianism) in a given population of individuals may be achieved by a distribution of pleasures and pains between individuals which inflicts major harms on some for the benefit of the others. There is no reason in principle (though most utilitarians would presumably argue it would not generally be the case in practice) why the utilitarian calculus should not commend an action which gave mild pleasure to a great many individuals as a consequence of torturing a small number of innocents. The outcome of a utilitarian calculation can be radically inegalitarian despite its 'predistributive' egalitarianism. To apply these considerations to non-human animals, there would seem to be nothing, in principle, to rule out on utilitarian grounds the infliction of extreme and prolonged pain on animals so long as the consequences for all affected individuals included a greater balance of pleasure over pain than any other available course of action.

Convinced of the inadequacy of utilitarianism as a source of protection of animals against abuse, Regan turns to the alternative, non-consequentialist, deontological traditions of moral theory. A deontological moral view is one according to which the difference between morally right and wrong action is not, or at least is not *solely*, a matter of consequences. Independent of the consequences, some acts may be morally required or forbidden. To be effective where utilitarianism is ineffective, a moral theory would have to forbid sacrificing the well-being of some individuals purely to benefit the majority. Regan's own rights view attempts to achieve this in a way which includes (some) animals as bearers of rights. There are three main elements in Regan's case for animal rights. These are: an analysis of an appropriate concept of what it is to have a right, a justification of the claim that human moral agents have rights in this sense, and third, an extension of that justification to (some) non-human animals.

Regan distinguishes between legal and moral rights, and also between acquired and unacquired, or 'basic' rights. The concept of rights pertinent to animal rights is some version of unacquired, or 'basic' moral right. That is to say, if individuals have rights in this sense they have them whether or not there exists some legal guarantee of them (though the existence of a moral right may form part of the justification for the claim that there *ought* to be a legal right), and they have them independently of the prior voluntary acts of themselves or others ('basic' rights do not arise from contracts, promises and the like).

There is a fairly clear resonance in Regan's concept of a basic moral right with established 'anthroposcopic' concepts of 'natural' or 'human' rights. Equally clearly, Regan cannot endorse, unreconstructed, either of these concepts. However, but for the question of scope, Regan's concept of (non species-specific) 'basic' rights is so similar in its construction, and in the kind of moral/political work it is supposed to do, that it is susceptible to very much the same kinds of criticism. Some of these criticisms will be discussed later, in chapter 4, but one familiar line of criticism will be addressed here, since it plays a prominent part in Leahy's recent critique of animal rights.

Leahy endorses Jeremy Bentham's rejection of universal 'natural' rights as 'nonsense upon stilts', and also reminds us of R.M. Hare's warning that too obsessive a belief in moral rights can be a recipe for 'class war and civil war'.[40] Leahy does acknowledge some place for rights in moral discourse, but only in so far as it approximates the legal paradigm. Some basic rules, he agrees, are necessary for 'rational existence as we know it'.[41] The basis, or grounding, of these rules – and so of our duties and responsibilities to one another – is in our inherited or instinctive reactions to one another, the prototypes of which are found in other animals, too. Interestingly, Leahy includes keeping promises, treating others politely, and respecting property as the 'unwritten rules' that may be so grounded. However, no moral theory has any hope of incontestably demonstrating what these rules must be. Rather, our most reliable guide must be the established corpus of 'positive' law:

> The closest to an available touchstone will be those rights which, at any one time, have survived the rigours of debate and enjoy the protection of a legal system. This is not an acid test, far less a self-evident one, but, as I have tried to show, contenders that profess to be are sure to fail.[41]

The obvious rejoinder from the rights view to this position is to call attention to its question-begging conservatism. The whole point of the moral vocabulary of rights and justice in this debate is to call into question the rational, and therefore moral, justification of precisely that set of prohibitions and recognitions which has contingently come to be embodied in any actual legal system. But this rejoinder equally obviously misses the point. Leahy is not a blind, unreflective advocate of the legal *status quo*. He has reasons for commending it as a 'touchstone' of rights and responsibilities: in a democratic society, the law we have has 'survived the rigours of debate'. But it is here that the key weakness of Leahy's position reveals itself, for by his own admission much of that history of debate has involved the conversion into positive law of just the kind of claim to basic moral rights which he condemns as nonsense upon stilts: the struggle against slavery, for women's suffrage, for black civil rights in the USA and so on. Indeed, such claims often were a recipe for civil or class war, but such wars did, after all, form part of the history of our current 'touchstone' legal systems. Surely, it is an arbitrary and unreflective conservatism which would seek to call a halt to this process without further good reason? There may, indeed, as I shall concede a little later, be good reasons for not extending the concept of rights in an unqualified way beyond the species boundary, but these do not require us to wholly abandon, as Leahy seems to wish, the radical-critical heritage of appeal to moral rights for the oppressed and exploited in the human species.

The analysis of 'basic' moral rights offered by Regan is derived from that of Joel Feinberg.[42] According to this view of rights, a right is a kind of claim. For a claim to count as a right, the claimant must be able to show that (1) she or he has a claim to, for example, treatment of some sort which is justifiable according to a valid moral principle, and (2) there must be some assignable individual who is both able to meet the claim and responsible for doing so.

The next step is to show that human moral agents have rights in this sense. Regan's argument is that the claim to respectful treatment is such a right. It is a claim by (or on behalf of) an individual, it is a claim against some assignable individual(s) (for example, those with whom the claimant has moral dealings), and it is one they are able to meet. All that is left is to show that the claim is justifiable according to a valid moral principle. To simplify considerably, Regan's exposition relies on a further premise that those individuals who have a valid claim to respectful treatment are the bearers of what he calls 'inherent value'. It is because they have inherent value that they are morally entitled to respectful treatment. It would be arbitrary and therefore unjust to recognize inherent value in human moral agents and not to recognize it in human moral patients and, in turn, in non-human animals which are also moral patients. If we cannot consistently deny that (at least some) non-human animals have inherent value (and if the other criteria of basic rights also apply), then we cannot consistently attribute rights to human moral agents and refuse to recognize them in the case of non-human animals.

The postulate of 'inherent value' is one fairly obvious area of difficulty for Regan. He regards it as necessary if we are to account for 'reflective intuitions' such as the statement that it would be wrong to harm some individuals purely to produce a greater aggregate balance of pleasure over pain. For example, it might be shown that to execute an innocent person for a crime they were widely believed to have committed might have all manner of beneficial consequences – it might act as a deterrent to would-be criminals, give satisfaction to the law-abiding majority, and so on. But it would be wrong to treat an innocent person in this way. According to Regan, to show why it would be wrong requires the postulate of 'inherent value' and the associated right to treatment which respects that inherent value. It is, for Regan, the inherent value postulated to individuals which grounds the *prima facie* obligation not to harm them, and, just as that duty protects non-human animals which are moral patients, so they may be said to have *prima facie* a right not to be harmed.

Even if we find Regan's case for the postulate of 'inherent value' unconvincing, but nevertheless wish to assign 'basic' rights (for example, so-called 'human rights') to human moral agents on some other grounds, there is still some considerable force in Regan's argument for animal rights. Does the believer in 'basic' rights confine them to those individuals with unimpaired agency only, or acknowledge young children, the mentally enfeebled, and so on, as also having rights? If the answer is 'no' then the rights view fails to morally protect some of the most vulnerable in human society. If the answer is 'yes', then the onus is upon the believer in human rights to show some morally relevant difference to justify recognition of the rights of human moral patients while denying that recognition to non-humans.

The reader who may have been carried this far by the force of Regan's arguments, but whose moral intuitions may remain stubbornly anthropocentric might acknowledge that animals do, indeed, have inherent value, and therefore rights, but, surely, not equal value, and equal rights. Here again, Regan answers on behalf of animals. The available moral traditions face us with a choice between egalitarian and 'perfectionist' theories of justice. The latter (the moral perspectives of Aristotle and Nietzsche are influential examples) argue that what is due to individuals in justice, depends on the degree to which they possess certain virtues or excellences – more will be due to those who are better endowed – and less to others. Tom Regan simply rejects perfectionist theories of justice as morally unacceptable in their implications.[43] The alternative, egalitarian view of justice requires us not to regard differences in intelligence, taste or other attributes as grounds for discriminatory treatment. It follows that all individuals who have inherent value – including non-human moral patients – have it equally, and so are equal in their rights. This means, of course, that they are entitled to equal respect, not that they should always be treated in the same way, irrespective of differences between them.

Before I go on to a more systematic consideration of the rights view in relation both to humans and animals, it may be worth noting, in a preliminary way, some spontaneous responses to it. There are three significant considerations which tell in favour of it. First, it rests on a defensible, and, to my mind, largely convincing, view of the psychological complexity, capacities and needs of at least some non-human animals. In this respect it is also in accord with the best scientific knowledge available. Second, in terms of its own conceptual framework and substantive premisses, it is a remarkably consistent and rigorous moral view. This is not, of course, to deny that there are logical weaknesses, ambiguities and questionable inferences in it: a fully consistent, logically conclusive substantive moral argument would, indeed, be a rare find in the philosophical literature! The point is, rather, that it clearly reaches the standards of rigour required to be taken seriously within the analytical tradition, and, perhaps more importantly, presents a serious challenge to the intellect of any reflective would-be defender of an anthroposcopic moral view. Third, and connected with the last remark, in so far as the conclusions of the rights view are accepted they would offer significant moral protection to many animals currently suffering abuse of various kinds (though, as I shall suggest, they would be unlikely to offer protection against some of the most serious forms of abuse I mentioned above).

The Limits to Rights

1. *Overriding Rights*

Set against these (in my view) significant achievements of the rights view as Tom Regan presents it, are several difficulties and limitations. First, Regan considers, but rejects, the option of treating basic moral rights as absolute. For him, rights are held (by humans or animals) *prima facie* only: that is, circumstances may arise in which a right may be overridden. Typically, this will be the case when there are conflicting rights in a situation. The possibility exists that the rights of non-human animals may be acknowledged in theory, but overridden in practice by human moral agents when they judge that the circumstances warrant it. Since, as moral patients, animals are not in a position to contest these judgements, and since it is human moral agents who will stand to gain from them, the theory might end up not giving much protection in practice! To some extent, the situation between the *prima facie* right of an animal and the circumstantial overriding of its right parallels that between the utilitarian's 'predistributive' inclusion of the pleasures and pains of animals and their losing out in the aggregate redistribution of them. Some of the attraction of the rights view as a moral step forward is lost when it is recognized that rights are held only *prima facie*.

Regan clearly takes this danger seriously, arguing that rights may justifiably be overridden only on the basis of a valid moral principle, and in each case the 'bottom line' for him remains the insistence that animals must be treated as individual bearers of 'inherent value', never as replaceable 'receptacles' of value, or as mere means to human ends. Three such principles which may justify overriding the rights of individuals are: (1) the 'miniride' principle, according to which it is permissible to harm a small number of (innocent) individuals if thereby a larger number may be saved from harm, provided the harms concerned are of comparable magnitude; (2) the 'worse-off' principle, according to which major harms may not be inflicted on (or allowed to befall) individuals to save others from less serious harm, no matter what numbers are involved; and (3) the 'liberty' principle, according to which individuals may harm others if it is necessary to prevent harm to themselves. These principles, together with other qualifying considerations, are applied by Regan to yield firm conclusions against the rearing and killing of animals for food, the hunting and killing of wild animals, toxicity testing of drugs and other products on animals and the whole spectrum of educational and scientific uses of animals which involve harming them to meet some human purpose. But despite the strong moral defence of animals which these conclusions purport to offer, they have a dependence on debatable factual premisses, and reliance on auxiliary considerations which render them manifestly fragile by comparison with the 'core' argument for *prima facie* rights.

2. *The Scope of Rights*

A second area of difficulty in Regan's position concerns the range of beings which could be given moral protection from abuse – the scope of the rights view. There are several aspects here. First, the immense majority of animal species are offered no protection whatsoever from Regan's argument. The right to respectful treatment derives from possession of 'inherent value', and the criterion of this, for Regan, is that an individual counts as 'subject-of a-life'.[44] This applies to an individual capable of beliefs and desires, purposive action, experiencing pain and emotions, memory and some sense of the future, 'experiential welfare', and psychophysical identity. In order to take the moral concept of 'right' across the species-barrier, Regan has defined its conditions of application in such a way that only beings very like humans in their possession of this range of attributes can be included. While it may not be anthroposcopic, the rights view certainly remains anthropocentric. The teeming millions of insects and other invertebrates, amphibians, reptiles, fish, birds and mammals at the earliest stages of infancy all would appear to be objects of complete moral indifference. The difficulty is, indeed, sharpened by Regan's insistence that inherent value cannot be a matter of degree: either one has it or one does not, and anyone who has it has it equally with everyone else who has. For Regan, this requirement follows from the need to avoid any parley with the detested perfectionist views of justice. Either, therefore, a being does satisfy the subject-of-a-life criterion and so possesses equal rights with human individuals, or it does not, in which case it has no moral status at all.

Regan is, understandably, unhappy with this implication of his position. He has two lines of defence. One is to say that the subject-of-a-life criterion is a sufficient, but not a necessary condition for possession of inherent value. It remains possible that convincing arguments will be found which enable us to acknowledge a wider range of beings as bearers of rights. This being said, it has to be admitted that Regan himself makes short work of the most widely canvassed alternatives to his subject-of-a-life criterion. The second line of defence is to acknowledge that there is no sharp borderline between those beings which satisfy and those which fail to satisfy the subject-of-a-life criterion. This is especially obvious in the case of the early developmental stages of beings (including humans) in transition to subject-of-a-life status. Regan's view, here, is that the appropriate practical attitude is moral caution: when in doubt, treat such a being as if it were inherently valuable. But this is no solution for that immense range of species and developmental stages where there just is no reasonable doubt that they fall on the wrong side of Regan's criterion. In these cases, Regan hovers dangerously close to the brink of an 'indirect duty' view: that it is wise to discourage mistreatment of these animals, since it is likely to reduce our moral sensibility when we come to deal with animals which do have inherent value.

A second problem to do with the scope of the rights view is that it does not – and Regan is insistent on the point – assign any special place to the extinction of species. Regan supports efforts to protect endangered species, but only on the grounds that the individuals thus protected have rights, and in the same terms that he would support the protection of individuals of more common species. This is not, in itself, necessarily a failing in Regan's position, but it does complement what I just referred to as the anthropocentrism of the rights view as a further source of tension with any wider environmental ethic. This tension is further exemplified in Regan's direct treatment of environmental protection. He rejects as 'environmental Fascism' the view that moral value resides in properties such as stability, diversity and beauty of ecological communities: this would be to override the rights of individual living beings in favour of the collectivity. There is just a hint of a possible reconciliation between the rights view and the wider environmental movement in Regan's gesture towards a rights-based environmental ethic. However, there are reasons for thinking such an ethic would have adverse consequences for the cause of environmental conservation, and Regan himself has provided strong arguments against any such extension of the discourse of rights.

There are two important sources of these tensions between Regan's rights view and wider environmentalism. One, already noticed, is the clash between Regan's anthropocentrism and the widely held 'ecocentrism' of especially the 'deeper' end of the environmental movement. The other is the conflict between Regan's radical individualism and what he takes to be the 'holism' of much environmentalist moral thinking. In Regan's moral approach it is difficult to see how collectivities such as species or ecological communities could have value in their own right, independently of the 'inherent value' of the individuals who are their members. There are, of course, approaches in the philosophy of biology according to which both species and ecosystems may be regarded as individuals, but, presumably, these individuals would not be of the appropriate kind to be bearers of rights in Regan's sense. I shall, of course, need to return again to these issues.

3. *The Individualism of Animal Rights*

The question of individualism, indeed, does arise immediately in connection with a third area of difficulty in Regan's position: the specific analysis of rights which he advocates. As we have seen, possession of a right depends on having a valid claim against some assignable individual: that is, it depends on there being some identifiable individual who has the responsibility to meet one's claim. The paradigm in this concept of rights is that of an individual right-holder at risk of harm from the voluntary action of some other individual with whom he or she interacts. But some of the abuses of animals which have aroused most moral concern do not sit at all comfortably with this paradigm. The victims of intensive rearing practices are subject to highly routine and impersonal procedures in which the voluntary actions of directly involved human moral agents often have only marginal causal importance. Moreover, although human moral agents figure in the process and in the social structure which ensures its institutional continuity, assigning either causal or moral responsibility to any particular agent would be both arbitrary and practically inefficacious. Should we assign responsibility to the operatives who administer and maintain the animals and the physical plant, to their managers, or to the business executives who run the enterprise, or to the investors in the pension schemes who supply its capital, or to the food processors and retailers who demand standardized and predictable supplies of meat at set prices, or to consumers who demand cheap food and ask no questions, or to legislators who fail to outlaw these practices, to a civil service which fails to enforce what legislation there is, or to a citizenry that fails to act against abuse? If individual responsibility is shared, it is shared so thinly that no one may feel the issue is one of overriding priority.

The limitations of the individualism in Regan's proffered analysis of rights are also evident in cases where animals suffer harm as a result of the unintended, unforeseen, and often unrecognized effects of human social practices such as agricultural reclamation, economic development, primary appropriation and industrial pollution. If, for example, a seal dies because of the levels of PCB toxins in its diet, where the sources of these chemicals are widely dispersed and very numerous, how could individual responsibility be assigned? Given Regan's analysis of rights, inability to unequivocally assign responsibility to individual moral agents involves, at best, the prospect of low levels of practical recognition of rights, at worst, inability to make good the rights-claim at all. Of course this is familiar territory in the literature of human rights and I do not wish to be understood as pleading the case of the concentration camp guards that they were just obeying their supervisors, and so had no moral responsibility. Where individual responsibility is shared, or difficult to attribute, there are often good reasons for continuing to assign it and to seek redress. My point, rather, is that where an abuse is integral to a widespread and institutionally sustained social practice it is often more practically efficacious to seek abolition or transformation of the practice and its institutions than to selectively arraign particular individuals. The causal analysis and the moral language required to call into question a deeply embedded social practice and structure of relations may well include the recognition of the causal powers and rights of individuals but it will also require analytical and moral concepts not reducible to these.

4. Human Rights, Animal Rights and Philosophical Abstraction

Two further difficulties for the rights view arise from the part played by philosophical abstraction in Regan's argument. Regan is (commendably) concerned to develop a view of moral justice which is not only universal in its application to all human individuals, but crosses the species barrier to include all individuals, ('quasi-persons') who satisfy the subject-of-a-life criterion. This concept of justice, logically tied to the principle of equality of inherent value for all those individuals who possess it, is necessarily highly abstract: it must treat as morally irrelevant a host of individual and specific differences in physical constitution, intelligence, character, motivational disposition, needs and modes of life. The moral irrelevance of such differences plays a key role at two points in Regan's argument: first, in establishing that human moral patients, such as young children and the mentally enfeebled, have rights if human moral agents do, and, second, in establishing that non-human moral patients have rights if human moral patients do.

A number of difficult questions arise here. First, there is a factual premiss underlying Regan's argument which he never makes fully explicit. This is that at least some 'mentally enfeebled' humans, and young children, have the full range of subject-of-a-life attributes and powers, but lack the capacity for moral judgement and responsibility. This suggests a view of moral capacity as in some sense a separate faculty, added on, and as detachable by some misfortune, while everything else remains intact. A related structure of assumptions lies behind the thesis of the moral equivalence of human and non-human moral patients. Animals are thought of as like humans in a wide range of capacities and attributes, though they are generally less well developed in these respects, but, like human moral patients they lack only the specific capacities that go to make up moral agency.

Although it is not explicitly stated, the outlines of an anthropocentric 'evolutionary progressivism' are clearly discernible beneath the surface of this moral argument. Now, part of the difficulty is that these factual assumptions – the autonomy of the 'moral faculty' *vis-à-vis* the other human attributes, the view of individual development and psychological disability, and the doctrine of evolutionary progress – may be mistaken. Also it is arguable that the level of abstraction required to establish the appropriate notion of rights and justice has the effect of rendering the theory insensitive to just those features of particularity and difference which the rights view insists – against consequentialism – must be respected.

Of course, the rights view has an obvious reply to this: that equality of rights does not imply equivalence of treatment. In deciding what substantive treatment is due to an individual one has to arrive at an assessment of what according 'equal respect' amounts to for this particular individual in these particular circumstances. A human individual in a literate culture has a right to learn how to write, but to attempt to teach a dog how to write would be a torturous invasion of its rights. For beings whose constitution and mode of life are radically different, justice positively requires appropriate differences of treatment. This line of defence is, indeed, persuasive as far as it goes, but it does not go far enough. The gap between the level of abstraction at which the moral argument is pitched, and the practical contexts in which it has to be applied leave room (as we saw above) for rights well established in theory to be substantially overridden in practice. More tellingly the framework of abstraction required to make the extension of the moral vocabulary of rights simultaneously prevents any sensitivity to particularity and diversity, for instance, as between children and the psychologically disabled humans, and the many different species of non-human animals. Regan's style of argument, rejecting as it does human/animal dualism, asserts human/animal continuism in a way which preserves a major weakness of the dualist position – abstract insensitivity to the diversity of non-human animal species and their requirements.

A further area of difficulty, also connected with abstraction, is Regan's focus on human/animal similarities and differences. At its core, the argument claims that humans and animals are sufficiently similar to make it arbitrary and therefore unjust to acknowledge rights in the one case but not in the other. At one point in his argument – in the course of the 'cumulative' argument for animal consciousness – Regan acknowledges another kind of relation, that of kinship between humans and animals as postulated by evolutionary theory. Apart from this, however, Regan proceeds as if the moral status of animals were a function of the kinds of beings they are, independently of the diverse relations in which they stand to human moral agents and their social practices.

Since, as we have seen, these diverse practices pose a variety of different moral concerns and issues, it seems at least *prima facie* likely that these relations are pertinent to the question of the moral status of the animals which stand in them. Again, given the diversity of moral dilemmas posed by our relations to animals, it seems on the face of it unlikely that the single philosophical strategy of assigning universal rights of a very abstract kind to them would be a sufficient response. Is, for example, the moral status of a farm animal, a domestic pet, or a 'wild' animal to be conceptualized in identical terms? What place is there for acquired, as distinct from unacquired, rights in moral thinking about animals? How are responsibilities to, or for animals properly assigned to individual moral agents? What is the moral significance of human/animal ecological and social interdependence? These and other pertinent questions are difficult to pose, let alone answer, within the terms of Regan's rights view. This is primarily because that view considers the moral status of beings independently of the substantive social relations which hold between them.

5. *Rights and Self-definition*

Yet another difficulty with the rights view comes sharply into focus when we compare the campaigns for animal rights and liberation with those for racial and gender equality. Singer, for example, explicitly sets his case for equality of consideration (as distinct from sameness of treatment) for animals within this political context. For him speciesism is 'logically equivalent' to racism.

THE SOCIAL LIFE OF ANIMALS

But a quite crucial difference between the two is that in the liberation struggles of oppressed groups of humans, those who suffer oppression are able themselves to articulate and press the claims which constitute their moral rights. In the case of animals there is a necessary and permanent incapacity to recognize and articulate their own moral status as right-holders. The rights of animals must always be claims made on behalf of, and never by, animals themselves. There is an inescapable moment of paternalism in the attribution of rights to non-human animals. This is, indeed, no mere formal difficulty, since a crucial issue in the comparable intra-human struggles against racism and sexism is precisely the right to autonomous self-definition in the face of the denigration imposed by the available images within the dominant culture.

In some ways the contrast is less sharp than this might suggest. In, for example, struggles for the abolition of slavery, the denial of positive legal rights on the part of the oppressed is so total and universal that the moral rights of slaves have to be articulated and pursued by their sympathizers. A little more controversially, it is frequently argued that even where oppressed groups have legal rights, the negative weight of the dominant culture so cuts them off from a full recognition of their human potential that they are *de facto* unable to articulate and press their rights autonomously. But these cases are quite unlike the campaigns for animals in at least two important respects. First, while paternalistic or vicarious action on behalf of oppressed human groups may often be a necessary element, or moment in such campaigns it is hard to imagine such a campaign ever generating the moral momentum for success without the eventual active identification and involvement of the oppressed groups themselves. Significantly, when this phase in a liberation struggle is reached the autonomous definitions sought by the oppressed for themselves are often markedly different from those anticipated by their sympathizers, frequently to the point of sharp mutual alienation. No such political dynamic could emerge in the case of animal liberation. The second difference concerns the objectives of struggle. Whereas human liberation struggles frequently highlight the inferior educational opportunities, job prospects, housing priorities, health status and so on of the oppressed group, there is a general demand for equal respect as members of the community, self-definition and full rights of political participation. These are objectives which could make no sense in relation to non-human animals, considered as an oppressed class of individuals. This group of rights – civil rights, broadly conceived – do appear to be specific to human moral agents. They are rights which, for reasons quite independent of their institutional positions or individual biographies, non-human animals are intrinsically incapable of exercising.

But perhaps the contrast can be blunted from the other side of the species-boundary? Surely campaigns on behalf of young children and the mentally disabled also have a necessarily and permanently paternalistic character? Significantly, here as well, where the claim is made for rights, it is not, or not centrally, a claim for *civil* rights or liberties. As I have suggested above (pp. 90–92), the case for the moral equivalence of the mentally enfeebled adults, young children, and non-human animals which qualify as 'moral patients' is far from fully convincing. But even if it were accepted for the sake of argument, the evident differences in the relationships in which the human categories of moral patients stand to moral agents make a clear difference to the plausibility with which the latter can claim to represent authentically the interests of the former in specifying their rights. All human adult moral agents have been young children, and will have some memory of that state. Many adult human moral agents have close personal ties with children involving sufficiently high-quality communication for there to be a widespread adult comprehension of the 'experiential welfare' of human children. In the case of mentally disabled human adults there are, again, generally sufficiently powerful subject-to-subject affective bonds to give grounds for thinking that those who campaign on behalf of the mentally handicapped have an authentic sense of what it is the mentally handicapped would themselves campaign for if they were able to do so.

6. *Rights, Motivation and Enforcement*

My final reservation about the rights view is really the starting-point for a more thorough-going and distinctively socialist critical assessment. In general terms, a rights-based strategy for defending individuals against abuse encounters what is sometimes called the problem of motivation: rights are unlikely to be effective in practice unless those who have the power to abuse them are already benevolently disposed to their bearers. In the case of animal rights, it is only when those who would otherwise abuse animals already recognize them as subjects-of-a-life and are already disposed to compassionate, benevolent relations with them, that the rights view is likely to be persuasive. But it is precisely where such an acknowledgement is missing that the rights view is most required. Where humans gain their livelihood from a practice which presupposes a 'reification' of animals, or gain pleasure from sports which involve systematic animal suffering, it seems unlikely that a rational argument that this treatment is unjust to the animals concerned would be sufficient to make the humans involved change their ways. In part, this is a point about the power of rational argument, as compared with other kinds of motive, to change human conduct. But it also takes into account the socio-economic and cultural positions and formations of the human agents concerned. Workers or managers in intensive agriculture, huntsmen and the like are much less liable to feel the force of arguments like Regan's than are those of us with less of an economic or cultural stake in animal abuse.

The problem of motivation is, in fact, compounded by the further problem of unattributable or shared causal responsibility. If the abuse is not a matter of wilful individual wrong-doing, but, rather, a feature of a widespread social practice which has powerful institutional support, then individual moral agents caught up in it are unlikely to feel that their own self-sacrificial renunciation on behalf of abused animals will make enough of a difference to be worthwhile. But this is perhaps to mistake the strategic role intended for the rights view. Perhaps its point is not, or not solely, to persuade animal abusers and their accomplices to desist, but to provide grounds for legislation. In this event, the coercive power of the state complements that of rational persuasion to prevent those abuses which the latter is insufficient to end unaided.

Here, again, the rights view comes up against a problem shared with its parallels in the world of liberation struggles for oppressed human groups: even where the argument is won, and rights are written into the statute-book, there can be no guarantee that they will be enjoyed in practice. As both women's rights and black liberation campaigns have experienced, prevailing structures of economic, cultural and political power may continue to obstruct the realization of juridically acknowledged rights. A variety of mechanisms may be at work here – the deliberate application of pressure to weaken the force of the legislation itself, at the drafting stage; forms of legislation which (intentionally or not) outlaw discrimination without addressing the social-structural causes of disadvantage; inappropriately designed or inadequately resourced methods of enforcement; and numerous others.[45] It is at this point that the individualism inherent in the rights-view most clearly acts as a limit to its effectiveness. To the extent that an ontology of freely choosing and rationally active moral agents (and freely choosing moral patients) is inadequate to the task of accounting for the social-structural sources of injustice of rights-abuse, to that extent it is likely to issue in well-intended but ineffective remedies. This is not, of course, to deny that the ontology of freely choosing and rationally acting agents works well in some contexts, or that, for such contexts, the rights view may well offer effective protection from abuse.

PART II

Human Rights and Social Practice

= 4 =

The Radical Case against Rights

The present chapter marks a pause in our argument. It does not pretend to break new ground. Rather the aim is to rehearse, or take stock of, the main established lines of radical criticism of liberal rights discourse and practice. I begin by noting both affinities and differences between the form of socialist critique of rights which I provisionally endorse, and some currently influential strands of 'communitarian' criticism. I then investigate some of the unresolved tensions in Marx's classical critique of liberal rights: *On the Jewish Question*. The chapter then opens out into an attempted review of four distinct themes in what I take to be a well-established 'radical' (commonly, but not exclusively, socialist) critique of rights. This ordering of critical lines of argument serves both to structure the arguments of chapters 5, 6 and 7 and to pose, in a preliminary way, limits and dilemmas implicit in the radical critique. The larger claim, to be developed in those final chapters, is that the naturalistic view of human nature, the 'animal/human continuism' outlined in Part I, can both deepen and illuminate each facet of the established radical critique, and also begin to show ways of overcoming its limits and inner tensions. Above all, the aim is to provide a single framework for thinking about the moral status of both humans and non-humans. Predictably, the salience of embodiment and ecological interdependence figures centrally in this framework.

Communitarian and Socialist Critics of Rights

It is sometimes claimed (by both adherents and opponents) that Marxian socialism is necessarily a form of anti-moralism. Like Nietzsche and other moral relativists, the argument runs, Marx and Engels rejected the idea of universally valid moral principles. For them, moral concepts and principles arise in the context of specific, historically transitory social forms. In any historical epoch, the dominant moral concepts and principles are expressions of the interests of the dominant group in society, so that morality as such has a conservative, order-maintaining, oppressive social function. Breaking free of the prevailing moral constraints is an essential condition for the oppressed to establish themselves as an effective revolutionary force.

Persistent moral scepticism does indeed characterize much of the contemporary literature influenced by Nietzsche, but any attribution of anti-moralism to Marx and his followers must, whatever the textual support, be qualified by some important countervailing considerations. The most obvious of these is the undeniably moral tone of Marx and Engels's critique of capitalism and their advocacy of a communist future. Though they often spoke as if the future transition to socialism and communism were a scientifically predictable certainty, this was a 'fact' they undeniably welcomed, and welcomed as an immense moral advance in civilization. The very idea of such moral progress through historical transition to a new social form implies a commitment to historically transcendent moral concepts and principles. The vision of a communist future is a standpoint from which the present state of society stands condemned, not just in this or that particular feature, but as a total structure of social practices and relations.

This apparent paradox in Marxian approaches to morality may to a considerable extent be resolved by a two-fold qualification of its radical historicism in relation to morals. First, it may be acknowledged that moral concepts and principles have specific social and historical conditions of emergence, but it does not follow from this that they are limited in scope to those conditions, or to the periods of time during which they prevail. Second, it does not follow, either, that moral concepts and principles which emerge under definite prevailing social relations necessarily have an order-preserving, conservative social function. The discourse of the universal rights of man and citizen emerged and rose to prominence in early modern Europe, but played a role in the revolutionary overthrow of the social and political relations under which it emerged. The discourse of universal rights has subsequently played a critical and even revolutionary role in nineteenth- and twentieth-century struggles against specific forms of social and economic oppression and political tyranny. Notably, many thousands of socialists, including Marxists, have fought and given their lives in the name of those same moral ideals.

It is clear that a more qualified, nuanced approach is required if we are to understand the relation between socialism and morality. Steven Lukes, in his major recent clarification of the issues at stake here,[1] contrasts the morality of *Recht* (rights and justice) with that of positive freedom and emancipation. On Lukes's view, Marx was hostile, or at best equivocal, in his attitude to the discourse of rights and justice, in favour of an alternative morality of human emancipation through social transformation. Leaving on one side, for the moment, the question of an emancipatory morality, I shall consider the sources of Marxian and, more broadly, socialist reservations about the morality of rights and justice. To what extent are those reservations sustainable, and should they take us in the direction of a radically alternative moral vision, or towards a more generous, socialist re-construction of the ideas of rights and justice themselves?

But, since there are significant affinities between a distinctively socialist tradition of criticism of liberal individualist views of rights and justice and a recently refurbished 'communitarian' critique, some brief comments on the contemporary state of the debate on rights may be in order. It is generally true of the liberal tradition that it assigns moral priority to securing the integrity and autonomy of the individual person, or 'subject'. This moral priority is expressed in Regan's preparedness to assign inherent value to subjects-of-a-life, and to recognize inherent value as grounding rights as *prima facie* valid moral claims. As will become clearer in the course of this work, I do not take this order of moral priorities to be exclusive to the liberal traditions, or as definitive of it. Indeed, assigning moral priority to the well-being of individuals is, I think, widely shared by both liberals and their communitarian critics. It is also shared with the socialist critique of liberal rights theory, at least in the version I am here prepared to defend.

What I do take to be definitive of liberal views of rights and justice are a certain range of answers to two further questions: (1) What is presupposed in the integrity or autonomy of the individual subject? and (2) What is the relationship between the moral discourse of rights and justice, on the one hand, and the protection of the integrity and autonomy of the individual subject, on the other? Both contemporary communitarian and 'traditional' socialist critics of liberal rights find liberalism wanting primarily because of its distinctive, and in their view unsatisfactory ways of answering these two questions. Kant's transcendental arguments for a 'noumenal' self, presupposed as the unifying subject of experience, and the autonomous subject of moral duty have been paradigmatic for the liberal tradition's responses to the first question. But, more recently, attempts have been made to preserve a broadly Kantian moral framework, with its commitment to a categorical priority for universal rights and justice over substantive and particular versions of virtue and the good life, without commitment to Kant's metaphysics of transcendental idealism. By far the most influential such attempt has been Rawls's[2] theory of justice, with its conception of the 'original position' in which subjects consider principles of justice from behind a 'veil of ignorance', unencumbered by accidents and contingencies of actual life, much as the Kantian transcendental self is unencumbered by the contingencies of experience and desire which determine the empirical self.

Whereas, as we shall see, Marx's critique focused upon the imputed self-interestedness of the subjects of liberal rights-theory, the contemporary communitarian view goes deeper. It calls into question the possibility of individuation of the self, independently of, or prior to, community membership. Michael Sandel,[3] for example, distinguishes three concepts of community (more precisely, I think, three concepts of the relationship between personal identity and community). In the first, self-interested individuals cooperate with one another because it is in their interests to do so. This is the 'instrumental' concept, and it is a proper target for Marxist and other critics of the self-interest view of human nature and motivation. The second concept is the one Sandel attributes to Rawls, and which he calls the 'sentimental' account of community. On this view, it is conceded that individuals may be benevolently motivated, and may come to attach value to the good of the community. However, this account of community remains individualist in that it takes the individuation of selves as given independently of their membership of a community. The third account of community, favoured by Sandel himself, is one in which 'community would describe not just a feeling, but a mode of self-understanding partly constitutive of the agent's identity'.[4] This view of the relation between personal identity and community membership takes the former as not (or, at least, not wholly) pre-given, but as something acquired or achieved by individuals in the course of self-reflective engagement in social life. The 'boundaries' of the self, so to speak, are open-endedly constituted and revised in the light of the individual's ability to reflect on the question 'Who am I?' as distinct from (merely) 'What do I want?'

Sandel argues convincingly that Rawls's theory of justice illicitly draws upon a tacit recognition that individuals are situated in this sense, that his theory of justice cannot be sustained without reference to some substantive account of the good. Otherwise, the 'thin', unencumbered self would be a being whose choice of a substantive content for the good life would be arbitrary, and so lacking in moral relevance. Either way, the categorical priority of rights and justice cannot be sustained.

However, Sandel does concede that the character of our social life is such that there are likely always to be some contexts in which justice remains necessary. 'Justice', he says 'finds its occasion because we cannot know each other, or our ends, well enough to govern by the common good alone.'[5] In this respect, at least, Sandel is at one with Hume, whose 'radically situated' concept of the self he rejects no less clearly than the 'deontological' self of the liberal tradition. Like Sandel, Hume regarded rights and justice as necessitated only by unfortunate contingencies of human life: 'Encrease to a sufficient degree the benevolence of men, or the bounty of nature, and you render justice useless by supplying its place with much nobler virtues, and more valuable blessings.'[6]

Since Sandel, like Hume, acknowledges the necessity of justice where such conditions as community, benevolence or abundance are absent, and since he rejects a deontological grounding for the moral priority of the integrity and autonomy of the individual, we must suppose that he includes this priority within his substantive conception of the good. Adherence to this moral priority, quite independently of its philosophical foundations in liberal theory, is now widely shared as a deeply ingrained feature of modern moral sensibility, even if grotesquely abused in the practice of many modern political regimes. This state of affairs is one bequeathed to us as a kind of practical moral condensate by classical liberalism's philosophical response to the competing demands of stable and legitimate political order and the recognition of irreducible moral plurality.

The approach which governs this chapter, and the rest of this book, has no quarrel with that order of moral priorities. However, it seeks to take further than Sandel himself does the criticism of liberal conceptions of self-identity and its presuppositions. Sandel's analysis of community as a framework of relations and commitments through which self-identity is continually formed and re-formed is of a piece with the long tradition of socialist and radical criticism of liberal individualism and it is endorsed in what follows. However, the naturalistic view of the human which emerges from sustained human/animal comparison extends this view of the nature of personal identity and its conditions in two directions: first, in the analysis of the implications of human embodiment for identity, autonomy and well-being, and, second, in the analysis of the part played by physical location and the non-human environment in sustainable personal identity and integrity.

Humans are necessarily *embodied* and also, doubly, ecologically and socially *embedded*, and these aspects of their being are indissolubly bound up both with their sense of self and with their capacity for the pursuit of the good for themselves. If this can be shown, then to give moral priority to the autonomy and integrity of the individual is also to give moral priority to securing those social, ecological and organic-bodily conditions for it. The 'unencumbered' self of the liberal tradition allowed for an open vista of unconstrained individual choice only on condition that it remained unencumbered by the vulnerabilities, requirements and commitments of material and social existence.

Of course, a pattern of life which secured for each individual these social and material conditions of autonomy, integrity and choice would also impose constraints on the range of choices each could make consistently with the opportunity of others to do the same. This view of the conditions of the liberty of individuals clearly imposes strong constraints on its scope. But, as we shall see, this is not an argument against the protection of liberties by a discourse of rights. On the contrary, it favours a more powerfully entrenched practice of rights to sustain the exercise of liberties over the widest scope reconcilable with universality and sustainability. Moral pluralism is a condition which may not be transcended. Indeed, it is a condition which we should not wish to transcend. However, to think through the implications of human 'embodiment' and 'embeddedness' is to reduce the range of defensible visions of the good life in ways which may begin to offer the possibility of an ordered but still plural social life beyond the material unsustainabilities and social oppressions of the present.

So, the account I shall be offering here attempts to go beyond the communitarian critique of the philosophical basis of liberalism, while at the same time continuing to share with liberalism the moral priority it accords to the integrity and autonomy of the individual. However, it must now be recognized that this moral priority forms the centrepiece of a positive moral vision of the good life, rather than figuring as an abstract and unrealizable substitute for such a positive vision. Moreover, to be committed to the moral priority of individual integrity and autonomy is not necessarily to be committed to any particular view of the discourse of rights and justice as indispensable to the achievement of this moral priority. It may turn out that rights and justice are neither necessary nor sufficient for the securing of personal autonomy. As we saw, both Hume and Sandel have been less than enthusiastic about rights and justice. But this was not because they cared little for the individual. Rather, it was because they were less than enthusiastic about the moral texture of a society in which individuals stand in need of the protection promised by the discourse of rights.

What I shall be trying to develop in Part III of this book is a more complex, multi-dimensional view of the conditions and contexts of personal autonomy and well-being than is characteristic of either liberalism or its communitarian critics. Given that more complex view, the question is posed still more acutely: can we imagine any society in which those conditions would be satisfied, as a matter of course? Only if the answer to that question is 'yes' can we consistently pursue the moral priority of individual autonomy *and* dispense with the discourse and practices of rights and justice (or some functional equivalent). If the answer is 'no', then the search must be on for some version of rights and justice which escapes the limits and defects apparent in the liberal-individualist heritage. This question is a continuing preoccupation of Part III of this book and is addressed directly in chapter 7. Throughout, the discussion is interwoven with the parallel question as applied to the autonomy and well-being of non-human animals. My hope is that keeping a cross-species comparison in view will illuminate such answers as are forthcoming.

Finally, after endorsing so much of the communitarian critique of liberalism, at least in so far as Sandel is representative of it, it is still necessary to establish a critical distance from some influential communitarian arguments. These derive not so much from the critique of liberal conceptions of personal identity and its conditions, as from a certain view of the conditions of significance and authority of moral discourse itself. Alasdair MacIntyre is our exemplar here.

On MacIntyre's view moral claims presuppose a socially established set of roles. In the absence of these, to make such claims is not 'an intelligible type of human performance'.[7] Lacking the appropriate institutional setting, 'the making of a claim to a right would be like presenting a cheque for payment in a social order that lacked the institution of money'. So, MacIntyre has no objection on these grounds to 'those rights confirmed by positive law or custom on specified classes of person'. But he does object to 'those rights which are alleged to belong to human beings as such and which are cited as a reason for holding that people ought not to be interfered with in their pursuit of life, liberty and happiness'. He concludes: 'there are no such rights, and belief in them is one with belief in witches and in unicorns'.[8]

There is an interesting convergence between MacIntyre's idea that as distinctively modern concepts, moral fictions such as human rights provide a moral cover for 'arbitrary will and desire',[9] and Sandel's demonstration of the arbitrariness of the choices of the 'deontological' self. Neither writer recognizes, or seeks to preserve in this moral vocabulary, any emancipatory content. When MacIntyre locates significant moral claims within sets of socially established rules, and when he tells us that rights-claims 'always have a highly specific and socially local character',[10] he appears insensitive to the respects in which rights-claims have been made as claims not so much within as against such local communities. Communities can stifle and suppress individuality, just as they can also provide an indispensable means and context for self-definition and the flourishing of individuality. The claims of individuals against such oppressive 'socially established' sets of rules were given their first outlet in the very universalizing moral discourse of rights which MacIntyre puts on a level with witches and unicorns.

One obvious way, within the communitarian tradition, of retaining this critical, emancipatory aspect of the discourse of universal rights is to see it as making its moral appeal not to any extant 'socially local' community, but to the notion of a real or hypothetical universal human community. I have already, in chapter 1, indicated some scepticism towards this idea in its use as a means of defending preferential treatment of humans over animals. Another attempt at a solution of this dilemma is offered by Jay Bernstein,[11] in the notion of an open-ended, partially self-defining community as characteristic of modernity. Bernstein sustains his commitment to the view that rights are expressions of, rather than grounds for, mutual recognition in communities, but retains the critical, universalistic dimension of the liberal discourse of rights. He considers the obvious objection that the self-defining community may simply exercise its power of self-definition by exclusion, and denial of recognition. One line of response is to distinguish implicit from explicit recognition, grounding struggles for rights as primarily about rendering already implicit recognitions explicit. The other is to make use of the contested concept of human rights. As 'substantial entities' these are, for Bernstein as for MacIntyre, fictions. But some indeterminate concept of human rights has a role as a 'moment of excess' in virtue of which any particular, empirical community can call into question its boundaries: 'Human rights, we might say, are never fully within or fully outside political community.'[12]

But this concept of human rights is so indeterminate, we might wonder whence its critical force comes. Unless some substantive grounds can be given for acknowledging membership of a political community independently of the bare fact, implicit or explicit, of actual acknowledgement, it is hard to see how either of Bernstein's responses to the central difficulty of his device can be effective. To make this further step would be for Bernstein to accept some consideration of what he calls 'characteristics' of individuals as having some part to play in establishing the moral validity of rights claims. Otherwise, why speak of the rights of humans, rather than of sexes, or races, or, indeed, of (other) species? However, these disagreements aside, Bernstein's attempt to sustain the core of Marx's critique of liberal conceptions of justice, while insisting that this critique must be complemented not by a rejection of rights *tout court* but, rather, by a positive conceptualization of socialist rights is a laudable one. To see why this must be so, I will begin by returning, like Bernstein, to an analysis of Marx's ambiguities on the question of rights.

Marx and the Critique of Rights

The *locus classicus* for Marx's alleged hostility to individual rights is his early text *On the Jewish Question*. Central to that text is Marx's distinction between human emancipation and political emancipation. The latter is achieved with the formation of the modern democratic state, with the institution of universal rights of citizenship. This political revolution established a public sphere in which 'Public affairs as such ... became the general affair of each individual, and the political function became the individual's general function.'[13] Marx is quite unequivocal as to the historically progressive character of political emancipation:

Political emancipation is, of course, a big step forward. True, it is not the final form of human emancipation in general, but it is the final form of human emancipation *within* the hitherto existing world order.[14]

Turning to a closer analysis of the constitutional declarations of the most nearly perfected modern states – French and North American – Marx exposes a real content which betrays the limitations and presuppositions of these grand proclamations. General human rights are in part political, pertaining to the relation of the individual to the community, and fall under the category of political freedom, or civil rights. The remainder are the rights of 'man' – liberty, including liberty of conscience and religion, equality, security and property. But these rights of 'man' are expressed in a way which presupposes a certain view of individual human nature and of the relations between humans: liberty is the power to do anything which does not harm others, while its 'practical application' is the right to property – 'to enjoy one's property and to dispose of it at one's discretion, without regard to other men'.[15] Equality and security, too, involve the same notion of individual persons as 'self-sufficient monads'. Self-sufficient, egoistic individuals who are for one another boundaries, or limits to freedom, and who meet their needs through ownership and exchange of property: these are the conditions which form the basis of 'civil society'. As Marx puts it:

None of the so-called rights of man, therefore, go beyond egoistic man, beyond man as a member of civil society, that is, an individual withdrawn into himself, into the confines of his private interests and private caprice, and separated from the community. In the rights of man, he is far from being conceived as a species-being; on the contrary, species-life itself, society, appears as a framework external to the individuals, as a restriction of their original independence. The sole bond holding them together is natural necessity, need and private interest, the preservation of their property and their egoistic selves.[16]

So, the establishment of the modern democratic state, as an ideal expression of the communal, species-life of humans also entails the formation, as an autonomous sphere, of 'civil society' in which particular individuals live as mutually alienated, egoistic, 'natural' beings. But the problem is not solely that political emancipation is an incomplete, partial prefiguring of all-round human emancipation. Marx also views the quasi-natural, mutually estranged relations of civil society as presuppositions of the modern state and its civil rights:[17]

Feudal society was resolved into its basic element – *man*, but man as he really formed its basis – *egoistic* man. This *man*, the member of civil society, is thus the basis, the precondition, of the *political* state. He is recognized as such by this state in the rights of man.[18]

Further, the primacy of the egoistic individual of civil society over the abstract-ideal citizen, participant in the communal species-life, is manifest in the claim in the French *Declaration of the Rights of Man and Citizen* that 'Government is instituted to guarantee man the enjoyment of his natural and imprescriptible rights.' Political emancipation and civil rights, it is acknowledged, serve only to protect and maintain the rights of the individual, egoistic man of bourgeois civil society. The progressive moment of political emancipation as an ideal expression of human community, of species-being is itself offset and corrupted by the foundations of the modern state in the egoism of bourgeois civil society, and the reduction of civil rights to the status of means to the preservation of the conditions of that egoistic material existence.

Complete human emancipation would involve a transformation in the relations of civil society, the establishment of communal human nature in those areas of life excluded from political society in the current order; and with it the transcending of the opposition between civil society and the state itself:

> Only when the real, individual man re-absorbs in himself the abstract citizen, and as an individual human being has become a *species-being* in his everyday life, in his particular work, and in his particular situation, only when man has recognized and organized his 'forces propres' (own powers) as *social* forces, and consequently no longer separates social power from himself in the shape of *political* power, only then will human emancipation have been accomplished.[19]

A widespread reading of these arguments in *On the Jewish Question* presents Marx as a rather unequivocal opponent of individual rights, whether as 'rights of man' or as civil rights, political freedoms. Rights of man represent the forms of human nature (self-sufficiency, egoism, instrumental rationality) and of human relations (mutual alienation, external-instrumentalism, the requirement for external regulation) which characterize bourgeois civil society as the 'natural' state. Civil rights provide for an institution of those political relations necessary to protect and preserve the egoistic individuals, their property and their transactions as conceived under the category 'rights of man'. Both sub-divisions of human rights presuppose, legitimize and preserve the basic unit of bourgeois civil society – the self-sufficient egoistic individual and his possessions.

Since, indeed, the rights of property and of property-owners have been deeply entrenched in the constitutional forms of liberal capitalist regimes and since the necessity of that entrenchment has often been argued in the face of the threat posed by extensions of political democracy to those without property, the reduction of liberal rights to their 'essence', the right to property, has gained plausibility on the left.[20] Whether or not Marx's text must or should be read in this way, the pressures in favour of so reading it have been considerable. The questions remain, however, do rights protect something which it is important to protect, other than property? And is property itself not something that it is right to protect?

For the moment, I will simply allow these questions to stand, only returning to consider them in the context of my re-valuation of the animal-rights perspective from the standpoint of the socialist critique of individual rights. Meanwhile, it is to the further elaboration of that socialist critique that I shall turn. Many of Marx's own early, formative political battles were fought against state censorship, and he recognized early on how central were the 'bourgeois' rights of freedom of expression, of publication and assembly to the spread of socialism itself. But such acknowledgements of the utility of 'bourgeois' civil liberties do not necessarily amount to a full moral endorsement of them. For one thing, the moral declarations of bourgeois society can be effectively turned against the reality of inequality, injustice and oppression for which they provide a cover. This can be done by way of an 'immanent' critique, by showing that in practice bourgeois society stamps on the very moral precepts it proclaims, without necessarily adopting those moral precepts as one's own. For another thing, Marx and Engels and their followers may have welcomed, and fought for, bourgeois political rights in a purely instrumental, or 'cynical' mode, recognizing only that their institution provided more fertile ground for the development of their communist transcendence.

But this is unsatisfactory as a reading of the evident affective tone, the sense of authentic outrage which characterizes so much of the critical writing of Marx and Engels, and it does no justice to the part genuinely played by subsequent generations of Marxists in popular struggles against injustice and tyranny (including tyrannies established in the name of Marx himself). In particular, this reading is not consistent with the position clearly enough stated in *On the Jewish Question* that 'political emancipation is of course a big step forward'. These considerations suggest the possibility of alternative readings of Marx's position in *On the Jewish Question*, and, independently of the viability of such readings, they call for the development of a more nuanced critical socialist view of the discourse and practice of rights.

A plausible reading of Marx which would take us some distance along this road would be to take his critique of the rights discourse of the bourgeois constitutional declarations as a critique of a specific discourse of rights in its specific complex of relations to a set of historically transient socio-economic and political forms. That is, as a critique of the theory and practice of bourgeois rights, not of rights as such. The modern democratic state is emancipatory, but its emancipatory form is vitiated by its basis in bourgeois socio-economic relations. The emancipation represented in ideal form in the

109

democratic state must be extended to the practices and relations of civil society, a process which would itself entail a transcendence of the state/civil society opposition. But since Marx is unclear about the precise relation between civil rights and the (albeit limited) emancipatory content of political (as distinct from human) emancipation, it remains also unclear whether human emancipation itself entails the transcendence of bourgeois rights in some richer, socially content-full realization of human rights, or whether it entails the transcendence of rights as such.

I think this is a genuinely unresolved ambiguity in Marx's text, and its source is in an inadequacy in his account of individual human nature and of relations under conditions he characterizes as 'bourgeois civil society'. Marx's view of the self-sufficient, egoistic, possessive individuals of capitalism includes within it, undifferentiated, two distinct analytical moments. On the one hand, these individuals are social beings whose sociality is suppressed, or 'sublimated' into their ideal being as political citizens, and who are pressed by their conditions of life into mutually antagonistic, competitive relations with one another: they are individualized social beings. On the other hand, they are quasi-natural beings, the bearers of individual needs, appetites and rational powers, whose full social potential has yet to be acknowledged, gathered and realized: they are as-yet-unsocialized individuals. Both aspects of bourgeois individuality are, I think, present in Marx's analysis, but it is the predominance of the former which favours the confusion of bourgeois rights with rights as such. The individualized social being is one who claims and exercises rights against his fellows, whose liberty is bounded by the modern state's recognition of the equal rights of others (just as, Marx says, the 'boundary between two fields is defined by a boundary post'[21]). This is a form of egoistic, competitive antagonism established and sustained by historically specific socio-economic and juridico-political forms. In so far as the discourse of rights is conditioned by and is a regulative moment within these historical forms, then to that extent will the discourse of rights be transcended as and when these historical forms are themselves transcended in practice.

But what of the as-yet-unsocialized individuals of bourgeois civil society? What of those aspects or attributes of individuals, whether of bourgeois, feudal or communist society, which are the ground, or condition, of their acquisition and exercise of their social, communal powers? When Marx speaks of 'security' as a right, his irony is bitter:

> Security is the highest social concept of civil society, the concept of *police*, expressing the fact that the whole of society exists only in order to guarantee to each of its members the preservation of his person, his rights, and his property. ... The concept of security does not raise civil society above its egoism. ... None of the so-called rights of man, therefore, go beyond egoistic man, beyond man as a member

of civil society, that is, an individual withdrawn into himself, into the confines of his private interests and private caprice.[22]

Here, Marx gives the game away with such expression as: 'exists only in order' and 'none ... go beyond', and 'does not raise civil society above'. Here, the aspects of individuality and the relations at stake are not denounced as distortions or degradations of human sociality, but, on the contrary, are given a lukewarm endorsement. What bourgeois rights protect is not something inimical to the emancipated condition, an obstacle to its realization, but, rather, something acceptable enough in itself, but falling far short of the full richness of human social potentiality. Mere *security*, is that all bourgeois society claims to offer? And Marx shows elsewhere that it cannot deliver on even this impoverished, minimal, miserly offer. The mention of 'private interests', too, is capable of more than one interpretation. The withdrawal behind private interests and separation from the community is clearly the state of the individualized social being of bourgeois civil society. But will the emancipated individual of communist society be one who no longer needs to hide behind private interests, one whose private interests no longer separate her or him from the community, or will this individual be one who has transcended the domain of 'private interests' altogether? Russell Keat beautifully exposes the consequences of this conflation in Marx's hostility to 'egoism':

> Marx was mistakenly adopting a simple, mutually exclusive and exhaustive dichotomy between self-interested and other-interested motivations. ... The danger in using egoism as a purely negative category is the implicit endorsement of altruism as its preferred alternative. For this is to remain trapped in a form of 'moralism' in which any kind of self-concern is automatically rejected as morally unacceptable, and to take as one's ideal a society of selfless other-regarding agents. Such an ideal does, of course, have the apparent virtue of guaranteeing co-operative harmony as the general condition of society; but at the cost, it could be argued, of any genuine differentiation and sense of autonomy amongst its individual members.[23]

Depending on whether we emphasize 'egoism' as atomized sociality, or as stunted potential for sociality, two alternative (but, possibly, reconcilable) views of the discourse of rights can be sustained. According to the first, the discourse of rights emerges with, and as an integral moment of, the socio-economic and political forms of the bourgeois epoch. Rights are necessary to regulate the lives of mutually competitive, egoistic, individualized social beings. With the coming of full human emancipation new forms of individuality and social relations will arise which will render rights not only unnecessary, but even insusceptible of coherent application. According to the second

111

view, the historical achievement of political emancipation in the modern state provides conditions for a recognition of universal moral rights of individuals, the full meaning or content of which cannot, however, be realized without profound further socio-economic and political transformations. As the rights of as-yet-unsocialized individuals, bourgeois rights are both conceptually limited by the bounds of bourgeois socio-economic relations and are substantively unrealizable within the bounds of those social relations. I shall, for the time being, work with this second view of the rights discourse as limited and flawed by its status as a discourse of *bourgeois* rights, leaving until later the question of what might form the content of a socialist right, continuous with, but enriching and transcending the terms of liberal individualism.

The Radical Critique of Rights

So far I have mentioned two strands of 'communitarian' criticism of the liberal discourse of 'natural' or 'human' rights. Bentham's utilitarian scepticism of rights as 'nonsense upon stilts' is echoed in recent 'anti-essentialist'[24] criticism, while Burke's[25] conservative revulsion against rights also has its contemporary advocates.[26] The socialist, or, more broadly, radical critique which is central to my investigations in this book does, as we have seen, have something in common with the communitarian position. Nevertheless, it is a tradition of thought with its own distinctive features, and which deserves critical exploration in its own terms. This is what I shall try to offer in the rest of this chapter. Subsequently, in chapters 5, 6, and 7 I shall test the resources of both this socialist view and the liberal tradition of rights against the challenge of human/animal continuism, and its associated naturalistic view of the human.

This socialist or radical critique of the liberal-individualist concept and practice of rights has four interrelated strands. The first I shall simply call the 'sociological' critique. The various elements within it are so many ways of showing that the actual structure of social relationships (the economic, cultural and political inequalities of capitalist societies, the forms of institutional separation of state and civil society, and so on) render the equal rights proclaimed in the liberal discourse incapable of substantive realization. In Marxian and democratic socialist versions of this argument the concepts of class structure and inequality are central. More recently, feminist critics of legal discourse, and, specifically, of the discourse of rights, have either displaced or complemented the analysis of class domination with an analysis of gender relations as a pertinent dimension of social stratification.[27] Ethnicity, disability and various forms of pervasive cultural taboo can also be assimilated to the general terms of this sociological critique of 'bourgeois' rights.

Though as it stands this critique is a purely contingent one – that is, it measures a certain legitimating moral or legal discourse against the real relations and conditions of life of those to whom it is applied – it has a practical political effectiveness which outweighs its relative lack of conceptual or philosophical complexity. Moreover, the radical conceptual critique of rights which constitutes the remaining three strands in the radical case against rights is in important respects grounded in the sociological considerations advanced in the first.

The Sociological Critique: Formal and Substantive Rights

Central to the sociological dimension of socialist and other radical critiques of liberal rights is a contrast between formal and substantive rights. It is one thing to be formally recognized by the law as having a right, but quite another to be in a position to exercise it. The most obvious case is the right to property. For those who have property, the law will protect their possession by punishing theft, restraining public authority, and guaranteeing the right to free enjoyment and disposal of it:

> Property being an inviolable and sacred right, no one may be deprived of it unless public necessity, legally determined, clearly requires such an action, and then only on condition of a just and prior indemnity.[28]

But this right offers nothing to the person without property, save to place obstacles in the way of obtaining some share of the property of those who already have some!

The right to free communication of thoughts is another case. Article 11 of the French *Declaration* (1789) states:

> The free communication of thoughts and opinions is one of the most precious rights of man: every citizen can therefore freely speak, write and print: he is answerable for abuses of this liberty in cases determined by the law.

But on what grounds is this right asserted? Is it simply an acknowledgement of the intrinsic satisfactions to be obtained from conversation, or of a human need to communicate? The listing of media of communication suggests more than this – or why should freedom to write and to print one's views get specific mention? Only, one must suppose, because freedom of communication is an indispensable *civil* right, a freedom to enter on equal terms into the public process of democratic determination of the terms and objects of law and government. The right of freedom to communicate is a right not only to speak, but to be heard, and to have a place for one's opinions in whatever form in the exchange of ideas in the public sphere. In the recently emancipated modern state, this meant literate communication and publication. In our day it would be necessary to include the electronic media.

Once all this is understood, then it is clear that the legal right to free communication means one thing for the owner or editor of a newspaper or printing press, quite another for the reader; one thing for the literate, another for the illiterate; one thing for the trained and skilled public orator, another for the uneducated and inarticulate. With the right to free communication, as with the right to property, substantive inequalities of condition (such as are presupposed by and reproduced in the socio-economic structure of bourgeois societies) have a clear bearing on the differential capacities of individual citizens to exercise whatever rights are attributed to them in law.

Formal equality between individuals is, at least in these areas, quite consistent with substantive inequality. And not only 'consistent with', since the law regulates and so sustains the social and economic relations of bourgeois society it may be plausibly argued that formal rights *perpetuate* substantive inequality. As Marx put it, all rights are rights to be unequal. This is true also of equality under the law ('it must be the same for all, whether it protects or punishes' – Article 6 of the French *Declaration*). We have seen how inequalities in substantive powers to enter and be effective within the public sphere entail inequalities of participation in the formation of law. But the application of the law, as well, in taking no account of substantive inequalities, must necessarily perpetuate them. Legal rights are formally codified and accessible only to the educated and literate. To the extent that effective defence or prosecution depends upon specialist knowledge of law, and trained advocacy, to that extent differential access to the professional bearers of these qualifications implies substantive inequality in access to justice under the law.

The difference between formal and substantive rights is also apparent where rights conflict. Article 4 of the French *Declaration* defines liberty in a way which acknowledges the possibility of a conflict of rights:

> Liberty consists in being able to do anything that does not harm another person. Thus the exercise of the natural rights of each has no limits except those which assure to the other members of society the enjoyment of these same rights; these limits can be determined only by law.

Each individual is here conceptualized as autonomous and self-sufficient, each exercising liberties within a personal 'territory', the law operating, as Marx put it, as a 'boundary post' between these territories. One question socialist criticism has raised concerns the notion of a personal territory – an inviolable private space – implicit in liberal conceptions of liberty. This is an important dispute and I will return to it later,[29] but my focus here is on a second question concerning the way liberal rights discourse abstracts from the substantive social relations in which the individual right-holders stand to one another.

If we consider one central category of such relations, that of employers to employees, it is clear that exercise of liberty by one party is often *ipso facto* restriction on the liberties of the other. For example, social researchers or other public or private employees often acquire knowledge, the publication of which may be considered damaging to the interests of the state organization or firm concerned. One response to this is for the employer to insist upon a contract of employment (or research contract) through which the employee renounces his or her normal rights of freedom of expression. Where the knowledge concerned is claimed as 'property' by the employer, this may be seen as a conflict between the right to freedom of expression and the right to property.

Alternatively, and more generally, the conflict may be conceptualized as between the rights of differently placed individuals (or groups of agents). The employer has a property right to dispose of wealth as he or she chooses – one such option is to purchase the labour-time of individuals who thereby become employees. But the individual who has agreed to sell his or her labour-time, in doing so, renounces the full range of substantive liberties inconsistent with being an employee: depending on the kind of employment these may include liberty of movement, freedom of association, free communication of thoughts and opinions, and others. In these respects the relation between employee and employer is by its nature conflictual: exercise of liberties by the one implies loss of liberties by the other. Freedom for the pike is death to the minnow. As Keat succinctly puts it: 'the exercise of private property rights (unless these are hedged around with such extensive qualifications as to render them practically meaningless) is incompatible with the maintenance of an (equal) right to liberty'.[30]

In such cases what the liberal rights discourse proposes is equal consideration of the rights of each party, and the use of law to define the 'boundary' between them. If each party is, as the discourse of the French *Declaration* suggests, autonomous and self-sufficient, then the role of the law is simply to ensure compliance with the contract they freely enter into with one another. Though he does not endorse it, Tom Campbell recognizes the force of the socialist criticism of 'legalism', the point being that depending on the material circumstances, a perfectly fair and dispassionate application of a rule may be unjust in its outcome:

> not only may particular decisions made according to rules result in material injustice, but a rule may systematically discriminate against the poor and the

oppressed. In such circumstances, to be committed to applying the rules, however fairly or impartially administered, come what may, is to ignore the more obvious and direct demands of justice and human welfare which socialism is intended to serve.[31]

But if one acknowledges the differential power of employee and employer prior to their contract, the dependence of the former upon employment for meeting their most basic needs, and the freedom of the latter from any such immediate exigency, then the status of the contract as a voluntary agreement, entered into by equal partners, looks questionable. Where, under pressure from organized workers and their supporters in liberal democracies, legal immunities[32] are granted to employees' organizations this constitutes an acknowledgement of the relative vulnerability of individual employees in entering into contracts with their employers. The incompatibility of such recognitions with the ontology of the liberal rights discourse is reflected in the common complaint that they put trade unions 'above the law'.

Where basic rights are in conflict, and positive law adjudicates, the likelihood is that socially, economically and politically powerful groups will be successful in ensuring that their interests predominate in the drawing of the 'boundary' between their liberties and those of the less powerful. The opportunities for the less powerful to enjoy their 'imprescriptible rights' will be severely circumscribed by the requirement that they do not conflict with the more extensively entrenched rights of the powerful. This limit to the equality conferred by citizenship rights upon individuals who are simultaneously unequally placed in their material conditions of life is acknowledged by Rawls, the most widely cited of all modern liberal theorists of justice: 'the worth of liberty is not the same for everyone. Some have greater authority and wealth, and therefore greater means to achieve their aims'.[33] As Keat[34] points out, however, Rawls's proposals to deal with this dilemma are reforms aimed at instituting fair competition for access to privileged positions, rather than constraints on liberty-denying social inequalities themselves.

Finally, as we saw in the latter part of chapter 3, the enjoyment of rights has motivational and social structural conditions. The bearer of rights may, under hostile social or cultural conditions, lack the will or the skills to exercise them, or the self-respect to claim them. Powerful groups may ensure that legally defined rights may be abused with impunity by obstructing enforcement, influencing the choice of mode of enforcement, or by the underfunding of enforcement. In each of these respects in which agents may be assigned formal rights but be unable to exercise them, the liberal-individualist discourse has ways of resolving the simultaneous presence and absence of rights in a non-contradictory way, a way which, in effect, legitimates continuing inequality and lack of rights.

In the liberal-individualist paradigm, rights are generally defined 'negatively': as restraints on others.[35] My freedom of expression is the non-right of anyone else to silence me, my freedom of movement the non-right of anyone else to obstruct it. Two aspects of this conceptualization are of particular significance here. First the intrinsic ability of the self-sufficient individual subject of liberal rights to exercise his or her liberties is taken as a 'given' attribute. Second, the sources of obstacles to the exercise of these liberties are assigned to two categories only: other individual agents and public authorities (also conceived as analogous to, if not identical with, individual intentional agents).

As I have tried to show, the sociological critique of rights sees the hiatus between negative, or formal, rights and their positive, or substantive, realization as having its source in a systematic mismatch between the actual conditions of existence and action of individuals in this range of societies, on the one hand, and, on the other, these underlying presuppositions of the negative definition of rights. Where abilities (effective communication in writing or in print, legal knowledge and skills of advocacy, and so on) rest upon unequally distributed aptitudes or require unequally distributed resources for their acquisition or exercise, then injustice results from proceeding as though they were 'given' intrinsic abilities. And where the acquisition or exercise of an ability is dependent upon the vagaries of individual biography or upon position in an unequal social structure, to treat obstacles to the enjoyment of rights as exhausted by the categories of individual agent and public authority is to ignore some of the most pervasive forces which shape the individual and her or his life chances in capitalist societies.

Of course, the possibility exists that space can be made for these considerations to be addressed within the terms of the liberal rights discourse itself. The *Virginia Bill of Rights* (1776), for example, speaks (Article 1) of an inherent right of 'pursuing and obtaining happiness and safety'. Happiness is not a 'given' state, it must be pursued, and, having pursued it, is something we have a right to retain. This suggests something not fully definable within the bounds of a 'negative' right: it suggests a right not just to be free from obstruction in the pursuit of happiness, but a right to be enabled, or empowered, to obtain it.

However, the systematic incorporation of such considerations into a revitalized discourse of rights did not come until the present century. During the nineteenth century, in the most economically developed nations of the West, extensions of rights of citizenship – most notably of the franchise – were won, piecemeal, by successive waves of working-class, popular and feminist agitation. Ameliorative reform in the social, industrial and cultural spheres generally accompanied the extension of the franchise: if the newly won

117

franchise was not to be used for revolutionary purposes, the masses must be 'gentled'. Central to the new reforms was an extension of working-class education as 'the means by which the mass of the people, the "labouring poor" would be brought to understand their identity of interest with capital'.[36] In Britain, progressive liberals such as John Stuart Mill who had supported the extension of the franchise, and opponents, such as Robert Lowe, were united by the 1867 Reform Act, in seeing educational and broader social reform as vital to order and stability:

> should the working class legislate in their own interests, 'our entire system of industry and commerce would undergo a revolution, and with it every institution of property'; if the manual labour class 'usurped such a predominance as to give it the practical control of the house of commons', the resultant evils would 'assume the monstrous proportions of a destructive revolution'. The workers must, then, be educated to vote for their betters.[37]

But only with the turn of the present century did progressive liberals, under the influence of socialist agitation, begin to conceptualize such social and economic developments as positive rights of citizenship. The real watershed for the idea of human rights, however, was the Second World War. The victors had mobilized popular support for the war-effort by way of an egalitarian and inclusive appeal to a future safe from the atrocities and abuses of Nazism, but also with a firm commitment that there could be no going back to the unemployment, hardships and insecurities of the 1930s. When it emerged, as the theoretical underpinning of the post-war welfare state, and in the United Nations *Universal Declaration of Human Rights* (1948) the new discourse on rights affirmed more than the traditional liberal agenda inherited from the early modern period. Not only were civil liberties and the traditional 'rights of man' re-affirmed, but universal rights to full democratic participation in the political sphere were consolidated, and a range of new rights to economic and social security was added, not merely as conditions for the 'positive' exercise of legal and political rights, but as morally valid claims in their own right.

This radicalized version of the liberal discourse of rights retains its links with that of the early modern period, in continuing to regard the human individual as the sovereign bearer of moral value, the paradigm locus of rights, but simultaneously acknowledges key elements in the socialist critique of that earlier discourse and practice of rights. Rights are purely formal, ineffective, if the individual is in practice unable to acquire the necessary skills or resources to exercise them. Any strategy designed to enable or empower individuals in the appropriate ways must necessarily acknowledge the socially conditioned character of individual skills and capacities, acquisition and exercise of which are presupposed in negative rights. Legal and political rights, in particular, cannot be exercised equally by individual citizens, unless certain social, economic and cultural conditions also obtain: universal literacy and political education, economic independence, self-respect, personal autonomy, and so on.

Indeed, the earlier tradition of liberal rights had also acknowledged this, in an inverted form. Restrictions on the political rights of women, domestic servants and others whose state of social or economic dependence was held to militate against their formation of an autonomous judgement of public affairs eventually gave way, in most liberal capitalist regimes, to a universal franchise only after prolonged and bitter political struggles. But to make these newly-won political rights effective, to fully emancipate the political citizen, would necessitate a further social, cultural and economic emancipation: the full cultural, financial and economic independence of women, an end to ethnic and racial disadvantage, the securing of occupational rights of several kinds, and so on.[38]

As my last sentence indicates, this radicalization of the liberal tradition, taking seriously the notion of effective, positive rights does entail, as Marx foresaw, a certain transcendence of the division between state and civil society. Social, economic and cultural rights come to be recognized as both necessary to the realization of legal and political rights and as, in their own terms, independently valid claims. The classic statement of this form of modern, radicalized liberalism is T.H. Marshall's (1949) 'Citizenship and Social Class'.[39] It is important to notice, however, that Marshall did not anticipate a reconciliation between the class inequalities of a capitalist society and the socially integrative, egalitarian connotations of an extension of citizenship into the social sphere. Welfare capitalism was, for him, an institutional framework within which an unavoidable tension between incompatible organizational principles might be contained.

More or less simultaneous with Marshall's work, in the aftermath of the Second World War, the United Nations *Universal Declaration of Human Rights* reiterated each of the 'negative' rights of man and citizen but, significantly, added a series of articles explicitly specifying a series of economic, social and cultural rights:

> Everyone has the right to a standard of living adequate for the health and well-being of himself and of his family, including food, clothing, housing and medical care and necessary social services, and the right to security in the event of unemployment, sickness, disability, widowhood, old age or other lack of livelihood in circumstances beyond his control. [from Article 25]

> Everyone has the right to education. Education shall be free, at least in the elementary and fundamental stages. Elementary education shall be compulsory. [from Article 26]

Everyone has the right freely to participate in the cultural life of the community, to enjoy the arts and to share in scientific advancement and its benefits. [from Article 27]

But to acknowledge the social, economic and cultural requirements for effective rights is not the same thing as to bring those requirements into existence. As Laqueur and Rubin point out, 'while millions of men and women have indeed turned to the Universal Declaration of Human Rights, they have received very little guidance and no help from the organization that propagated it'.[40] The problem of a hiatus between formally declared rights and the actual conditions of life of many millions of people remains. Nevertheless, the terms of the radicalized liberal discourse of the *Universal Declaration* mark a major shift from those of the great constitutional statements of the eighteenth century. Two points are especially worthy of note. One is that the shift from a negative to a positive view of rights as implying enablements, or empowerments, directs our attention to the resource requirements of this shift.[41] This is explicit in Article 22:

Everyone, as a member of society, has the right to social security and is entitled to realization, through national effort and international co-operation and in accordance with the organization and resources of each state, of the economic, social and cultural rights indispensable for his dignity and the free development of his personality.

And if the creation, appropriation and direction of social wealth is a precondition for the realization of rights, this poses the further question of the institutional locus of responsibility for this task, its organizational capacities and its will to perform the duties imposed upon it. This goes a long way beyond Tom Regan's (and Feinberg's) view of rights as a claim on some assignable individual moral agent to respectful treatment. A new set of questions is posed concerning the status of public institutions – either of nation states or international organizations – as bearers of moral responsibilities, their relationship to moral and political communities, their social, economic and political conditions of existence, and the interests they serve. Adequate answers to these questions would, of course, be necessary to any adequate understanding of the relative failure of implementation of the UN *Declaration*. Marx's insistence upon the pertinence of the relation between the state and civil society is, again, vindicated. This time, however, the radicalized discourse of rights does not legitimate, but rather exposes to view, both the hiatus between promise and reality, and its institutional sources.

A Conceptual Critique: The Bourgeois Limits of Bourgeois Rights

So far I have reviewed some of the well-established radical criticism of rights as merely formal, and so ineffective in the protection of individuals, as long as the profound social and economic inequalities of capitalist societies persist.

I have also suggested that the liberal-individualist discourse of rights has responded to these criticisms by moving towards a positive rather than negative conceptualization of rights and by adding social, economic and cultural rights to the early modern list of rights of 'man and citizen'. Arguably, however, in the absence of profound alterations in social and economic relations, these advances in the discourse of rights serve only to render more evident the gap between aspiration and reality.

I now turn to a second set of radical criticisms of the rights discourse. These have to do not with the realizability of rights under capitalism, but with the limited, defective character of the liberal view of rights itself. Since my main source is Marx, I shall focus on the socialist view of the limitations of the early modern discourse of rights, but much of the argument applies also to its later, radicalized version. There are three distinguishable threads, or 'themes' in this conceptual critique of liberal rights. The first, and most fundamental, is the socialist challenge to the liberal-individualist view of individual persons, the nature of their interests, and the kinds of harm to which they are peculiarly liable. Socialists characteristically criticize the liberal tendency to abstract individuals from their social-relational setting when they come to define basic interests and to assign priorities for protection in the form of moral or legal rights. There is much in common between this strand of socialist argument and the case made out by contemporary critics such as Michael Sandel. My discussion will endorse this line of socialist criticism, but also seeks to extend it by bringing into focus human liability to basic harms in virtue of our embodiment and our dependence on an appropriate bio-physical environment. These features of the human condition are, I shall suggest, unjustifiably occluded or marginalized in the main liberal-individualist traditions of rights.

The second strand or theme in the conceptual critique challenges liberal-individualist views of the sources of harm to which individuals are vulnerable. In the liberal-individualist view the obligations correlative to rights are requirements placed upon other individuals to act, or refrain from acting, in ways which affect the basic interests of right-holders. But what if those basic interests are susceptible to forms of damage or destruction from which they *can* be protected, but yet which are not reducible to the voluntary actions, or inactions, of identifiable individuals? It is arguable that a great deal of the risk, danger and harm suffered by individuals in society falls into this category. What purchase does the liberal-individualist discourse of rights have upon it? The third and last theme in the radical conceptual critique is really an extension of the first. If a discourse and practice of rights is required to protect the basic interests and well-being of individuals, it is argued, this can only be because they live under conditions of social life in which autonomy, mutual respect, compassion and benevolence in people's spontaneous relations with

121

one another cannot be relied upon. An emancipatory transformation of society would realize these virtues and relations in ways which would further individual flourishing. These relations would render the practice of rights superfluous, while the newly emerging forms of individuality, or selfhood, would render the terms of the *discourse* of rights itself inapplicable. This question is given only a very preliminary treatment towards the end of this chapter, and the theme is taken up again in chapter 7.

The Conceptual Critique (1)
Persons, their Interests and Vulnerabilities

As we saw, Marx objected to the French *Declaration* for its protection of the private interests of the 'egoistic' individuals of civil society, for its representation of such 'egoistic' individuals as 'natural' man, for its separation of natural man from political man, the acknowledged member of the political community, and for its subordination of political man to the prior interests and purposes of 'natural' man. The rights discourse of the eighteenth-century constitutional documents, then, presupposes and endorses a certain view of the human individual and her or his well-being to which Marx objects.

What are the attributes of this 'egoistic' individual? Each individual has, as 'natural' attributes, personal autonomy, a capacity to reason and to use language, to recognize moral requirements and to act in conformity to or defiance of them, to reach voluntary agreements with others, to acquire and dispose of property, and to be harmed or benefited with respect to these various attributes, the protection of which constitutes their 'private interest'. Marx's comments suggest that this way of conceptualizing the individual and her or his capacities and interests is defective in several important ways.

First, individuals are recognized as 'self-sufficient' or 'monadic' in the sense that they are the bearers of these attributes, abilities and interests independently of their relations to other individuals (though the exercise of some of their abilities may put them into such relations). From a socialist standpoint, this view of the individual may be questioned in several ways. First, abilities such as language-use, reasoning, moral action, and attributes such as personal autonomy have complex social-relational and cultural presuppositions. They are not developed as attributes or abilities of individuals unless these external presuppositions are present in their social milieu. Second, once acquired, these attributes and abilities are not self-sustaining. Abilities and attributes of individuals may be lost or become atrophied if individuals are deprived of means of maintaining their intrinsic conditions (mental and physical health) or extrinsic conditions (cultural and institutional forms and relations). Third, abilities possessed by individuals may not be exercised independently of an appropriate cultural and institutional setting: property ownership and reaching voluntary agreements are obvious cases, but the point is no less true of reason, language and morality. These lines of argument, as we have seen, flow directly from the claim that rights are unrealizable under conditions of social and economic deprivation, and to a considerable extent the discourse of liberal rights can be appropriately radicalized to take account of them, at least at the level of their theoretical representation.

More intractable, from the standpoint of liberal individualism, are the problems surrounding the individualist notion of 'interests'. The primary objections here are inherited by the socialist tradition from a much older and broader tradition of civic humanism. According to this view it is both absurd and demeaning to attribute to individuals an interest in preserving only their own individual qualities, abilities and property.[42] The bonds of affection individuals establish with one another, and the attachments they form to common goods of many kinds are such that a harm to such common goods or other persons is experienced as a harm to those to whom they are attached. Our individual identities are, in other words, indissolubly bound up with our social-relational setting in ways which make a nonsense of the individualist conception of interests. This conclusion can, indeed, be reached by way of a reflection on the implications of the socially conditioned character of individual attributes and abilities themselves. If these are valued, and so part of the interests of individuals, then so, too, must be the preservation of their external, social and cultural, conditions of existence. If this view of the interests of individuals is taken seriously, then the protection of these interests would take the form of preservating certain aspects of their communal life rather than erecting fences, or boundaries between the territories of each.

Another line of criticism of this view of individual interests is especially plausible as an objection to its eighteenth-century version. The list of interest-constituting attributes singled out for special protection as rights of the individual is a rather select list. What are the principles and criteria involved in this selection? Why are certain sorts of harm explicitly ruled out? Singularly lacking in explicit acknowledgement, for example, are a range of bodily harms: though freedom from arbitrary arrest is a cardinal principle in virtually all of the eighteenth-century declarations, little or nothing is explicitly said about health, physical shelter, bodily integrity, reproduction, nutrition or work. Surely, deprivation or abuse in any of these respects would constitute a harm to the individual of a very fundamental kind, both in its own terms, and in its implications for the individual's capacity to exercise rights – such as freedom of conscience, of association, and so on – which *are* explicitly mentioned.

How should this lack in the eighteenth-century rights discourse be understood? One way of understanding it would be very much in line with at least one strand of Marx's critique: an abstract view of individual interests which gives priority to 'ideal' attributes and powers, independently of both their material, bodily and social-relational conditions of fulfilment is precisely what would be required for the discourse of rights to play its ideological role. Only such an abstract conception of individual interests and rights could sustain the ethical legitimacy of a social form characterized by such profound social and economic inequalities and such widespread material deprivation and suffering. There is, undoubtedly, considerable truth in this as a bald statement of the legitimating role of the eighteenth-century rights discourse once it had become established as the juridical and constitutional framework of the nineteenth-century European and American capitalist states. However, it does nothing to make intelligible the immense critical power of the rights discourse in the eighteenth century and since.

The interests which that discourse foregrounded as requiring firm protection in the form of rights were precisely those which were perceived as most requiring assertion as conditions of political emancipation from feudal and monarchical forms of authority and dependence; hence the centrality of specifically civil liberties and political rights. Marx, of course, acknowledged this in recognizing that these rights did constitute 'a big step forward': but they did not go far enough in their recognition of the range of relations or conditions of life from which individuals required emancipation. I shall, a little later, say something more on this limitation of scope in the rights discourse.

Finally, in a provisional defence of the eighteenth-century rights discourse, it might be argued that those attributes of the person which it singles out for special protection as rights – freedom of conscience and of speech, the political rights, to consent, or withhold consent, and so on – are precisely those which distinguish the human from the animal. Rights are there to protect not merely the animal being, but to underwrite the living of a life fully in accord with the *human* value and potential of the individual. In the light of this interpretation, the foregrounding of personal autonomy, psychological powers and political rights as against mere bodily requirements is a symptom of the depth of the radicalism of this discourse – the height of its aspirations. This, too, would make intelligible the nineteenth-century 'positivist' rejection of the discourse of rights because of its grounding in a speculative, metaphysical theory of human nature.[43]

But, in so far as the discourse and practice of human rights has been sustained into the twentieth century it has, as we have seen, undergone a radicalization in the face of these and other critical challenges. It could certainly be claimed, with justice, that such international documents as the United Nations *Universal Declaration of Human Rights*, the *International*

Covenant on Economic, Social and Cultural Rights (1966) and the European *Convention for the Protection of Human Rights* and *Fundamental Convention for the Protection of Human Rights and Fundamental Freedoms* (1953) do, as a consequence of their shift to a more 'positive', concrete specification of rights, acknowledge bodily well-being, social belonging and cultural identity as germane to the interests of individuals. As we saw above (pp. 119–20) the *Universal Declaration* speaks explicitly of rights to health, medical care, social security in the event of unemployment or other causes of loss of livelihood, to education, freedom from sexual or racial discrimination, and so on. Article 24 asserts a right to 'reasonable limitation of working hours and periodic holidays with pay', whilst Article 23 proclaims rights to 'form and join trade unions' and to 'equal pay for equal work'.

I have already mentioned the continuing hiatus between the declaration of the more positive, concretely specified rights and their implementation. But it is also worth noticing a further consequence of the way in which these rights are specified is that the lineaments of a definite type of social order are clearly visible. The limitation of working hours, the provision of paid holidays, the organization of trade unions, and equal pay all presuppose the institution of wage-labour, or some analogous system of social organization of labour and production, whilst the linkage of health with medical care and social security with unemployment insurance strongly suggests the institutional framework of the welfare state. Though the *Universal Declaration* and the other documents proclaim universality, they broaden and deepen the eighteenth-century rights discourse only at the cost of a conceptual restriction of the scope of rights to those societies in which the institutions of liberal-democratic welfare-state capitalism (or their close analogues) are present. It remains to be seen whether the limitations of abstract, liberal-individualist rights discourse can be overcome without, in this way, relativizing rights-claims to specific social forms, and thereby blunting their critical cutting-edge.[44]

There remain two further features of the eighteenth-century rights discourse to which Marx took exception, and which have become commonplaces of the radical critique of rights. These are, first, the presumption of a division among the interests of the individual between those which are a matter of private concern, and those which appertain to public life. This is at least part of the content of Marx's denunciation of the 'egoism' of the individual of bourgeois civil society, and also bears on his critique of the division between state and civil society itself. Second, and also connected with the charge of 'egoism', is the mutual antagonism of individual interests which Marx takes to be presupposed as a feature of human nature in the rights discourse.

First the private/public distinction, which is expressed, in the rights discourse, in the distinction between, on the one hand, the rights of man, and, on the other, the political rights of the citizen. The rights of man are the rights of the individual of civil society, 'an individual withdrawn into himself, into the confines of his private interest and private caprice, and separated from the community' (see note 16). As far as these non-political aspects of life are concerned, society, the 'species-life itself', appears as external to the individual, and as a limit to autonomy and self-sufficiency. In part this is a matter of mere appearance: individuals are already, as we have seen, social beings, but the rights discourse is ideological in its representation of individuals under a form of abstraction in which their sociality is invisible. But this discourse gets its plausibility from a form of social life which also in practice 'individualizes' the social beings who live it, and it also remains conceptually tied to a stage in the historical development of human society at which the potential for all-round human sociability is still unactualized. A transcendence of the division between state and civil society will make possible a comparable transcendence of the division within the life of each individual between the private and the public self. That which is now withdrawn from society as a private domain will become an area for full social participation.

If we bear in mind Marx's tendency to think of the 'rights of man' as centring upon, if not reducible to, property rights, this is readily defensible. For at least one category of property, ownership of means and conditions of production, the rights of property-owners decisively affect the conditions of life and well-being of many non-owners of such property. In Marx's view, the way these property rights are exercised has a profound bearing upon the shape and dynamics of social life as a whole. To regard it as a merely private matter, as the eighteenth-century rights discourse does, is to sweep these dimensions of the social character of property rights out of sight. Subsequent attempts, in radicalized rights discourses, to define rights of economic and industrial citizenship are responses to this line of criticism, and in effect they impose restrictions on the primary right of private ownership for those categories of property whose broader social weight and significance is recognized.

But does every non-political right of the individual come into this category: liberty of thought and conscience, freedom of movement and association, and personal security; the right, in short, to do what one pleases in those aspects of life in which the rights of others to do likewise are not affected? Undoubtedly, the assertion of such a 'private' sphere has a historical and cultural dimension to it. Also, it must be recognized that much of what has gone on under cover of the inviolability of the 'household' as the institutional locus of the private has been profoundly oppressive: much of the history and some of the continuing sources of oppression of women reside here, along with the often enforced subordination and dependence of a class of domestic servants. A whole range of abuses of women, children and servants only now is being brought into the light of public scrutiny.[45] No one should take the assertion of a right to privacy at its face value, as an innocent request to be left to get on with one's own life without interference. Set against this, however, is a critical and, arguably, emancipatory side to the demand for a private sphere, free from public interference. Freedom of thought, conscience, religious worship, expression and association, for example, are not freedoms whose exercise by one individual generally involves the oppression of anyone else. In those more-or-less exceptional cases where it does, boundary fences, as Marx recognizes, can be drawn.

But if there is admitted to exist a class of individual freedoms whose exercise does not in general infringe the freedoms of others, then what is to be said against a moral and legal framework which protects these freedoms as 'rights'? Again, depending upon whether we give priority to 'bourgeois' individuality as 'individualized' sociality or 'as-yet-undeveloped' sociality the answer will be different. If the former aspect is emphasized, then what is wrong with a discourse which singles out these freedoms for protection is that it does not call into question the form of society in which such aspects of individual well-being *require* protection. Only because individuals have come to see themselves as islands unto themselves, constantly at risk of invading one another's territory, has it become necessary to impose an authoritative restraint upon them. I will return to explore this thesis further, in chapter 7, but, for now, it should suffice to note that a society in which universal and spontaneous mutual benevolence could be relied upon seems to be a somewhat remote prospect from our vantage point at the end of the twentieth century.

If, on the other hand, as-yet-undeveloped sociality is emphasized, then what is wrong with the rights discourse is that it 'freezes' a conception of the conditions of individual well-being at a primitive stage of human social development. The possibility exists, at least, that the valuing of a private sphere of self-regarding activity as intrinsic to a fulfilled life, and a necessary medium for personal development, is a transitory historical product, co-terminous with bourgeois society and transcendable along with it. The post-bourgeois, socialist or communist society may, therefore, be able to dispense with these 'rights of man', the freedoms of the individual within a private sphere, for either of two quite distinct reasons: either individuals will so relate to one another in such a society that enjoyment of these freedoms will be a matter of course, will not require the protection of a discourse or juridical apparatus of rights, or individuals will be so altered in their connection to the communal life they share that they will cease to experience a 'private sphere' as essential to their well-being and personal development.[46] Again, more of this later.

So far, then, I have rehearsed some socialist (and, more generally, 'radical' lines of criticism of the liberal-individualist conception of rights, lines of criticism having to do not solely with the alleged unrealizability of rights in capitalist societies, but also with limitations or distortions in the liberal-individualist concept of 'right' itself. The criticisms have centred on the way in which, in liberal rights discourse, individuals, their attributes, interests and mutual relations are conceptualized. In particular, a certain decontextualized view of the individual and her or his well-being is fostered, together with an associated view of the relations between such individuals as 'naturally' external-instrumental, and essentially competitive/conflictual. Authoritative regulation of individual conduct is required both to secure each individual in her or his enjoyment of a legitimate sphere of free action, and to restrain each individual's tendency to encroach on the territory of her or his neighbour.

The Conceptual Critique (2) Sources of Harm

The next step is to consider the way in which the liberal discourse of rights conceptualizes the sources of those harms to individuals which constitute abuses of rights. These sources are two-fold. First, individuals are vulnerable to invasion, or abuses of their rights perpetrated by their fellow individual citizens. Indeed, in the contractarian tradition, it is the requirement to provide a defence against this expectation which serves as the main rational basis for the establishment of public authority itself. The conception of individuals as naturally relating to one another as means rather than as ends, as competitors or antagonists rather than as collaborators, is the ontological basis for the expectation.

The second source of potential abuse or invasion of rights is the sovereign power itself, or the bearers of the delegated powers of the sovereign. In the eighteenth-century constitutional declarations, for example, the right to property is clearly stated not, primarily, as an obligation on the part of the public authority to safeguard the possessions of citizens from theft, but, rather, as a limit on the public power itself, *vis-à-vis* the property of individuals. Article 17 of the French *Declaration* (1789), for example, licenses the deprivation of property only where 'public necessity, legally determined, clearly requires such action, and then only on condition of a just and prior indemnity'. The legal rights of individuals, too, come primarily within this category: the presumption of innocence until shown guilty, the bans on arbitrary arrest and retrospective judgement are all designed to protect the interest of individual citizens from abuses of the power by public authorities.

Again, the socialist tradition sees in this conceptual limitation on the range of possible sources of abuse to rights a further instance of complicity between the liberal-individualist rights discourse and attempts tolegitimate of the liberal-democratic capitalist form of social order. It is, indeed, the other face of the coin from the negative concept of rights. The socialist view recognizes three broad categories of sources of harm to individuals which are irreducible either to intentional acts of other persons or to deliberate acts of public authorities. First, there are harms which result from acts of commission or omission on the part of private or public organizations – business corporations, state enterprises, trade unions, voluntary associations, and so on. Where these organizations are large, and are characterized by a complex division of labour and a diffuse structure of delegated causal powers and decision-making responsibilities, it may be impossible to authoritatively assign individual responsibility for harms caused by institutional acts. As Celia Wells puts it:

> Crime is subject to a form of legal construction which excludes corporate or collective harm. The analysis of crime into an 'act' and a 'state of mind' immediately marginalizes corporate behaviour which is typically much more diverse in its behaviour and diffuse in its chains of decision-making.[47]

Wells argues that there are symbolic relationships between common-sense notions of 'crimes' as violent acts committed by individuals causing harm to others and legal constructions of crime which are similarly individualist in their conceptualization. Field and Jörg, similarly, note the influence of individualist notions of responsibility, such as H.L.A. Hart's depiction of 'aims', 'intentions', 'knowledge', and so on as 'psychological characteristics'.[48]

The effect of this pressure to conceptualize the locus of moral and legal responsibility in the individual human person is to obstruct the recognition of collective agents such as corporations as criminally responsible for harms which result from their activities or failures of action. Recent episodes such as the capsizing of the ferry *Herald of Free Enterprise* at Zeebrugge, the King's Cross fire and the Charing Cross railway crash have all served to renew controversy about the capacity of the UK legal system to recognize corporate manslaughter and effectively prosecute it. The world's worst industrial disaster, the Union Carbide chemical plant explosion at Bhopal, raises further issues about the legal accountability of multi-nationals operating across the boundaries of legal jurisdictions and of cultural, ethnic, economic and environmental contexts.

In their analysis of the workings of law on corporate liability in England and Wales, Field and Jörg show how rulings against 'aggregation' of individual responsibility, combined with the doctrine of 'identification' protect corporations from the full force of criminal law. According to the doctrine of identification, 'in every corporation there are certain people who control and direct its activities and who are considered, when they act on the company's business, to be the embodiment of the company'.[49] In other words, if culpability cannot be assigned to an individual 'controlling officer' of a corporation, then the corporation evades criminal liability. If corporate structure is diffuse and responsibilities are not clearly assigned, or delegated, precisely the sort of situation in which health and safety is particularly at risk, the corporation concerned is *more* likely to evade criminal liability. As Field and Jörg point out, it is 'clearly in the interest of shrewd and unscrupulous management' to decentralize safety services, contract-out safety research and so on as a strategy for avoiding successful prosecution. In the case of the *Herald of Free Enterprise* disaster, Field and Jörg show why it is that organizational criteria, not reducible to individual action or inaction, need to be taken into account if a construction of corporate liability is to overcome these problems:

> The sinking of the *Herald of Free Enterprise* can be directly, if narrowly, attributed to the failure of individuals. One could blame the Assistant Bosun who failed to shut the bow door as the ship sailed or the Loading Officer formally entrusted by a general corporate instruction with a duty to ensure that bow doors were secure when leaving port. But as the Sheen Report recognised, the corporate management may also be regarded as morally responsible for allowing pressure to build on crew to improve turn around time, for failure to scrutinise the enforcement of corporate instructions on bow doors and for not properly considering alternative checks or properly defining responsibility for safety. The collapse of the P & O trial merely serves to demonstrate the way that the individual British criteria do not reflect this collective responsibility.[50]

Field and Jörg use recent developments in Dutch law as a basis for developing workable criteria for a non-individualist construal of corporate criminal responsibility. According to them, corporations have 'policies, standing orders, regulations and institutionalised practices' which are evidence of corporate aims, intentions and knowledge that are not reducible to the aims, intentions and knowledge of individuals within the corporation.[51] Arguably, such attempts to revise moral and legal precepts go beyond liberal-individualist views of rights, in assigning positive rights to victims of corporate harms *vis-à-vis* the responsible collective agents. However, in so far as they are proposals for reform to legal systems in societies still marked by great concentrations of economic and political power, all of the standard sociological arguments concerning dilution of actual legislation, ineffective monitoring and reluctant enforcement continue to apply.[52]

The second class of sources of harm not assimilable to the liberal-individualist paradigm are those which result from the position of an individual in a social structure, or practical routine of life. These are the harms to which the more catastrophic and headline-catching cases just discussed 'represent the fluorescent tip of a submerged but ever present iceberg', to use Celia Wells's words.[53] They are the hidden injuries of class.[54] In their analysis of Bhopal, Pearce and Tombs[55] recognize that accidents may be caused by 'careless', 'irresponsible' or 'reckless' actions (of individuals or corporations) but they also point to the importance of 'normal accidents',[56] the results of 'those hazards and risks intrinsic to any particular production processes that we consider indispensable in any complex industrial economy'. They continue:

> One can make the confident generalization that whenever industrial plant is subject to close scrutiny, it will be discovered that violations of health and safety or environmental pollution laws are extensive and routine and thus a normal part of production. The non-detection of these violations allows the firm's accountants to ignore them as mere 'externalities' and its engineers to discount them as the price of progress.[57]

There remain massive class-differentials in life-expectancy and in liability to chronic or life-threatening illness in all of the advanced industrial societies.[58] There are, too, significant correlations between causes of death and occupation, for example, between mining and lung diseases, nuclear reprocessing and leukaemia, and so on. How do we conceptualize such occupational hazards and 'injuries of class'? Two broad approaches are available for conceptualizing such harms in ways amenable to the liberal-individualist vocabulary of rights. One, the 'bio-medical' model, acknowledges both the dependence of personal well-being on organic, bodily functioning, and the liability of the body to exogenous harms. Abstracting from the socio-economically patterned incidence of these harms, the bio-medical model licenses a conception of health rights and justice as a matter of equal access to a socially provided apparatus of diagnosis and treatment. Though I am a long way from endorsing some currently fashionable critiques of contemporary scientific medicine and bureaucratic health-care provision, it must be equally clear that the model of health rights it presupposes is very limited. It is very important to be assured, in the event of becoming ill, that one has access to the best available diagnosis and treatment, provided without regard to social status, political influence, or ability to pay. But most of us would, I think, prefer not to become ill in the first place.

The second way of conceptualizing these socially caused harms acknowledges this point. It licenses an extension of the notion of rights from the area of diagnosis and treatment to that of liability to harm itself. This way of thinking has given rise to the legislation and practices of environmental health, and, in a more specifically occupational context, 'health and safety'. Significant though these advances are, they continue to be limited in their *de facto* power to protect. The familiar problem of dilution of legislation, exemptions, ineffective or inadequately resourced enforcement, and so on, which are associated with the power of vested interests, apply here, as elsewhere. An additional feature in this context is the dependence of effective health protection measures on acquisition and publication of often quite recondite knowledge. Again vested interests may be at work in excluding available knowledge from the public sphere, actively blocking necessary research, or, simply, failing to resource it.[59]

More germane to my main argument, however, is the conceptual pressure in these forms of legislation and enforcement towards assigning individuals as loci of responsibility, both as causal agents affecting liability to harm and as bearers of moral/legal responsibility for health protection. This is, of course, a necessity if the liberal-rights discourse is to have any purchase at all on this range of problems. It is, within limits, a desirable and justifiable practice. Whatever the power of structural constraints and pressures which shape life on a building site, a North Sea oil rig, an open-cast mine or an agro-chemicals plant there are always areas of discretion within which the difference between good and bad individual or group practice can be a difference of life and death. It follows that legislation which requires, facilitates or encourages awareness of risk and the taking of personal responsibility for minimizing it has some purchase on those conditions of life it addresses.

But how much purchase? One limit has to do with the relative scale and influence of countervailing pressures on the ways individuals exercise choice within the area of discretion available to them. Where safety precautions cost time and other resources, employers and managers facing a harsh competitive environment have strong motives for overlooking their responsibilities, and, reciprocally, workers frequently face powerful short-term economic incentives to sacrifice longer-term health and safety considerations. Another, more intractable limit has to do with inherent constraints built into social practices themselves, limits beyond which even 'best practice' cannot offer adequate protection. The appropriate question here is not, for example, 'how can the health of workers in nuclear reprocessing be best protected?' but 'given that nuclear reprocessing is inherently dangerous, what good reasons are there for continuing to practise it?'

The third general category of sources of harm to individuals which puts conceptual pressure on the liberal discourse of rights is that of 'natural' disasters. When massive human suffering arises from a flood, an earthquake, or from crop failure, this may be seen by those not directly affected as mere misfortune – as something for which no one bears responsibility, and so as a situation in which questions of right or justice simply do not arise. Onora O'Neill criticizes neo-Malthusian responses to both famine and endemic hunger for their attempt to narrow the scope of ethical reasoning on these grounds:

> These neo-Malthusian perspectives suggest that ethical reasoning about famine has a severely restricted task. The starkest claims insist that famine and hunger cannot

be prevented, at least in the long run, and that attempts to intervene are likely to produce unsustainable population growth and so lead to more deaths. *Laissez faire* is then the only ethically responsible approach to problems of famine and hunger.[60]

As O'Neill points out, even if the neo-Malthusians were right about the ultimate causes of hunger and famine, there would still be far more room for ethical deliberation and responsibility than this picture suggests – about, for example, the ways in which supposedly unavoidable suffering is distributed or shared. But by far the most widespread response on the left to this range of problems has been to reject neo-Malthusian or other naturalistic causal accounts of 'natural' disasters. Human social and economic practices are often held to play a decisive causal role in precipitating what are subsequently perceived as catastrophic natural events. Deforestation of upland, for example, may play a key role in increasing the likelihood of adjacent lowland flooding; over-exploitation of poor soil by agriculturalists may induce local climatic change and desertification, and so on. Even where such a causal story cannot plausibly be told, the link between a natural event and the human suffering that results from it can be shown always to have some social mediations. An earthquake differentially affects the poor whose housing is more vulnerable to damage, who have less options in their choice of residence, and whose well-being is less likely to be a priority when emergency aid comes. Liberal-individualist conceptions of justice and rights come under pressure from two directions in such cases – individual agency has too little scope to make a difference, either because natural mechanisms are at work whose character and scale rule out significant individual human intervention, or because socio-economic structures are at work, which are, likewise, unamenable to significant intentional modification, no matter how well-meaning the individual.

In sum, the liberal-individualist discourse of rights gives priority to certain attributes of individuals as deserving of protection, and relies on a certain conception of the principal sources of harm (other individuals and public authorities) from which the individual deserves protection. I have so far explored three main grounds upon which this discourse has been criticized by the socialist and other traditions of radical thought: first, that rights proclaimed by these liberal-individualist discourses are not realizable in capitalist societies because of their endemic inequalities of wealth and power. To the extent that moral thinking in such societies remains confined to the terms of the liberal-individualist discourse, it has the status of an ideological mystification of those relations of substantive inequality and injustice. The second line of socialist criticism is that the list of individual attributes and abilities foregrounded in the liberal-individualist discourse as particularly deserving of protection is both selected and conceptualized in ways which render marginal or unrecognizable the social-relational content of individual well-being, as well as its social-relational causal conditions (both in the sense of sustainability, and in that of individual personal development). This line of criticism goes further than the first, in challenging not just the realizability of liberal rights within a capitalist socio-economic framework, but also the very concept of individual well-being which such a realization might entail. The socialist claim that the liberal discourse of rights is limited because of its impoverished and distorted vision of what is essential to the well-being of its individuals may be a stepping-stone towards a richer, authentic version of individual well-being as the basis for an alternative, socialist discourse of rights and justice, or it may (as, according to some commentators, in the case of the Marx of *On the Jewish Question*) be a step in the direction of abandoning the moral framework of rights and justice as such.

The third line of socialist criticism is to draw attention to the ways in which even the attributes and abilities taken by the liberal discourse itself to be definitive of individual well-being are vulnerable to sources of harms not readily assimilable to the two categories of moral agent (public authorities and other persons) capable of bearing the responsibilities correlative to the rights of the individual. For a wide range of harms to which individuals are liable – often peculiarly liable – in capitalist societies, and to which they are unequally liable, the conditions of applicability of liberal-individualist concepts of rights and justice are absent. There are important – and, for many, tragic and catastrophic – conditions of life which the liberal discourse may be extended to acknowledge, but which remain to some significant degree beyond its reach. At its least accommodating, for example, in neo-Malthusianism, anti-institutional approaches to social policy, and free market economics, the liberal-individualist discourse rationalizes the withdrawal of moral sensibility and renders whole categories of injustice literally unthinkable.

The Conceptual Critique (3)
Emancipation from Rights and Justice?

Now I turn, briefly, to a fourth line of socialist criticism – one associated particularly strongly with Marx by his critics. The liberal-individualist view of rights, as we have seen, carries with it an account of individual well-being and its conditions which is seen as impoverished and distorted when viewed from a socialist standpoint. But the impoverishment is not merely an intellectual 'mistake'. If these ways of thinking about human individuals are not actually motivated by a vested interest in order to preserve a society of a certain (questionable) sort, then at least they bear the marks of the influence of such a society as it shapes and limits the intellectual imagination. The concept of the individual as a self-sufficiently thinking, believing, speaking, fearful, pleasure-seeking and possessing subject, related only contingently and by acts of will to other such selves, in dire need of protection from the excess of sovereign power, and from the transgressions of 'his' neighbour is not simply false. It has, from the socialist point of view, a provisional, local truth: the forms of social life imposed by private ownership of productive resources, the market, and the separation of civil society and the state render this version, if not true, then at least plausible. We can recognize in it, although it is represented as a universal statement about individual human nature, a characterization of some salient features of life under capitalism.[61]

In this perspective, the liberal discourse of rights and justice appears as a framework for the regulation of the lives and interactions of individuals as they are shaped and experienced by the institutional forms of just such societies. Abstract individuality and external relations of mutual utility, exploitation and antagonism together make up a social ontology which is presupposed in the liberal discourse of rights and justice. On the one hand, the promises of liberal rights cannot be met under capitalism, but, on the other, it is only under capitalism that such promises need to be made in the first place. The extension of community from the abstract idealized form of the state to embrace all social and economic life, the creation of mutually affirmative, identity-recognizing, co-operative relations between individuals – taken together, these features of the historical transformation envisaged by the young Marx do, indeed, imply a transcendence of the very presuppositions of the rights discourse. If each emancipated self sees in her or his relationship to every other only a condition of their mutual well-being, and if public life has become solely a co-ordinating, or pooling of the purposes and powers of each individual, then the two paradigmatic sources of harm to the individual acknowledged by the liberal discourse of rights have been abolished. No longer threatened, we may dispense with the moral apparatus which promised (but generally failed) to keep us out of harm's way.

And what of those sources of harm – effects of oppressive social structures, dangerous social practices, institutional effects where individual responsibility is difficult to assign – which lie at or beyond the limits of liberal-individualist moral concepts? There are plausible – if partial – readings of especially the early Marx according to which such 'reified' structures of social existence could be transformed in ways which would render social life itself both transparent and susceptible to human agency. As we saw in chapter 2, Marx even envisioned a surpassing of the estrangement between socialized humanity and its natural conditions, a 'humanization of nature'.

According to this view, the requirement for an authoritative set of rules, establishing the rights of individuals *vis-à-vis* one another and the public power, and adjudicating between competing claims is a consequence of a certain state of human society and stage of historical development. This state of human society is one in which private property and market relations set up mutual estrangement and utilitarian calculation as the dominant form of personal interconnection, and the institutional separation of public, political life from the private sphere of individual need and exchange renders the latter vulnerable to transgressions by the former. This stage of historical development is one in which the immense transformative power of human cognitive and co-operative potentials is as yet unrealized.

The effectiveness of this line of socialist argument against the discourses and practices of liberal-individualist rights and justice is dependent on three sets of premises. First, there is a claim that a specific set of social-historical conditions necessitates the discourses and practices of bourgeois rights and justice. Second is the claim that transcendence of those social-historical conditions would render those discourses and practices superfluous (that is, there are no other conditions which necessitate the discourses and practices of bourgeois rights). Third, the realizability of a society in which the 'justice-and-rights-necessitating' conditions were abolished has to be rendered plausible. As we shall see, an ambiguity in the conclusion of this socialist argument must also be addressed: is it the socialist claim that (1) a socialist society makes possible the conceptualization and practice of a superior, non-bourgeois view of rights and justice,[62] or (2) that the need for the whole apparatus of rights and justice as such can be rendered superfluous? Clearly, our evaluation of the subsidiary claims in the socialist argument will have to take account of this ambiguity.

Steven Lukes has provided one of the most clearly and powerfully argued recent critiques of the Marxian view of rights. My argument here draws on Lukes's argument, but I differ from his at certain significant points. Lukes argues that there are four conditions which, taken together, make justice and rights necessary. These are: scarcity (in relation to desires), 'egoism' (or lack of complete altruism), conflicting conceptions of the good, and (Lukes's own addition) imperfect knowledge and understanding. Marx and Engels tend to emphasize the first two conditions, but, as Lukes argues, even if we were to imagine a society of limitless abundance and unconditional benevolence, individuals would still require protection from the well-intentioned abuses of others with different and conflicting moral or political values. And, even if complete moral and political consensus were to be achieved, there would still be a threat from the unintended consequences of ill-informed but well-meant actions.

On Lukes's reading, the Marxian vision of communism implies the surpassing of all these conditions and, as we have seen, there is textual support for such a reading, especially in the early writings. According to Lukes:

> Marxism supposes that a transparent and unified society of abundance – a society in which the very distinctions between egoism and altruism, and between the public sphere of politics and the private sphere of civil society, and the 'division of the human being into a *public man* and a *private man*' have been overcome – is not merely capable of being brought about, but is on the historical agenda, and indeed that the working class is in principle motivated to bring it about, and is capable of doing so.[63]

So much is, I think, at least plausibly, attributed to Marx and Engels, but Lukes goes on to make a still stronger claim, namely 'Marxists hold that, broadly, all significant conflicts are to be traced back to class divisions'. He continues:

> Certainly the Marxist canon has virtually nothing to say about any bases of conflict, whether social or psychological, other than class. It is virtually innocent (and totally so at the level of theory) of any serious consideration of all the inter-personal and intra-personal sources of conflict and frustration that cannot, or can no longer, plausibly be traced, even remotely, to class divisions.[64]

Here, I think Lukes's judgement is excessively harsh. If the 'Marxist canon' includes within it all the richness and diversity of the twentieth-century Western Marxisms, from Luxemburg and Gramsci to Habermas, Marcuse and Althusser, the claim is simply not sustainable. The repeated engagements between Marxism and psychoanalysis, Marxism and feminism, and, more recently, Marxism and ecology are a testimony to the acknowledgement on the part of Marxists of the requirement to both enrich and complement class analysis with an understanding of other sources both of lack of fulfilment and of social conflict. Of course, Lukes could reasonably respond by pointing out that in each case Marxists have had to draw on arguments and conceptual resources produced independently of historical materialism. To some extent this is true, but if the outcome of these encounters is a correction and enrichment of the historical-materialist tradition, then that tradition would appear to be an open and creative endeavour rather than, as Lukes sometimes seems to suggest, a closed system deaf to some of the obvious facts of personal and inter-personal life.

More central to our concern here, however, is Lukes's apparent view that for Marx and Engels the conditions which set up the need for rights and justice are, centrally, class domination and its consequences. This seems to me misleading. The target of Marx and Engels's critique is clearly that conception of universal rights and justice proclaimed in the course of the modern political revolutions. This modern bourgeois society and its associated state is, certainly, a form of class society, but so, according to Marx and Engels, were the pre-bourgeois societies and regimes against which the revolutions were made. In so far as these earlier societies employed a morality of rights and justice, it was in reference to tradition, the particularities of birth and social position, locality and hierarchy, and far removed from the abstract and universal individualism of such texts as the revolutionary French and American statements.

It is this abstract individualism and the economic and political forces which sustain it which are the central objects of the Marxian critique. This is, at least analytically, distinguishable from the specific forms of class domination peculiar to capitalist societies (consider, here, Marx's analysis of petty commodity production in volume 1 of *Capital*, as the material support for the key categories of 'bourgeois' social thought). Class was centrally important, for Marx and Engels, not as an explication for the discourse of bourgeois rights and justice, but as the source of what they hoped and expected would be a historical dynamic of change and transcendence. We must now acknowledge that this expectation was unfounded, but it does not directly follow that the critique of rights and justice was similarly flawed.

So, it is to that question that I now return. As we saw above (p. 136), that critique contains three main claims. The first is that the discourses and practices of liberal rights and justice are necessitated by conditions historically established by bourgeois social and political forms. Much of the argumentation of this chapter has been devoted to sustaining that claim – or, at least, a somewhat weaker version of it: that there are strong functional connections between the discourses of liberal rights and the social conditions and legitimation-requirements of bourgeois societies. I have no doubt that many readers will have found this less than convincing, and I acknowledge that to make it so would require a fuller and more empirically instanced discussion than I have space for. However, for my central purposes here, it is the second and third claims which are the most interesting. The second claim implicit in the Marxian critique is that once the institutional sources of interpersonal estrangement and lack of fulfilment in bourgeois societies were transcended, the requirement for a discourse of universal (bourgeois) rights and justice would fall away. The third claim is that a form of society which transcends the requirements for a discourse and practice of rights and justice is a realizable historical project.

I want to emphasize that there is a morally and politically very important logical gap between the first of these claims, on the one hand, and the second and third, taken together, on the other. That is to say, we may find (as I do) a large part of the Marxian critique of liberal-individualist rights convincing without being thereby committed to the possibility of an altogether rights-transcending form of social life. More specifically, the institutional forms, relations of social domination, inequality and estrangement characteristic of capitalist societies do necessitate a discourse of rights which, in turn, legitimates those forms without being able to deliver the substantive guarantees to individuals which it promises. If this case can be made out, then it is a powerful case against the liberal-individualist views of rights and justice quite independently of the truth or falsity of the second and third Marxian claims. It may not be possible to build a society marked by universal spontaneous benevolence, or which transcends all sources of human estrangement and suffering: such a prospect seems hardly, if at all, imaginable. But if the specific forms of abuse, exploitation and deprivation which characterize capitalist social forms, and which necessitate the discourse of liberal rights, are removable, then the Marxian critique retains its purchase. We do not need to believe perfection is possible to think it worth trying to make things better.

It is one thing to argue that individuals are rendered liable to fundamental and pervasive harms because of their location in specifically capitalist systems of social and economic relations, and that social transformations may emancipate them from such threatening circumstances more substantively and reliably than can the discourse of liberal rights. It is another, and much more ambitious claim that such post-capitalist, emancipated conditions of life would render those individuals who benefited from them 'sublimely proof' against all the sources of harm and suffering to which human kind is susceptible. Even if we follow Lukes (as I am inclined to do), in rejecting this more ambitious claim, conceding that an important residue of sources of conflict and suffering is likely to survive all efforts of ameliorative social change, none of this detracts from the Marxian case against the liberal discourse of rights and the institutional forms with which it is implicated. To the extent that Lukes's discussion effects an elision between the stronger and weaker claims for a post-bourgeois, socialist society it fails to do justice to the Marxian case.

However, Lukes is right in pointing out that the stronger Marxian claim is mistaken. To the extent that, especially in his early writings, Marx tended to see all the most fundamental forms of human suffering and antagonism as rooted in defective, or insufficiently developed, human social forms, to that extent his vision was utopian and idealist. Not only are there general features of the human predicament which must figure as a limit to any emancipatory project, but also any specific post-bourgeois society would be liable to develop its own, perhaps distinctive, sources of antagonism and harm. This is not, of course, an argument against emancipatory politics but, rather, one for trying to be realistic about what they can hope to achieve. This is, in turn, an indication of scepticism about Marx's early vision of communism as 'the riddle of history solved' (the third claim involved in the early Marxian critique of rights and justice – the possibility of a society in which the discourse of rights and justice would no longer be required).

But already I am anticipating too much. In the remaining chapters of this book, I aim to use a discussion of the moral status of non-human animals, together with a naturalistic view of human nature itself, as a way of exploring further the issues posed by all four strands of the radical/socialist critique of the discourse and practice of liberal rights. Chapter 5 is mainly concerned with the extension of the sociological critique of rights. Given that animals, as well as humans, are subject to risks and harms as a result of their location in socio-economic structures of power and domination, how does this fact undermine the possibility that the discourse of animal rights might offer substantive protection? Chapter 6 uses human/animal comparison to deepen and extend the socialist critique of liberal conceptions of the person. At the same time, a case is made for a positive view of rights, taking into account not only social belonging but also embodiment and environmental requirements as grounding basic interests worthy of protection. Chapter 7 begins with a further consideration of non-individualist ways of analysing sources of harm to individuals, both human and non-human. The argument returns to the concluding topic of the present chapter. How far, and in what ways are (relative) scarcity, mutual antagonism, liability to value-dissensus and to unintended mutual harm untranscendable features of the human (or animal) condition? To the extent that they are, what broad moral principles and institutional forms might be best suited to the twin aims of acknowledging these realities and living well? If *some* discourse of rights and justice is unavoidable, then what form might it take in a society no longer marked by the specific discontents of late bourgeois civilization?

PART III

Rights, Justice and Benevolence in a Finite World

5

Beyond the Sociological Critique: Rights, Human and Animal

In this chapter, and the two following it, I arrange an encounter between the philosophy of animal rights and the radical critique of (human) rights. Each discourse is used as a provisional standpoint from which to gain a critical appreciation of its partner. The four main strands of the socialist/radical critique of the liberal-individualist discourse on rights will be tested against the extension of that discourse to include non-human animals. Are the likenesses and continuities between humans and other animals such that the radical critique is equally effective against the attribution of rights to them, or, perhaps, do limitations of the radical critique stand out more sharply when the moral status of non-human animals is brought into focus? Alternatively, are the discontinuities and differences between humans and other animals so deep that either the rights discourse itself or its radical critique is rendered ineffective across the species-boundary? Clearly, my intention is to hold open the possibility that each philosophical position may be corrected in the light of its encounter with the other. The argument takes the form of an open-ended dialogue between two partially incompatible positions, rather than that of a deduction from 'first principles': I am enough of a historicist to acknowledge that we must start from where we happen to be, but enough of a foundationalist to believe that it may still be possible to get somewhere.

At least in the early stages of the argument, I deliberately leave open the question whether the radical critique of the discourse and practice of rights amounts to a critique of rights as such, or only of the limited realization and defective conceptualizations of liberal-individualist rights. I shall start by leaving open, therefore, the further question as to whether a richer, fuller and realizable vision of rights and justice appropriate to post-bourgeois society may be the ultimate standpoint from which the liberal discourse is found wanting, or whether this standpoint may be a society which has transcended the very conditions of life which necessitate rights and justice. However, my hope is that by bringing into the picture both the moral status of non-human animals and its ontological presupposition, a naturalistic view of human nature itself, we may be able to get a clearer view of this crucial question as the dialogue proceeds.

Social Inequalities and the Rights of Animals

I'll begin, then, with the first strand of the socialist/radical critique of the rights discourse. In societies governed by deep inequalities of political power, economic wealth, social standing and cultural accomplishment the promise of equal rights is delusory, with the consequence that for the majority, rights are merely abstract, formal entitlements with little or no *de facto* purchase on the realities of social life. In so far as social life is regulated by these abstract principles and in so far as the promise is mistaken for its fulfilment, then the discourse of rights and justice is an ideology, a form of mystification which has a causal role in binding individuals to the very conditions of dependence and impoverishment from which it purports to offer emancipation.

How much of this, our first line of criticism of the discourse of rights, applies to the liberal-individualist argument for the recognition of rights in the case of (non-human) animals? First, we can dispense rather quickly with the contention attributed to the early Marx that all (bourgeois) rights amount, in effect, to property rights. Except in rather special legal contexts (which do not, anyway, affect my argument) non-human animals cannot be property-owners. This is not a merely contingent, historical-cultural fact, but is rooted in a recognition of real differences of psychological constitution and moral attributes as between (most) humans and individuals of all currently known non-human animal species. The capacities to exercise ownership rights are, if not identical with, then closely allied with those that constitute moral agency.

If the claim that animals have rights amounts to the claim that they have a right to acquire property, then it directly falls. But those interests of animals which advocates of animal rights seek to protect remain unaffected by this argument. Whatever force the argument for animal rights has, it cannot derive from any claim that animals have a basic interest in the protection of their property. If there is moral force in that argument, it must derive from an acknowledgement that non-human animals have basic interests, other than property ownership, which ought to be protected. If this is so for animals, then the ontology of human/animal continuism suggests that humans, too, may have such right-grounding basic interests, irreducible to those of property. This consideration tells against any Marxian temptation to reduce even liberal-individualist rights to property rights. However, the serious point of Marx's association of rights with property is still sustainable.

For some categories of property – most obviously property in the means of production – ownership rights are simultaneously powers to affect the basic interests of non-owners: to give or withhold the means of livelihood, health, safety and personal liberty.

Just as economically dependent or relatively powerless humans are at risk of harm from the exercise of property rights by other humans, so, too, are non-human animals which live within human social relations and practices involving property rights, such as intensive livestock farming. Here, as we have seen, an analysis can be given of the distortion and fragmentation of the mode of life of animals in such regimes which parallels that given by the young Marx of the consequences for wage labourers of capitalist private property. Also, however, animals may suffer harm as a result of the exercise of property rights in land, as when land-use changes result in habitat destruction. Again, there are parallels with the effects on human rural society wrought by the extension of commercial agriculture, enclosure of common land, and the destruction of natural and semi-natural biotopes used as traditional sources of food and fuel resources. In each of these cases, animals suffer harms as a result of the exercise by humans of property rights in ways which parallel the effects on relatively powerless humans, but, of course, animals are significantly less well placed then even the most disadvantaged humans.

A Role for Rights?

However, there are also situations in which the discourse of rights appears to offer a good chance of substantive protection to animals. One implication of the radical criticism of rights as so far expounded is that we should expect the liberal discourse of rights to work best in protecting individuals from basic harms in real circumstances which approximate to what we might call the presumed social ontology of the rights discourse: that of autonomous individuals, contingently related, each resisting encroachment/interference on the part of the other, and seeking authoritative arbitration. For reasons I shall explore more fully later in this chapter, these conditions are never satisfied in the case of competing rights-claims across the species-divide. However, some moral controversies affecting animals are analogous in certain respects. In the case of blood-sports, for example, where the quarry is a wild animal, there is a (highly qualified) sense in which the hunters and the hunted are autonomous, contingently related beings: they are not bound together, as in the case of farmers and stock animals, for example, in socio-economic relations of power and dependency. Moreover, the right of the quarry-animal (asserted on its behalf by human allies) is a claim not to be interfered with in its own, non-right-infringing activity. This is a right closely assimilable to the liberal paradigm of negative liberty, and the situation is, *ex hypothesi*, one in which it does make sense to think of the wild animal's enjoyment of its freedom as something which can be taken for granted, given non-interference on the part of the hunters.

Of course, the situation is not an exact parallel. Most obviously, the rights attributed to quarry-animals conflict with those claimed by hunters to enjoy traditional rural sports which do not infringe the rights of other humans. These rights are aggressively asserted when they are threatened either by the direct action of 'hunt saboteurs' or by attempts at legislation. The disanalogy with the human case is, of course, that the countervailing rights of animals not to be hunted cannot be claimed by the animals themselves. The outcome then depends on the respective powers of advocacy and access to political and legal institutions of rival human social groups. Notwithstanding this disanalogy, however, this is one type of situation in which an extension of the liberal-individualist notion of rights to non-human animals could have some hope not only of carrying rational conviction, but also of being practically effective in protecting some categories of animals from substantive harms to which they would otherwise be vulnerable.

Another area in which practical efficacy on the part of the liberal-rights discourse might be hoped for is that of acts of cruelty committed by human individuals against animals kept in confinement. The deliberate infliction of unnecessary pain on domestic pets will serve as an example here. Although differentials of power and dependency are intrinsic to the relation between a pet-owner and pet, this situation is unlike the employer/employee one with respect to freedom of speech in that the right to inflict unnecessary pain cannot reasonably be claimed as a part of what it is to be a pet-owner. Cruel practices are a contingent, and not an essential feature of the relationship. On the contrary, the widely shared cultural norms which prescribe and regulate pet-keeping include a strong presumption against cruelty. In such a case, where a powerful consensus favours a presumption against causing unnecessary pain, where causal and moral responsibility for causing pain can be readily placed at the door of an identifiable (human) moral agent, and where there are no countervailing powerful socio-economic interests, the prospects for an effective defence of the rights of the animals concerned against the rival claims of pet-owners to privacy and rights of property in their pets are relatively good.

But even in these two cases, there is a point to the radical critique. First, in the case of blood-sports, the sense in which the quarry are 'wild' animals will generally need to be highly qualified. Commonly, game animals are deliberately hand-reared, or, in some cases, allowed to breed under highly protected 'semi-wild' conditions for sporting purposes. Even where this is not done,

146

links between landowners and blood-sports interests are generally crucial in sustaining conditions for the practice. Only if sufficient areas of suitable habitat are left free of incompatible commercial management or development will enough game animals survive to make the sport worthwhile. The relation between hunters and quarry, in this perspective, looks less like a 'contingent' relation between autonomous beings, but more like a systemically structured relation of differential socio-economic power and dependency, albeit an ecologically mediated one. To the extent that this is true, the practical effectiveness of the rights strategy in getting the sport abolished could well have the self-defeating outcome of undermining the conditions under which it was reasonable to take as 'given' the ability of the animals concerned to enjoy their freedom once protected from the depredations of the hunters. These conditions are, precisely, the preservation of the general ecological conditions for the living of the life appropriate to that species over a sufficiently large geographical extent to sustain its population. The often quite cynical use of this argument to give a 'conservationist' cover to blood sports interests does not affect its validity, so far as it goes.[1]

Application of the radical critique to this kind of case, at first sight one very amenable to the 'rights' approach, suggests that under prevailing patterns of social and economic relationship the objectives of protecting the basic interests of the animals concerned are more likely to be achieved by complementing – or even replacing – a rights-based strategy with a broader strategy for large-scale shifts in patterns of land ownership, and redistributed powers and altered criteria for regulating land-use and land-management. This strategy would, in turn, presuppose integrated socio-economic and ecological analysis, and involve animal rights and welfare campaigners entering into coalitions with other social groups which might favour such changes on other grounds: amenity access, nature conservation, aesthetics, social justice and so on.

The second kind of case – that of cruelty to animals kept in confinement by humans – is also to a degree vulnerable to considerations of a socialist or radical kind. For one thing, notwithstanding the power of the cultural consensus against cruelty, it would be a mistake to underestimate the rival cultural power of the appeal to privacy and property rights. The privacy of the pet-owner is not only the ground for powerful 'non-interference' rights but is also a major barrier against both detection of abuses and collection of reliable evidence. In this respect there are strong parallels between the situation of 'privately' abused non-human animals, and humans – usually children and women – abused in domestic contexts. To the extent that property-rights may be adduced to defend cruelty to animals, the advocates of the ascription of rights to animals have two options. One would be to argue for a limitation of property-rights in this case on grounds of the nature of the property: as the subject-of-a-life the pet animal has a right to respectful treatment. But it is difficult to see how this line of argument could stop short of a second option, calling into question the institution of private property itself in relation to this class of being. From a 'fully fledged' animal rights perspective the keeping of pets – even at its most benign – would be seen as a form of slavery.

However, we might reasonably ask whether the rights-perspective, if it has these implications, offers the best strategy for achieving its own objectives: protecting the individual animals concerned from harms to their basic interests. In this case, as often elsewhere, the rhetoric of rights (of the pet-owner) is implicated as both a substantive condition (privacy) of abuse and its legitimation (private property). The extension of rights to those vulnerable to abuse, though *prima facie* an attractive option, is liable to be limited in its practical effectiveness. What the radical line of argument suggests in this kind of case, too, is that a transformation of the social relations of power and dependency which characterize the private, domestic sphere would be likely both to be effective on its own account and also to provide conditions under which the extension of moral concern could begin to offer effective rather than merely formal 'protections'.

Animal Rights and Human Interests: In the Lab and on the Farm

Other kinds of case which give rise to moral concern over the treatment of animals in captivity include the use of captive animals in medical experimentation or in safety-testing of new commodities and also modern regimes of intensive rearing of livestock in meat production. Here, the liberal-individualist moral framework of rights and justice can be shown to be still more directly vulnerable to criticisms which foreground the social-relational and economic conditions under which such rights are conceptualized and are to be recognized.

Animal Experimentation

The use of animals as experimental subjects is in some respects analogous to the case of cruelty to pet animals. In both cases the animal is kept in confinement, and in both cases the concept of ownership plays a part in the moral justification of the disposal over the conditions of life of the animal by some individual or group of humans. However, there are also significant disanalogies. The keeping of animals as pets has as its central point the intrinsic value of the relationship itself. The relation is asymmetrical in terms of the social powers, communicative competences and so on of the human individuals and animals involved, but it is, nonetheless, a 'quasi-personal' relationship in which each takes pleasure in the company of the other and has regard to the other's desires as well as needs. If these features are not present, the relation is not one of pet-owner to pet, but, perhaps, more closely assimilable to a utilitarian one, in which the animal is kept as a protection for the household from burglary, to keep vermin at bay, or for some other purpose extrinsic to the social relation involved. By contrast, keeping animals for use as experimental subjects involves humans and animals in just such external, utilitarian relations with one another, and this is, moreover, the *point* of keeping the animals in confinement.

This is not, of course, to overlook the fact that moral and/or legal regulation is typically present in these situations.[2] For one thing, many experiments on animals make sense only if there are believed to be good reasons for thinking human/animal comparisons are valid with respect to the characteristics or responses under test. Depending on what those are, some degree or other of practical recognition of their conditions of well-being will have to be accorded in the way the test-animals are kept and treated. Also, there is often a tendency for those human individuals whose work-tasks include caring for the animals to develop affective ties and a sense of moral responsibility for the well-being of those animals. Finally, the whole situation will be bounded by broader cultural predispositions against maltreatment of captive animals, and a juridical framework which, to varying degrees, sets conditions and limits on the range of legally tolerable treatments and interventions.[3]

However, these regulations are themselves an implicit acknowledgement that the point of the practice of animal experimentation is that human experimenters intervene in the lives of the animals under their control in ways which are liable to cause them harm. This is a morally significant difference between the practice of animal experimentation and the keeping of pets. Standards of care which would be acknowledged and routinely maintained in the one sphere are deliberately, but conditionally and within limits, suspended in the other. So, for example, the deliberate causing of unnecessary pain, from which animal rights advocacy would seek to protect the pet animal, becomes a problematic concept in the case of animal experimentation. Difficulty focuses on both the terms 'deliberate' and 'unnecessary'. Let us suppose that a specific intervention be deemed necessary to achieve the purpose of an experiment, but that it is incidental to the experiment whether the intervention causes suffering to the animal. We could say in this sort of case that the intervention is deliberate, but not under the description 'causing suffering'. Here it would be morally relevant to ask whether the experiment would retain its epistemic value if some available anaesthetic were used, to spare the animal's suffering, and, if so, whether care had been taken to administer it. Where suffering really is, and is known by the experimenters to be an unavoidable concomitant of the experiment they wish to carry out, then the moral focus is on the term 'unnecessary': if the suffering is necessary to the experiment, is the experiment *itself* necessary?

In the terms available to the liberal-individualist rights discourse, it is of course possible to hold that individuals, including individual (non-human) animals have absolute rights. This position does, however, have implications which are difficult to square with the reflective moral intuitions of most supporters of the idea of individual rights, who tend to regard rights rather as *prima facie* morally valid claims. From this standpoint, an experiment which caused suffering to an animal (or person) might in some circumstances be justified, though an infringement of its (*prima facie*) rights. If the moral grounds (for example, competing rights of other individuals) are strong enough, then rights may be overridden. On the rights perspective, a utilitarian calculation of possible benefits to humans (or, indeed, other animals) in the form of cures to major diseases or the like cannot justify an infringement of basic rights. However, competing rights *could* do so.

Steven Rose, for example, advocates a high priority for research to replace animals in safety-testing, and in medical research. But, he argues, there will always be some areas where the use of animals is unavoidable:

> There is no way, for instance, that the biochemical causes of the lethal disease diabetes, or its treatment with insulin, could have been discovered, without experiments on mammals. And we can't use tissue-cultures, or bacteria, or plants, to develop and test the treatments needed to alleviate epilepsy, Parkinsonism or manic depression.[4]

This sort of argument, on the face of it, is flatly opposed to the rights perspective in its preparedness to license basic harms to members of the other species for the benefit of members of our own.

However it is quite possible to cast such arguments in the language of countervailing rights – those of human sufferers from terminal or chronically disabling diseases to some hope of alleviation, or of research scientists to intellectual liberty. For example, a recent newspaper article on the case for animal research combined both. Focusing on a sufferer from an inherited disabling disease called Friedreich's ataxia, the article went on:

> In the years that he has left, he hopes to further the chances of a cure for his and other disabling conditions by campaigning for the right of doctors and scientists to use animals in scientific research. ... He has founded Seriously Ill for Medical Research, an organization which places the human right to health above any claim animals may have on our consciences.[5]

Animal experimentation is an area, then, where the rights perspective is limited in its power to protect animals at risk due to several prevailing features of the social-relational conditions under which such experimentation is conducted. First, the rights of the experimental subjects have to be balanced against countervailing 'basic' rights of experimenters *and* against powerful popular moral sentiments which differentiate in ways not available to the rights perspective between a range of different benefits which may or may not result from experimentation (between, say, attempts to find a cure for cancer, and testing of novelty cosmetics). Both these countervailing social forces have access to political representation and therefore to legislative influence.

Second, the character of the *practice* is one within which such rights as are ascribed to experimental subjects are liable to be overridden or abused in pursuit of the intrinsic purposes of the practice. This contrasts with pet-keeping, in which the power and opportunity to abuse are structurally present, but in which the practice of abuse runs counter to the intrinsic normative order and 'spirit' of the practice. Third, the institutional framework – whether public-institution research science, or private corporation research-and-development – within which animal experimentation takes place is one which resembles the domestic sphere in its relative imperviousness to external monitoring and, in the event of suspicion of abuse, to the gathering of reliable evidence leading to successful prosecution. Though the rights perspective is not consensual among animal welfare pressure-groups, it is nonetheless true that widespread popular opposition to animal abuse in experimental laboratories has not yet been effective in preventing extreme suffering, often with quite trivial justification.[6] The socialist argument's emphasis on the social-relational conditions and contexts under which formal rights may or may not be substantively enjoyed is, I claim, a persuasive diagnosis of this state of affairs.

But, more than this, it places on the agenda alternative strategies for, firstly, changing the social and economic relations which enable and foster abuse, and, secondly, developing moral perspectives on the status of animals which may have more purchase on the complex social realities of animal research than does the rights-view on its own. Recent feminist work points in a promising direction here, linking laboratory abuse of animals with a broader critique of the culture and institutions of contemporary science. Lynda Birke, for example, is both critical of the abuse of animals in the name of science and sceptical of the value of the attribution of rights. Desensitization to animal suffering, she points out, is an established part of science education, a condition of the appropriate attitude of dispassionate 'objectivity' required to become 'real' scientists. She continues:

In our critiques, we have stressed the social context of contemporary science. Within that context of capitalism and patriarchy, specific forms of science have developed, and with them, specific ways of conceptualising animals and using them in science. But those forms are not inevitable. At present, our biological knowledge is grounded in a material base that includes the bodies of experimental animals. A science that did not see animals as expendable (if sometimes expensive) bits of apparatus might, then, have a somewhat different understanding of the material world.

A more humane and egalitarian society would be one in which many current laboratory uses of animals would no longer have any point, but 'even if that more humane society still sanctioned the use of some animals in research in specified conditions, it would see the ethical issues as centrally important'.[7]

The Costs of Food

In many cases of animal abuse in experimental situations, and quite generally in yet another area – modern intensive stock-rearing, or 'factory' farming – many of the above social-relational impediments to the substantive enjoyment of formal rights (even where they are juridically acknowledged) are complemented by yet another obstacle: an economic or commercial dynamic and its effects on the priorities and intentional attitudes of the human agents bound up in it.

There are several aspects of these processes which deserve some analytical differentiation. Whenever animals are reared to meet human organic needs – primarily food, but also clothing and shelter – the social practices involved have what might be called an 'intentional structure'[8] different from that which I indicated as 'quasi-personal' and illustrated with the practice of pet-keeping. In all these cases of keeping animals to meet some human organic need, animals are incorporated into some form of normatively and pragmatically ordered social practice, including an asymmetrical relation of social power between human agents and the animals involved. However, the overriding intentional structure is one in which activities are distributed and organized in relation to the provision by the animals of the means to satisfy some independently identifiable human organic need (for food, clothing etc.): the relation is, in other words, a 'utilitarian' or external-instrumental one, by contrast with the intrinsic value paradigmatically accorded to the relations between pet-keeper and pet.

Still, as a normatively ordered social practice, even if dominated by asymmetrical and instrumental relations, this broad category of animal-including human social practices still has room for both affective and normative dimensions within which the well-being of the animals themselves can be recognized and practically acknowledged. Not only is there, so to speak, 'room' for such acknowledgement, but it may be practically required as a condition of effectively meeting the external-instrumental purposes of the practice. For example, traditional practices of sheep-rearing generally involve a practical recognition that there are positive links between the capacity of the flock to develop its own stable social structure, for sheep to be able to form associations with their own lambs, and so on, and the success of the flock in lambing and general yield.

In general, traditional practices of animal husbandry involve a practical acknowledgement that more-or-less autonomous animal social-processes are a precondition of the achievement of human purposes. Socially organized human intervention is therefore deployed to optimize the conditions of those animal social-processes (where they are open to human-intentional modification) and selectively to appropriate their outcomes in ways which do not offset the long-run sustainability of the practice. That the animals incorporated into these human social practices are themselves living natural beings, with organic, social and ecological conditions of survival and thriving is therefore a practical recognition built into their intentional structure. It may also be, and generally is, experienced by the human agents involved as an affective disposition – something they choose to acknowledge, and gain satisfaction from – as well as a normative requirement.[9]

Now, a sub-set of such practices of animal-husbandry are also practices of commercial agriculture. Superimposed upon their character as human organic need-meeting labour-processes is a second intentional structure as processes whereby capital resources are deployed with the purpose of maximizing an economic return. The superimposition of such forms of economic calculation upon animal husbandry labour-processes exerts pressures on the latter towards cost-reduction, yield-maximization and overall process-control. The existing debate on capitalist development and labour-processes concentrates, understandably enough, on the relations between three broad terms – capital, labour and technology. Central questions at issue concern the status of supposed inherent tendencies in capitalist development for labour-displacing technical innovation, towards de-skilling of the labour-force and towards 'material', as opposed to merely 'formal', subsumption of labour.

However, the pattern of capital accumulation and its relation to re-organization of labour-processes take distinctive forms in the case of agriculture. Recent work by David Goodman, Michael Redclift[10] and others constitutes a major step forward in our understanding of this specificity. In their account, mechanization in the form of tractors and harvesters, as well as the application of artificial chemical fertilizers, was already well established in the latter part of the nineteenth century. However, farming at that stage was still integrated with what Goodman and Redclift (following Aglietta[11]) refer to as an 'extensive' regime of capital accumulation, in which agriculture provides cheap food for urban populations, and especially for the industrial labour force. Transition to the 'Fordist', intensive regime took place in the USA in the 1930s, was consolidated in Western Europe after 1945 and subsequently 'exported' to parts of the Third World. Characteristics of the intensive regime include:

> the interdependent expansion of capital and consumer goods industries, rapid technical change and productivity growth, monopoly market structures, the transnationalization of production and exchange, and mass consumption of standardized commodities.[12]

Aspects of this process which have the most direct bearing on agriculture and food production include the commercialization of much domestic labour, and the increased participation of women in the industrial labour force. These processes were crucial for the rise of what Goodman and Redclift call 'the modern agri-food system' characterized by increasing dependence upon chemical, genetic and mechanical 'inputs', and the rise of new consumer markets for 'processed or "industrial" food products, including the expansion of catering and fast-food outlets, which have revolutionised what, how, and where we eat'.[13]

While acknowledging the importance of the relation between the post-war transition to a 'Fordist' regime of accumulation and the rise of the agri-food system, Goodman and Redclift reject any attempt to assimilate the two processes – to represent the new agricultural and food-processing technologies as the rural equivalent of industrial mass-production. The role of pervasive state intervention in agriculture, according to them, has to be understood as a response o the failure of industrial capital to apply 'Fordist' principles to agricultural labour processes: 'Agriculture remains an unstable, volatile sector of activity, with a pronounced tendency in the absence of state intervention towards low returns and over-production crises.'[14] The fundamental causes of this distinctive pattern of capital accumulation in the 'agri-food system' have to do with biological constraints, in terms of human consumption requirements, and in terms of ecological conditions and the biological nature of crop plants and animals.

This dual pattern of biological constraint has led to a dynamic of accumulation in which innovations and concentrations of capital have taken place primarily outside the sphere of immediate production. Farming has become increasingly locked into a structure of 'upstream' concentration of capital in chemicals, engineering and genetic innovation and supply, and 'downstream' concentration in food processing, distribution and retailing.[15] Individual rural activities have been 'appropriated' by industrial capitals in an *ad hoc* and uneven way, fragmenting innovation in a way which has brought about the familiar problems of rural ecological degradation. At the same time, despite an increase in average farm size, 'family norms of production' have been retained:

> These relations of production are capitalist, but the labour process retains recognizable links with inherited, artisan-based pre-industrial activity. Direct producers continue to bring their individual blend of skills, experience and judgement to bear on the organization of the immediate production process.[16]

The focus in Goodman and Redclift's analysis is, however, on cereal production, and they concede that livestock production and horticulture show a pattern of industrialization in which labour-processes have, indeed, been revolutionized. The approach I adopt here is broadly complementary to that of Goodman and Redclift, but I offer a provisional analysis of forms of organization of specifically animal husbandry labour-processes. My analysis shares their emphasis on integrating both human-social relations and ecological considerations into a single interpretive framework and, in doing so, shows that biological processes continue to impose constraints on labour-process organization in livestock production as well.

The establishment and extension of commercial relations into animal husbandry exerts pressures both on the forms of co-operation and subordination of the labour force and upon the organization of the relations between human labour, stock animals and their ecological conditions of life.[17] In analysing these pressures, questions of economic surplus appropriation as well as control, regulation and predictability need to be simultaneously kept in mind.

The 'formal' subsumption of labour to agricultural capital is achieved with the establishment of the wage-relation between rural workers, bereft of land and of traditional rights of common, and commercially oriented landowners. Enclosure is significant not only as an aspect of the process whereby 'free' labour is created as a condition of the wage-relation, but also as a condition of the reorganization of the relations between labour, stock animals and ecological conditions. Along with the formal subsumption of labour goes an extension of the powers of the landowner to control and regulate both the activity of farm labour and the organic-developmental and social aspects of the lives of stock animals. Ratios of stocks to grazing land available can be calculated, stock can be more effectively monitored and protected, intensities of grazing in different seasons and on different parcels of land can be regulated, and so on. Output and economic return can be directly enhanced by technical innovations, for example, to 'improve' the quality of grazing land by drainage, fertilization, introduction of more nutritious grass species, and so on. It makes sense, I think, to extend the concept of 'formal subsumption' to this whole complex of wage-labour, stock animals, and ecological conditions, whose interrelations are reorganized and subjected to distinctive forms of regulation under commercial pressures.

Though there is some room within this broad pattern of traditional-cum-commercial animal husbandry for a piecemeal displacement of labour by technology, the 'material' subsumption of labour takes place primarily through a socio-technical transformation of the whole labour-process including the stock animals and their ecological conditions: this technical reorganization is, in effect, the 'factory' farm.[18] Stock animals are reared in enclosed pens, their movements and interactions severely restricted or entirely prevented, their nutritional requirements supplied in carefully calculated and regulated quotas, and other 'ambient' conditions artificially maintained and regulated. Traditional skills of animal husbandry are, under this reorganization, largely dispensed with, in favour of a quantitatively reduced labour force divided between routine, unskilled tasks and technically qualified supervisory work in relation to the various operating conditions of the intensive unit.

The 'material' subsumption thus achieved is in some respects analogous to industrial mechanization (hence the popular term 'factory' farming) but it is important to keep in mind a number of distinguishing features. First, the socio-technical organization of the labour-process involves not just the 'material' subsumption of wage-labour to capital, but also the stock animals and their conditions of life (we should, perhaps, speak of the ecologico-socio-technical organization of the labour-process). Second, the distinctive character of agricultural labour-processes as eco-regulative practices, in which human intentionality is primarily restricted to enhancing the conditions under which autonomous organic processes take place, is preserved into the intensive regime and continues to operate as a limit to the full subordination of the labour-process to the prevailing mode of economic calculation.[19] There are, then, economically, politically and ecologically significant biological constraints in even the 'factory' farm, though there clearly is, as Goodman and Redclift acknowledge, a considerable difference in the way these constraints operate as between animal husbandry and arable agriculture.

However, the project of overriding even these limits is already on the horizon. A new wave of biotechnological innovation threatens to enable interventions into the organic-developmental biological-reproductive processes of stock animals themselves. This programme, if realized, would tendentially eliminate eco-regulative aspects of stock breeding and rearing, assimilating it to the intentional structure of an industrial production. To some extent the process is already in train with routine administration of

156

growth hormones, antibiotics, and so on. The technology of genetic manip-
ulation is also well advanced and seems likely to rapidly accelerate the rate and
extent of human control over biological innovation. Though I do not have
space here to argue the point at length, there are strong grounds for thinking
that claims made on behalf of the new biotechnologies are likely not to be
fulfilled. Organic form will turn out to be less manipulable than is often
imagined, and the new technologies will turn out (like all other technologies)
to have important unintended and counter-intentional consequences.[20]

So, what is the bearing of this prolonged discussion of the meat production
industry on the question of animal rights? First, it suggests that the development of commercial and, then, fully capitalist agriculture exerts contradictory
pressures with respect to the treatment of stock animals. For any specific
technical organization of agricultural labour-processes there are pressures
towards an instrumental treatment of animals as mere 'things' whose output
is to be maximized by whatever technical means are available, but there are
also countervailing obstacles and restraints on the full realization of these
pressures, which derive from the organic, psychological and social requirements of the stock animals themselves. These restraints are not, or are not
necessarily, of a normative kind, but are ontological. If the social needs of
captive animals are not met, they cease to breed, they show developmental
anomalies, become ill, behave aggressively or self-destructively, and so on. In
his description of the early stages of intensive rearing in the poultry industry,
for example, Jim Mason notes:

> Large-scale indoor production caught on fast around the urban market centres, but
> the new methods created a host of problems. Nightmarish scenes began to occur
> in the crowded sheds. Birds pecked others to death and ate their remains. In the
> poorly ventilated poultry sheds contagious diseases were rampant and losses
> multiplied.[21]

Of course, as Mason also points out, research science was able to come up with
technical responses to many of these problems – automatic 'debeaking'
machines for reducing the damage birds could do to one another, antibiotics
and other drugs to reduce losses through disease, and so on. However, none
of these responses was free either of costs or of undesirable unintended
consequences. Obstacles and constraints deriving from the biological nature
and psychological and social requirements of confined animals remain as
limits to 'reifying' commercial pressures whatever technical reorganization of
animal 'husbandry' is adopted.

However, there are qualitative differences both in the extent to which needs
are acknowledged and the ways in which they are met by different production
regimes. Traditional, non-commercial pastoralism requires human/animal

communicative interaction, extensive sharing by humans of the conditions of life of herd animals, and human adaptation to those conditions. There are generally deeply held affective dispositions and culturally authoritative moral regulations at work in these practices, even though the animals are commonly being reared to be killed as food. Commercial agriculture, with the 'formal' subsumption of ecological conditions, animals and human labour, retains many of these features, though the requirement for humans to adapt to the conditions of life of stock animals is reduced or eliminated with physical confinement and eco-regulation.

A sharp differentiation in the affective and normative content of human/ animal relations comes with intensive rearing. The fragmentation, distortion and partial suppression of the mode of life of the stock animal is paralleled by an elimination of 'quasi-personal' elements in the relation between humans and animals in the labour-process. The human social division of labour and specialization of tasks imposed by the overriding intentionality of value-maximization fragments, de-skills and 'operationalizes' necessary human/ animal contacts in ways which give them the character of episodic interventions and routines as distinct from long-run relationships, as in other husbandry modes.

The paradox for the rights perspective is that it is precisely this animal 'husbandry' regime whose predominance in modern agriculture has led to the most intense moral outrage. Yet, at the same time, the forms of human/animal interaction at the core of these practices are precisely the ones which are least likely to be responsive to moral appeals. There are several reasons why this is likely to be so. First, the appeal to the rights of the animals involved can be effective only if the moral agents to whom it is addressed are already able to recognize or acknowledge these animals as subjects-of-a-life, or as bearers of inherent value. The mode of involvement of human agents in these labour-processes is one which, as we have seen, obstructs the formation of long-run, 'quasi-personal', communicative relations between humans and animals. In this respect intensive rearing of livestock is quite unlike traditional animal husbandry, pet-keeping and other such social practices which combine humans and animals. To the extent that intensive stock-rearing regimes do acknowledge or recognize the subject-of-a-life status of the animals involved (and I have suggested that they do necessarily do so to some extent) they do so in a sense not reducible to the forms of calculation employed by individual human actors in the process. Such recognitions are, rather, built into the design of the overall structure of the labour-process, for which no single individual is likely to be wholly responsible:

'I am just a small cog in a big industry', Mr Turton said. 'Today poultry management is dictated by the company accountant rather than the stockman, but the big companies are not so much villains, as victims of a system that dictates that only the economically ruthless shall survive.'[22]

A second reason why the appeal to rights in the case of intensive stock-rearing regimes is unlikely to be effective is closely related to the first. Even if an argument in favour of the rights of animals subjected to these regimes could be made rationally convincing to the human moral agents involved, the affective conditions under which such a conviction might issue in relevantly altered conduct are liable to be missing. In the absence of long-run, quasi-personal, communicative relations between humans and animals, the affective ties of trust, loyalty, compassion and responsibility cannot develop either. This is still more significant if we take into account the powerful socio-economic interests of the workers in these regimes which run strongly counter to their giving subjective recognition to any feelings of repugnance or moral disquiet they may have about the nature of their work.

Finally, the human-social structure of these regimes is one in which a division of labour and hierarchy of authority diffuses both the causal and moral responsibility of the individual human agents involved. An electrical maintenance worker at an intensive plant may well strongly disapprove of the regime, but quite sensibly take the view that there is very little she can do to alter it. She has no access to top management, withdrawal of her labour would make the situation of the animals even worse, while giving up the job would deprive her of an income without helping the animals at all: another electrician with less of a conscience will be employed to replace her. As in my discussion of corporate liability in chapter 4, I am not, of course, arguing that where individual causal responsibility is diffused by the structure of an oppressive practice there is no moral responsibility on individuals. The point is that, in such a case, the bare moral appeal is liable to be ineffective. It needs to be complemented by a critique of the social-relational structure of the practice and a strategy for transforming it. This is precisely what is obstructed by the abstract-individualist social ontology which underpins the most influential animal rights arguments.

It could reasonably be argued against me that I have proceeded under a mistaken assumption about the addressee of the animal rights case. It can be acknowledged that it is unlikely to appeal to those who have a direct economic or practical involvement in the meat production industry. The argument is, rather, directed more widely to the citizens of democratic political systems, in the hope that they will use their electoral power to see appropriate legislation for the protection of farm-animals enacted.[23] But there are several problems which arise if the situation is conceptualized like this. One is that the rights argument is very difficult to square with the practice of killing animals for food at all – most advocates of animal rights think that it implies an obligation to vegetarianism (I think they are wrong about this – growing vegetable crops involves habitat changes which cause the deaths of animals which would otherwise live where crops are grown, so that the rights of these animals have to be put into the balance, too: it is a fact about the human predicament that we cannot live without causing the deaths of other animals).[24] This rights-based opposition to all animal agriculture desensitizes the rights perspective to the profound, and widely popularly perceived, moral differentiation between different kinds of stock-rearing regimes. From the point of view of achieving the kinds of protection sought by the advocates of animal rights, it seems likely that a more consequence-sensitive moral perspective might be more effective on this issue.

A second reason why the rights view is likely to be ineffective, even on this broader conception of its strategic place, is that it relies on a general view of citizenship and political order which is also vulnerable to pressing criticisms from socialist and other radical sources. Intensive regimes of stock-rearing are labour-processes which only become generally established under economic conditions of large-scale accumulations of capital which integrate food production, processing and distribution in large transnational corporations. These vast concentrations of economic power have privileged access to opinion-forming (and diet-shaping) media, and to the state apparatuses which develop agricultural policy and legislation.

In Britain, Howard Newby refers to the National Farmers' Union as 'undoubtedly one of the most successful pressure groups':

> Over the years the NFU and the Ministry have developed an almost symbiotic relationship. The Ministry needs the NFU in order to have a representative organization to negotiate with, one which can 'deliver' its membership on any agreed deal over prices and guarantees. The presence of the NFU also enables the Ministry to sound out farming opinion on any issue before developing a definite policy on the matter. ... The NFU is also a past master at publicity. ... By utilizing this panoply of publicity the NFU hopes both to influence wider public opinion and to apply pressure on the relevant authorities to implement policies beneficial to farmers.[25]

And this picture is not unique to Britain. Michael Tracy, writing about Western Europe as a whole, argues that:

> The influence of farmers' organizations was built up in all countries during and since the 1930s. The NFU in Britain, the FNSEA in France, the *Deutscher Bauernverband*, the *Union des Paysans Suisses* and similar organizations in other countries became powerful bodies generally committed to maintaining and improving the standard of living of their members.[26]

Where restrictive legislation does get parliamentary approval, the large agribusiness corporations are well placed to shift operations between national jurisdictions, influence or obstruct procedures for implementing and enforcing legislation, and, finally, to absorb any penalties which might accrue from whatever limited enforcement is achieved, while some though, of course, not all of these strategies are also open to specifically farming interests.

In short, there is no reason to suppose that well-meaning attempts to legislate for animal rights in the context of liberal-democratic regimes are any more likely to be effective than they have been in the case of women, the physically disabled, ethnic, religious or sexual minorities, and so on, where recognition of these rights runs counter to powerful vested interests (especially in the sphere of employment and economic production). Again, these considerations tell in favour of a broad strategy aimed at a re-structuring of economic and technical relations in the food production, processing and distribution industries. A coalition of forces committed to diverse but complementary aims – animal rights and welfare organizations, agricultural trade unions, organic farming interests, health and diet campaigners and others – would be likely to be more effective in realizing the kinds of protection sought by the rights view than would a campaign relying solely on the moral force of the argument for animal rights.

Needs, Paternalism and Benevolent Harms

So far my discussion has focused on ways in which the situation of animals with respect to human social practices is analogous to that of socially or economically disadvantaged or dependent human social groups. To the extent that these analogies can be made convincing, to that extent the socialist/radical critique of the (liberal-individualist) discourse of rights and justice can be applied also to that discourse in its extension to (non-human) animals. But, as I remarked above, animals are in some respects still less well placed to benefit from the ascription of rights than even the worst-off humans. Sometimes this is just a matter of degree, but in one respect there is a major qualitative difference of situation, and one which is radically inimical to modification. This is the fact, acknowledged in the animal-rights literature itself, that non-human animals are never moral agents. It is, perhaps, worth noting that this is a 'mere' fact – there could have been, and very likely have been, other species whose individuals may have possessed moral agency. No one, however, seriously argues that those animals with which humans now generally interact, or whose fate is bound up with human activity, are capable of apprehending moral principles, making moral judgements, acting according to or breaking moral rules, and so on.

One consequence of this, together with the closely connected lack of linguistic-communicative ability, is that ascription of rights to (non-human) animals is always other-ascription. If rights are analysed as justified claims, then the claim is never, in the case of animal rights, made by the bearer of the right but always, and necessarily, on its behalf by someone who is a moral agent. In the argument above I have implicitly acknowledged this in considering the strategies available to humans acting on behalf of animals. But this dependence of animals subject to the power of human social institutions upon other human agents and institutions to offer effective protection is yet another source of difficulties for the rights view. Though they are well worth further elaboration I will merely summarize these difficulties here.

1. In the liberal-individualist rights discourse in its paradigmatic application to the human case, personal autonomy and its preservation is a core value. This is transferred across the species-boundary by way of the attribution to animals of 'preference autonomy' and retention of the paradigm concept of rights as 'non-interference' rights. However, in this same discourse, the value of autonomy implies that the individual is the authoritative judge of his or her own interests. If rights are claims to treatment of a certain sort, then the value of autonomy requires that the bearer of the right is the one who authorizes the content of the claim (though, of course, that person will not necessarily have the last word on the validity of the claim). Making claims on behalf of beings unable to make or authorize claims on their own behalf is difficult to square with a core value in the liberal-individualist moral canon.

2. There are difficulties of an epistemic nature in attributing interests to members of another species for the purpose of defending their rights. We may be able to discover what conditions are necessary to their survival, and to their health and physical well-being, but lacking the kind of communicative relation to non-human animals which is available in the human case, access to a reliable view of the subjective aspects of animal well-being is peculiarly problematic. The risk of causing harm or suffering by action which is well-intended is, therefore, ever-present in animal/human relations where humans have power over animals. One moral consequence of this epistemic consideration is that to minimize the risk of 'benevolent harms', relations with animals, other things being equal, should be organized so as to maximize the 'preference autonomy' of the animals involved. This is a further argument against intensive rearing practices in animal husbandry. In more traditional forms of animal husbandry, stock animals meet their own psychological, social and physiological needs under conditions conserved or regulated by human intervention, while under intensive regimes such needs of the animal

as are met at all are met by direct human intervention rather than by the independent activity of the animal itself.

Superficially, this consideration may seem to favour a 'thin', negative, or non-interference view of rights in the case of non-human animals. However, the appropriation by humans of otherwise usable animal habitat, and the maintenance for human purposes of populations of animals which could not survive in the areas allocated to them without human eco-regulative activity, are two conditions which render stock animals dependent upon human activity for their well-being. As in the case of animals such as pets and laboratory subjects, there is a quasi-contractarian argument for attributing to humans a moral responsibility for the well-being of animals which they have by their past or present social activities rendered dependent. In such social-relational structures, mere non-interference cannot be seriously regarded as a fulfilment of the humans' acquired responsibility to the animals. To simply refrain from interfering out of respect for the animals' preference-autonomy would, under these circumstances, be to cause harm to the animals by neglect. There are, of course, close parallels to the limitations of this same non-interference view of rights as applied to psychologically, bodily, or economically dependent or dispossessed humans.

To clarify the moral issues at stake here, we need a three-fold classification to displace the positive/negative contrast which prevails in the literature, and which I have so far used. Conceding, for purposes of argument, the appropriateness of attributing rights of any sort to non-human animals,[27] we may distinguish:

a. negative, non-interferences rights, to which the correlative responsibility is to refrain from confining animals, or obstructing them in the exercise of their preference-autonomy;
b. enablement rights, to which the correlative responsibility is to preserve or provide those conditions of life necessary for the animals concerned to autonomously meet their needs, or secure their well-being;
c. security rights, to which the correlative responsibility is simply to ensure that needs are met, or well-being secured.

Enablement and security rights are both properly to be regarded as positive rights, in that they correlate with a responsibility to act where conditions of their fulfilment are absent. They cannot be construed as mere formal claims or entitlements. However, enablement rights are by definition autonomy-respecting, while security rights are defined in such a way as to leave open the mode of satisfaction of need or securing of well-being. The epistemic limit to cross-species recognition of need, and especially of the subjective aspects of well-being, favours the enablement construal of rights and/or responsibilities, since it reduces the risk of causing harm by well-intended action. In the case of human moral agents, and, arguably, in the case of some non-human animals, autonomy in the meeting of need and pursuit of well-being is itself a component of well-being. For these classes of being enablement rights are further favoured, as against mere security rights which may not be autonomy-respecting. These considerations, of course, while favouring enablement rights in these classes of case, are not necessarily overriding. Where resources are very scarce, in extreme emergency, or where autonomous agency is itself undeveloped or impaired, the 'security' construal of rights and responsibilities may be an appropriate one.

But this raises yet more difficulties for the attribution of rights to non-human animals, since key arguments for animal rights depend on the moral equivalence of non-human animals and human moral patients such as the severely mentally disabled and young infants. If we recognize rights in the case of human moral patients, the argument runs, we cannot consistently (or, therefore, justly) deny them in the case of non-human moral patients. But the epistemic limit, with its moral consequences, does not apply in the case of human moral patients, or, at least, does not apply in quite the same way. Where human individuals are impaired in their moral agency, or where this complex of capacities is as yet undeveloped, claims made on their behalf may be authorized by an appeal to counterfactuals. We can ask, and plausibly answer, questions as to what claims these individuals *would* make if they *were* able to make moral claims on their own behalf. The possibility of benevolent harm is, of course, still present, but the liability to it is much less than in cross-species contacts. Moreover, the inability of human moral patients (of the kinds generally addressed by the advocates of animal rights) to meet their needs autonomously implies the inappropriateness to their situation of both the 'thin', non-interference concept of rights and the enablement construal.

In these kinds of case, effective rights would have to be conceptualized in terms of direct obligations on the part of moral agents to meet the needs and ensure the provision of whatever level of well-being is attainable for the moral patient concerned. (This argument is, incidentally, *ad personem*: the likeness of the moral situation of human and non-human moral patients can be restored from the perspective of a needs-based view of rights which does not take self-avowal as the sole authoritative criterion of need. This is implicit, for example, in the way that contemporary family law makes use of the notion of 'the best interests of' the child. This may conflict with what the child wants, and cannot readily be made sense of in terms of counterfactuals such as 'what would the child want if it were, or had the agency of, an adult?')

3. Finally, the notion of an 'epistemic limit' adds yet another layer of sources

of vulnerability on the part of animals to human-generated harms. If, for example, humans have an interest in (or, simply, a desire for) a particular mode of treatment of an animal, then an acknowledgment of the 'epistemic limit' may facilitate interested dismissal of objections: if we have no authoritative access to the subjective states of animals, how do we know that this proposed activity is cruel?

Review (1) Against Rights?

So far I have tried to show that one broad radical/socialist line of criticism of the liberal-individualist notion of rights is at least equally pertinent to the extension of that concept to non-human animals. Indeed, the prospect that non-human animals might be effectively protected by an acknowledgement of them as bearers of rights is in several important respects less likely than in the case of disadvantaged or oppressed humans. Social, economic and political relations of power and dependency, dominance and subordination may serve to render rights, even where formally acknowledged, more-or-less ineffective. If we consider the variety of patterns of social relationship through which humans may be linked to animals, then even where the rights view might appear to be most promising, there are strong grounds for thinking it would offer only limited effective protection. In the more socially and economically central practices which involve non-human animals, most notably in intensive stock-rearing regimes, the prospects for an effective rights-based approach appear be very limited indeed, and for reasons which closely parallel the limitations of rights or citizenship-based approaches to work-place disadvantage or oppressions suffered by women, ethnic minorities, the disabled and other stigmatized groups in the human population.

Finally, the intrinsic incapacity of non-human animals to make rights-claims on their own behalf is a further source of difficulties for the rights view, specifically in its proposed extension beyond the species boundary. These difficulties do, indeed, take us a significant step beyond this phase of the argument. They suggest not only that significant practical and social-relational obstacles stand in the way of any hoped-for translation of the moral argument for animal rights into effective protection for non-human animals, but also call into question the conceptual basis of the argument for animal rights. So central is the value of individual autonomy and the authority of the individual in the judgement of her or his interests to the liberal tradition, that the attribution of rights to beings who by their nature cannot make rights-claims on their own behalf must induce conceptual strain, to say the least. Interestingly, this particular source of conceptual strain might turn out to be less telling for any re-constituted view of rights in which the value of individual autonomy were rendered less central than it is in the liberal canon.

Review (2) For Rights?

As well as tending to confirm the sociological basis of the radical/socialist line of criticism of the liberal-individualist morality of rights, the above exploration has yielded some considerations which point, rather, in the opposite direction. First, and most obviously, the case in favour of animal rights tends to tell against the view, often attributed to Marx, that 'bourgeois rights' amount to nothing more than property rights.

Second, a social ontology which takes seriously the social relations and structured social practices by which individuals are bound together, and which differentially shape their life chances, does not of itself demonstrate the practical ineffectiveness of the rights view – whether in its application to humans only, or across the species-divide. Consideration of the diversity of social relations and practices through which both humans and animals may be brought into interest-affecting relations with one another reveals a complex and differentiated moral scene. Where the real structure of social relations approximates, or is analogous to, the presumed social ontology (of 'atomic' individuals, contingently related by free choices) of the liberal-individualist rights discourse then that discourse may, indeed, have sufficient purchase to bring about effective protection from basic harms. Since humans are bound to one another by patterns of social relations still more diverse and complex than those through which they are bound to non-human animals, the likelihood is that the moral pertinence of the liberal-individualist concept of rights may be sustained for at least some aspects of the well-being of at least some human moral agents in at least some contexts of their lives, and even (perhaps especially) while capitalist social and economic relations prevail. In short, this radical/socialist line of criticism of the liberal-individualist rights discourse (whether applied to humans or across the species-divide) is strictly contingent upon sociological considerations of a broadly factual kind. It does not, and cannot, provide decisive arguments against the morality of liberal rights as such or in general.

The third consideration yielded by the above argument which tells against, or at least requires a response from, the radical/socialist critique itself concerns the value of autonomy. Epistemic limits to cross-species judgement of need and well-being render any practice of direct meeting of need across species boundaries especially susceptible to the unwitting infliction of harms. The moral importance of the distinction between a responsibility to provide or secure conditions under which bearers of correlative rights are able to autonomously meet their needs, and a responsibility to ensure that needs are met is brought sharply into focus by these considerations.

Where personal autonomy is itself viewed, as in the liberal tradition, as a need in its own right, and as an indispensable component of well-being, the moral importance of the distinction within the domain of the specifically human is in any case already clear. However, in contexts where the significance of the value of personal autonomy may not be uncontroversially given, the argument from epistemic limits may still be highly consequential. For example, in the provision of emergency aid, especially in contexts where there are wide cultural differences between donors and intended beneficiaries, there may be pressures to define need in terms which fail to recognize the autonomy of recipients. In these and analogous contexts, the argument from 'epistemic limits' (here applying across cultural, rather than species-boundaries) favours the autonomy-respecting 'enablement' construal of rights and responsibilities, as against mere 'security' rights and responsibilities.

6

The Limits of Liberal Rights
I: Individuals and Their Well-being

As we have just seen, the first, sociological line of radical/socialist criticism of the liberal-individualist discourse of rights readily passes into conceptual criticism. If structures of social and economic power tend systematically to obstruct the exercise or realization of formally acknowledged rights then this must put pressure on the conceptualization of rights themselves. If the discourse of liberal rights cannot, or cannot under prevailing social and economic relations, offer effective protection from basic harms, then there is a case for replacing it with either some more sociologically nuanced, and potentially more practically effective conception of rights and justice, or a moral discourse and strategy which dispenses with rights altogether (the position often attributed to Marx). But getting clearer about the significance of this latter dilemma will require us to look more analytically at the specifically conceptual limitations alleged against liberal-individualist constructions of the concept of rights (focusing, of course, on the version favoured by the leading advocates of animal rights). I shall deal first with the view of individuals (both persons and non-human animals) and their needs, interests and well-being presupposed or implied in the liberal discourse. Then, in chapter 7, I will consider critically the liberal-individualist conception of those sources of harm from which acknowledgement of rights would seek to protect individuals.

The Limits of Individualism

As we saw (in chapter 3), Tom Regan provides us with a set of arguments for attributing equal rights to all individual beings who possess inherent value. A sufficient (but not necessary) condition of possession of inherent value is to be a 'subject-of-a-life'. To be a subject-of-a-life, in turn, requires psychological complexity sufficient to ground some notion of 'preference-autonomy', a distinction between harm and well-being, and enough sense of self for the attribution of 'experiential welfare' to be coherent. Any individual, whether human or not, who satisfies these conditions has inherent value, and therefore a *prima facie* right to be treated with respect, not to be harmed, and so on. As we have seen, Regan's abstraction from the substantive social relational bonds between humans and animals, and his exclusive concern with what he calls 'basic' or unacquired rights tend to favour a negative conception of rights as imposing duties of non-interference, as restraining human moral agents with respect to potentially harmful acts they might otherwise have performed.

One way, as we have seen, of showing the inadequacy of this conception of rights is to bring into the picture the extent to which components of well-being such as autonomous pursuit of preferences and meeting of need are activities which require appropriate contexts, conditions and media. If individuals (human or animal) are deprived of *de facto* access to these conditions then a negative, or 'non-interference' right is no use to them. Acknowledgement of a negative right can only offer substantive protection if the necessary conditions of its exercise can be taken as unproblematically given.

So far, however, I have focused primarily on the extrinsic conditions, contexts and media necessary for the enjoyment of the 'experiential welfare' which the rights view seeks to protect. But the broad view of what it is to be a 'living natural being' which I advanced in chapter 2 suggests that the attributes, powers and potentials of individuals in virtue of which they are able to live the mode of life appropriate to their species have their own intrinsic as well as extrinsic conditions. Living beings acquire these attributes and powers, which are at first only potentials, in the course of developmental processes. Specifically psychological powers are dependent upon, but not reducible to, features of anatomical structure and physiological functioning. Continued organic functioning in the appropriate respects is a necessary intrinsic condition for the continued possession, and therefore exercise, of psychological powers. In the absence of extrinsic conditions for their exercise, some powers and capacities (though not all) either not may be acquired at all, may be only defectively acquired, or, having been acquired, may atrophy (those powers we recognize as 'skills' are my paradigm here). For an important subset of these powers, long-run continuity and frequency of social interaction within stable social relations are necessary both for their initial acquisition and for their long-term retention (skills underlying language-use are paradigmatic here).

This range of considerations, which bears upon living beings across species boundaries, nevertheless is appropriate to different extents and in different ways according to the differences of biological organization and mode of life of the species under consideration. Nevertheless, even for that range of species with which Regan is centrally concerned, we can now see a new 'layer', so to speak, of limitations in the radical individualism of his rights view. For animals to be able to pursue their preferences and meet their needs requires not only that the extrinsic conditions of the exercise of those abilities are present, but also that the conditions of initial acquisition and persistence of the abilities themselves are and continue to be satisfied. Individuals, as living organisms, are subject to complex and generally species-specific sets of reproductive and developmental conditions if they are to acquire the abilities necessary to the living of the mode of life appropriate to the species. Species differ greatly in the extent to which, and in the ways in which, social interactions and enduring social relations enter into reproductive success, and into the individual development of species-characteristic attributes and abilities.

However, for fairly obvious reasons, most species of animals which figure significantly in human social life are themselves highly social beings in this sense. It follows that to acknowledge their well-being as a value entails also acknowledging the social conditions of their reproductive and developmental needs as intrinsic to their well-being. The introduction, here, of reproductive and developmental needs sharply challenges the narrower focus of abstract-individualist views of the self. The skills and capacities which constitute personal autonomy, the ability to be harmed or benefited by the treatment of others are, in this perspective, seen not as 'given' attributes of individuals, but as achievements, often only partially and provisionally won, in the course of long developmental processes. These processes, in turn, are not self-sustaining, but rely on the continuous provision of nurturing practices, caring relationships and the presence of appropriately sustaining social and material environments. If, in the human case, a naturalistic view is to ground some notion of developmental rights as individual attributes, then what is required is a view of the developing individual as one who stands in need of the appropriate social and material conditions for personal development.

The case of reproductive needs and the associated grounds for rights-attribution are, of course, far more complex. To define well-being in terms of participation in the mode of life characteristic of the species would seem to imply reproductive activity as essential to well-being. However, this is not to specify any particular mode of participation in reproduction. Moreover, the concept of 'reproductive need' as a universal, or 'basic' need of individuals is much more difficult to sustain than, for example, health, or nutrition. Refraining from reproduction does not lead to premature death, nor even to any uncontroversially identifiable pathological consequences.[1] Nevertheless, in the human case, to be prevented from exercising reproductive choices is, arguably, an experience which could be genuinely identified as a deprivation, or as a harm to the individual.

It is, perhaps, in the area of reproduction that the universality implicit in a rights approach, even one explicitly pitched against the abstract and formal individualism of the liberal tradition, is at its limit of usefulness. While some notion of reproductive need in non-human animals may properly ground conceptions of welfare obligation to them, as moral patients, the moral implications of such a notion in the human case are likely to be very limited. This is for two basic reasons. The first is the (biologically rooted) dissociation of sexuality in the human case from its narrowly reproductive function. Sexual expression as a dimension in affective bonds between couples, independently of reproduction, allows for the foundation, in the human case, of diversity and complexity in sexual orientation and preference which would seem to deny all possibility of universal formulation. The second is that with respect to reproduction itself, primary sexual differences, which are in most cultures elaborated and embellished with normative content, and woven into most aspects of the social division of labour, constitute gender-specific, and often conflictual, problems of need and interest.

On this latter issue there is a lively and sophisticated feminist debate which has many striking parallels, in its recognition of both the appeal and the limitations of the rights discourse, to my own discussion here. Where, for example, reproductive rights have been claimed by pro-choice campaigners on the abortion issue, successes have been achieved in making abortion a public, political issue in new terms, defined, at least partly, by women themselves, and in extending women's access to abortion. But set against this has been the experience that to have a legally recognized formal right is not the same thing as to have a substantive right – one sufficiently resourced for women who need to exercise it to be, in practice, able to. Furthermore, as we have seen in the case of the use of the discourse of rights in defence of animals, rights-claims can generally be challenged by countervailing rights. In the abortion case, the conflict of rights involved is 'the claim by women that they must have a right to determine the reproductive capacities of their own bodies, and the counter-claim that such a right must take second place to the right of the foetus (usually referred to as a child) to life'.[2] For some participants in this controversy, the irresolvability of such conflicts of rights-claims, weighs, together with other considerations, against feminist use of appeals to reproductive rights.[3]

To give the issues the depth of treatment they evidently require is beyond my competence here, but simply to pose the issues is to indicate in a general way how our agenda for moral debate is set by a naturalistic perspective on human nature. The abstract-individualism of the liberal rights view, both in its paradigmatic application to the human case and in its proposed extension to non-human animals, renders invisible or marginalizes such fundamental aspects of living beings as reproduction and development. There is, in the abstract-individualist view, insufficient purchase for substantive moral significance to be assigned to such conditions and components of well-being. The strength of a naturalistic perspective is not that it offers a resolution of such conflict, some short-cut to bridging the gap between 'is' and 'ought', but, rather, that it enables us to get some sense of the significant landmarks in a human (or animal) life which must be mapped by any moral view with any hope of sustaining whatever potential for happiness such beings possess.

The individualism of the rights view, both in its paradigmatic liberal application to the human case and in its proposed extension to non-human animals, renders invisible or marginalizes such questions in ways which impoverish its moral force and weaken its practical impact. The widespread shift in emphasis in wildlife conservation, for example, away from protection by forbidding collecting or killing individuals of certain species and towards preserving or actively managing habitat is an acknowledgement of these limitations in the individualistic perspective. It should be noted that the point here is not, as Regan himself is sometimes inclined to suggest, a matter of replacing the centrality of the moral value of individuals with that of populations, ecosystems or species, but rather to suggest that the well-being of individuals is itself indissolubly bound up with their ecological and social conditions of life.

The socialist/radical critique of the rights view highlights the social-relational preconditions that enable individuals (whether human or animal) to acquire and sustain those attributes and abilities in virtue of which they are held to have inherent value. If humans have direct obligations to non-human animals which are moral patients, then these considerations point to the appropriateness of a broader conception of those obligations than is so far manifest in the animal rights literature. If animal husbandry is tolerable at all, these considerations tell in favour of husbandry regimes which preserve opportunities for animals to establish and maintain the broad patterns of social life which are peculiar to their species. Where physical and psychological development requires more-or-less prolonged relationships between juvenile animals and adults, conditions for those relationships need to be provided. Regan's exclusive focus on mammals above the age of one year, itself linked to his subject-of-a-life criterion, excludes such concerns from the rights view. In the absence of any moral vocabulary to complement that of rights, this implies excluding such considerations from moral concern altogether (except, for example, in so far as suffering is imposed upon adult animals by separation from their offspring).

However, focusing on the situation of non-human animals, the dependence of animal sociality upon the availability of appropriate environmental conditions is directly evident. In part we are prepared to recognize this by the tradition of popular ethological literature, and by the tendency for ethology itself to become increasingly integrated, as a scientific specialism, with ecology. Those animals who satisfy Regan's subject-of-a-life criterion are, in general, capable of considerable variation in their behavioural responses to one another, to members of other species (such as ourselves), and, more broadly, to their ecological conditions of life. Nevertheless, it remains a relatively straightforward matter to characterize their habitat requirements as falling within a definite range of variation. Clutton-Brock, for example, argues that the wolf, the wild ancestor of the domestic dog, shared much with human hunting populations with the same food sources. Moreover, communication between wolves by posture and facial expression made possible communication and therefore mutual co-ordination of activity across the species-divide. The strong development of patterns of submission and dominance among wolves also made it possible to train them and their domesticated descendants to obey human commands. These intersecting ethological and ecological features of the populations of both species provided the necessary conditions of possibility for initial domestication.[4] In the case of sheep, another species subject to early domestication, we again find a fortuitous coincidence of social and ecological features of their mode of life in relation to human populations. Unlike deer or gazelles, sheep are not territorial animals, and are not psychologically adapted to escape from predators, but are, rather, adapted to harsh, mountainous conditions with relatively little threat from mammalian predators; they maintain a home-range, rather than a territory which is defended. They are relatively placid, and also have a form of social life with strongly developed dominance, which 'predisposes them to leadership by a herdsman'.[5] These broad ethological and ecological generalizations carry implicit reference to the position of each species in the food-chain, its dependence on a certain kind of terrain and climate, and so on. As I suggested in chapter 5, when animals are kept by humans under confinement regimes, the design of the latter generally acknowledges these features of the mode of life of the species concerned, by actually protecting its conditions, by artificially replacing them, or by intervening with drugs or other technical innovations to offset the pathological consequences of overriding them.

Humanism or Naturalism?

This set of considerations, while taking further the criticism of the liberal-individualist tradition, also exposes an important limitation in the socialist–radical critique of rights: its focus on social-relational conditions of the development and maintenance of valued capacities and attributes at the expense of more broadly ecological ones. This is the legacy of a deep-rooted anti-naturalism in the humanist traditions of radical social theory, and facing up to the issue of the moral status of non-human animals may offer a valuable corrective to it: if habitat protection is demonstrably necessary to any strategy for preserving the well-being of non-human animals, why should this not follow in the human case?

Two broad lines of response to this question are open to humanist radicals. One is to argue that the rather direct relations of causal dependency which link habitat conditions, patterns of social life and individual well-being in the case of non-human animals, simply do not apply to humans. The other is to argue that the distinctively human attribute of culture establishes the possibility of a qualitatively different symbolic mode of relationship to the environment.

Both lines of argument are attractive and well grounded. In the case of the first, historical, archaeological and anthropological evidence does, indeed, suggest a degree of ecological adaptability in humans which is quite unique. However, it is equally clear that this adaptability is neither limitless nor devoid of definite causal conditions. The incidence of mass infectious diseases, drought, flooding and famine as causes of catastrophic loss of human populations are evidence enough of this. In each case, there is a complex causal interweaving of social-relational and ecological causal conditions, and the configuration of causal mechanisms will be different from episode to episode. Nevertheless, the immense diversity of forms of social relationship and technical means by which humans interact with external nature in the meeting of their needs and satisfying of their desires should not blind as to the vulnerability of each of those various socio-natural forms to ecological constraints.[6] The constraints may be different in each case, and may impinge upon social life in different ways in each case, but they are present none the less.

We are, I think, justified in speaking of environmental conditions as requirements for human well-being, and of humans as having basic interests in those conditions. However, the peculiarities of human ecology which ground the anti-naturalist response do have a profound moral significance: we cannot say, in advance of a serious analysis of the mode of life, and especially of the 'material culture' of a human community, what those conditions will be. This is partly a question of such features as the technologies locally deployed, the prevailing, culturally ordered scale and pattern of material consumption, and features of the local geology, climate and biotopes. For any given locally established socio-ecologico-technical order there will be limits to the adaptive power of that order with respect to variations in one or more components of the system: limits, as Habermas might put it, to the 'steering capacity' of the system.[7] It is important to notice, here, that such limits are defined by a specific intersection of ecological conditions and patterned socio-technical practices. Ecological conditions and limits, in the human case, cannot be defined independently of the specific patterns of social activity in relation to nature which approach and potentially exceed those limits. This remains true even in the ultimate case, recently acknowledged and debated, of global limits, whether in agricultural production, carbon dioxide emission, non-renewable resource use, or ozone depletion: in each case, the rate at which a limit is approached, the global distribution of the activities concerned, and their combination with other ecologically relevant activities are all significant variables in defining any potential 'limit'.[8]

The human/animal comparison, then, draws our attention to the extent to which humans, as living organisms, depend for their organic well-being on their (socially mediated) relation to their ecological conditions of life. If such basic requirements can ground rights, at least in the human case, then we are led to postulate appropriate environmental conditions for organic well-being as itself a right which ought to be acknowledged alongside, and presupposed by the rights to freedom of worship, of speech and so on. Since we are also social animals, and so depend for our individual well-being upon the opportunity to develop within, be sustained by, and to participate in the reproduction of the social life of our local sub-population of the species, this notion of environmental rights would have to extend to the preservation of the ecological integrity of a sufficient geographical terrain for the living of that social life.

This line of argument can most directly and clearly be applied to the situation of indigenous peoples whose traditional ways of life continue to be threatened and undermined by the ecological consequences of development strategies, especially in the Arctic and in the rain-forests of tropical South America and South East Asia. As small, relatively self-sufficient communities, whose technical achievements are primarily adaptive rather than transformative, they have well-defined local ecological conditions of life. The ascription of environmental rights here would posit a valid claim on the part of (members of) such local communities against interests such as cattle ranching, mineral exploitation, transportation, and logging whose projects would damage or destroy their ecological sustaining conditions. Again, the presence of a powerful moral and ontological case for the recognition of such rights is no guarantee either of their juridical acknowledgement or of the *de facto* power to exercise them on the part of the communities concerned.

Part of the problem here (but by no means the whole of it) has to do with how, in cases like this, the 'community' is to be defined. To the extent that such communities exist as socio-culturally and politically semi-detached enclaves within the territorial boundaries of nation states (and they generally do) the opportunity is ever-present for the boundaries of the relevant community to be drawn much more widely. If the nation state adopts a development strategy in which such projects play a central role, it may be argued that the short term interests of small populations of indigenous people may justifiably be subordinated to the benefit of the wider population which stand to benefit from generalized socio-economic and technical modernization.

There are two broad lines of response to this kind of argument. The first is to remind ourselves of Regan's key reasons for adopting a rights view against a utilitarian or consequentialist moral perspective for thinking about the moral status of non-human animals. To acknowledge some condition as a right is precisely to obstruct – at least in the context of moral argumentation – such 'playing off' of fundamental interests of some individuals for the sake of a net aggregate benefit. This would be, precisely, the point of arguing for a concept of environmental rights. The second line of response is to argue for a recognition of the identity and integrity of such indigenous local communities on the basis of their own shared symbolic universe, communal identity, and distinctive mode of social interaction with their local physico-chemical and biological environment.

The modernizing and modernist discourse of universal rights is, on the face of it, radically inimical to such recognitions. It was precisely against such traditional ties of individuals to community, and of community to land and locality that the rights-discourse of the seventeenth and eighteenth centuries was pitted. And, indeed, in so far as this modernizing project did succeed in breaking these fetters on the formation of free and autonomous individuality it was celebrated and endorsed by Marx and Engels as emancipatory. This is not, for course, the place to rehearse the long-running debate about the benefits and the price of modernity in the West. Wherever we stand on that great cluster of issues, it is clear that the historical configuration and the practical prospects which face indigenous peoples in, predominantly, third-world countries today is radically different from that of the European peoples in the early modern period. The life of the indigenous Amazonian peoples, for example, is rigorous, narrow and often dangerous. It is not a life that would be freely chosen by many of the readers of this book. But, equally, it is not the life of a feudal serf, and the practical alternative to it, given locally prevailing socio-economic and political institutions, is not the life of an affluent modern Westerner with secure citizenship rights. Bereft of access to the conditions of life which sustained them bodily and culturally, the victims of lost environmental rights are prey to catastrophic loss of identity, and to addiction, disease, humiliation and rampant exploitation.[9]

In mentioning, here, the cultural dislocation and loss of identity involved in ecological destruction I have already implicitly acknowledged the pertinence of the second source of 'humanist' resistance to human/animal continuism – the distinctively cultural, symbolic aspect or moment in human/environmental relationships. There are, indeed, distinctively human ways of relating to environmental conditions, but these strengthen and enrich the case for environmental rights, rather than the reverse. If we include within the concept of culture what some anthropologists refer to as 'material culture', the rule-governed social practices through which human groups act upon and interact with their environments in meeting their organic needs for food, shelter, clothing and so on, then this recognition of a cultural moment in our relationship to the environment has several direct consequences.

First, there is a diversity in such patterns of social/environmental relations across human sub-populations, which far exceeds that exhibited by any other animal species. Second, in virtue of human capacities for individual and collective reflective monitoring and transformation of the rules by which their practices are ordered, the range of this variation is open-ended, and may not be prescribed in advance. Perhaps one might say, here, that this potential variation is bounded but unlimited – each sustainable form must conform to requirements imposed by the nature of the physical and organic environment, by the adaptive capacities of individual humans and by specifically social constraints, but within those bounds (which are themselves manifested differently with each new variation) there are limitless creative possibilities. Third, as cultural forms, these practices are normatively ordered.

Typically, activity is normatively regulated with respect to three sets of relationships. These are, first, the division of labour between participating individuals and the associated forms of co-operation between them; second, the division of the material results of the practice both among the participating individuals themselves and between them and non-participants (allocation rules); and, third, rules governing the appropriateness and permissibility of the concrete types of intentional intervention into the natural world involved in the practices – taboos on the killing of certain kinds of birds or animals, ritual observances in modes of killing of others, ritually demarcated seasonality in the temporal distribution of various kinds of agriculture, and so on. Both Western capitalist and state-bureaucratic socialist forms of industrialization have shared an anthropologically quite exceptional suspension of normative regulations of the third sort. Both in their practice and in their dominant modes of philosophizing only the normative character of divisions of labour, forms of co-operation, and distributive justice have been fully acknowledged. The secular, mechanical view of the universe which emerged from the scientific revolution of the seventeenth century favoured the suspension, as superstitious, animistic cultural residues, of all normative regulation of the concrete forms of human/natural intervention.[10] Only in recent times, with the growing acknowledgement of environmental outer limits, has this dimension of material culture in the industrialized and industrializing countries been brought back into the scope of normative reflection and practical regulation. This book is, of course, one expression of this process. Finally, but certainly not least in importance, the acknowledgement of material culture as culture implies the collective, socially co-operative character of all human need-meeting interaction with environments.

These several features, then, are implicit in the distinctively cultural character of human need-meeting interaction with environments: social co-ordination of activity, complex normative ordering, bounded but limitless variation, and liability to transformation. Of course, this list by no means exhausts the importance of the culturally mediated character of human/environment relations for views of rights and justice. However, it is worth pausing here to explore further the significance of these features before moving on to consider more directly symbolic and identity-constituting aspects of cultural mediation. First, as I have suggested, there is a case for regarding some set of environmental conditions of well-being as valid objects of universal human rights claims, although the concrete content of these claims cannot be established independently both of some specification of the material culture of those on behalf of whom the claim is made and of the bio-physical sustaining conditions of that culture. But this does not imply a complete cultural relativism of the notion of environmental rights, of a kind which would subvert the universality of the claims involved.

The starting-point for our analysis was the idea of the well-being of the individual and its presuppositions, social-relational and environmental/ecological. An uncontroversial aspect of well-being is bodily health, though there are significant variations in normative standards of health from culture to culture. For my purposes here it is necessary only to accept that there is some common core of organic functioning and absence of developmental anomaly, disability or chronic disease which can be defended as a cross-culturally valid 'negative' conception of health.[11] Given only this, the appropriate location of an individual within *some* ecologically sustainable material culture can be recognized as a necessary condition for health and, therefore, in one important aspect at least, well-being: appropriate dietary requirements, such clothing and shelter as the climate necessitates, distributive norms which ensure the allocation to individuals of the material means of meeting these requirements, and so on, are all presuppositions of health in this very basic, 'core' meaning. The definite, but highly culturally variable, and open-endedly transformable ways in which these various requirements may be met do not need to be exhaustively specified for their status as necessary conditions for health, and therefore of the well-being, or basic interests, of the individual to recognized as a universal right. Nor does an acknowledgement of this cultural variability in any way blunt the critical cutting-edge of such a notion of universal environmental right.

Two other features of the culturally mediated character of human organic need-meeting interaction with environments – social co-ordination and complex normative ordering – bring us to a direct engagement with the conceptual limits of the liberal-individualist view of rights. I have so far used human/animal comparison as a resource for exploring the case for an acknowledgement of embodiment rights (such as health) and environmental rights as, so to speak, additions to the list of 'valid claims' which began in the seventeenth century with freedom of speech, worship and so on. These considerations arise from a certain shift in our conception of persons and the components and conditions of their well-being.

This shift can be taken further with the recognition of humans as 'embedded' as well as 'embodied'. The radical/socialist case against the liberal-individualist view already establishes this shift with its focus on social embedding. However, at least some of the force of that radical critique is lost if we see in it only a protest against ways in which structures of social domination and dependency or inequality and deprivation obstruct the substantive enjoyment of rights by individuals. Bringing into the account, as the above argument does, the necessity for humans to conduct their organic need-meeting activity in social co-operation with others, under authoritative forms of normative regulation, and within the affordances provided by their ecological conditions and contexts, calls into question the level of abstraction at which the individual of the liberal-individualist view is conceptualized. The subject of a rights claim is, indeed, (the liberal-individualist tradition is right about this) an individual person (not necessarily of the human species) but to the extent that a rights-claim is given substantive content, it must be specified in its application to that individual in relation to *some* cultural form and set of ecological conditions and contexts. And this is not merely a matter setting down the conditions under which an 'abstract' right can be exercised but, rather, a matter of giving substantive content and applicability to the rights-claim itself.

It should be clear from this that the alternative to the liberal-individualist view which is beginning to emerge here is not one in which rights (or any other moral status) are assigned to social collectivities. Such collectivities are, indeed, real, as sites of emergence of causal powers whose exercise affects (adversely or favourably) the well-being of individual persons, as well as the integrity of bio-physical mechanisms and systems. This is why individuals

179

position in relation to social structures and ecological conditions is so central to our consideration of their well-being and so to the concept of rights. But to consider an extension of the concept of a moral agent (or patient) to include either social structures or collectivities would require a further set of arguments over and above those required to establish their reality as sites of emergence of causal powers. Whatever view is taken on that nexus of problems, the case for rights attributions to collectivities is one which would take me well beyond the confines of this book. So, the alternative to the liberal-individualist view is one which shares with it the primary focus of ethical concern on the well-being of the individual person (or subject-of-a life, of whatever species), but disputes both the conception of personal well-being advanced within the liberal tradition and that tradition's conception of the categories of sources of harm to well-being which come up for moral consideration.

The challenge to the liberal-individualist view of sources of harm will come later. For the moment it will suffice to remind ourselves of the ways in which the human/animal comparison suggests to us the importance of aspects of bodily well-being (most especially health), of developmental requirements, and of both social and ecological embeddedness, or relatedness, as conditions and components of human well-being. To the extent that these conditions and components constitute basic interests of individuals they may ground morally valid claims, or rights. I leave aside, for the moment, the question of the bearers of the moral responsibilities which correlate with these claims. The individuals who are the subjects of rights, on this emerging view, are necessarily embodied, and are also to be conceptualized as 'individuals-in-relationship' both to other persons (and living beings) and to ecological conditions through the medium of (highly variable) cultural forms. So far we have considered the importance of including some of the social and ecological embeddedness of the individual as necessary to well-being in the conception of the person as moral agent (or patient). This is not to argue that one and only one set of such relations of embeddedness is necessary for any given individual. Rather, the claim is that embeddedness within some combination of such relations and conditions which is sufficient to secure the bodily health requirements of the individual is necessary for any individual.

Identity and Environment: A Sense of Place

So far as the argument has yet reached, social and ecological embeddedness figure as necessary conditions for individual well-being, though any one of an indefinitely large range of modes of such embeddedness may do: there is a contingent relation between the well-being of the individual and her or his embeddedness in any particular set of eco-social relations. But the case for culture as a uniquely human mode of relationship to environmental conditions of life carries with it a much stronger claim: that our interaction with and symbolic investment in stably identifiable and re-identifiable elements and configurations in our external environment are essential to the formation and maintenance of a stable personal identity. It is a commonplace of post-Hegelian philosophy that personal identity is acquired in the course of and only in the context of the mutual recognitions afforded by the inter-subjective encounters of social life. The argument here extends this claim to include the necessarily asymmetrical recognitions of non-human living and non-living beings which form the physical context and media of both individual and social activity. My sense of self is rooted not only in my regular monitorings of my face-to-face encounters with significant other persons, but also in my monitorings of my bodily trajectory, and my emotional, aesthetic and practical encounters with and responses to the non-human items in my experiential universe. The cultural forms, and especially the linguistic forms which enable, constrain and relate both these encounters and responses, and the range of self-reflective monitorings of them are, of course, indispensable mediations. There is no 'direct' or 'immediate' encounter that can, so to speak, by-pass the forms made possible by the cultural embedding of the experiencing subject.

If all of this is right, then it tends to show that personal identity is itself indissolubly bound up with both a particular, concrete configuration of environmental circumstances and the availability of symbolic means for making sense of, practically negotiating and reflecting critically upon those circumstances and the individual's relation to them. This is one (I would argue, persuasive) way of making intelligible the disorientation and loss of identity so characteristic of indigenous peoples in the face of ecological destruction and consequent cultural dislocation. But the implications may go much wider: the conservative critique of modernity, drawing upon powerful images of traditional communities bound by organic ties to one another and to land and locality; the classical sociological ambiguity expressed in the contrasts between *Gemeinschaft* and *Gesellschaft*, traditional and rational action, and in the pervasive themes of estrangement and anomie; and successive waves of romantic and mystical revaluation of nature – all of these may be more than passing, localized cultural expressions. Cultural expressions they certainly are, but their popular diffusion, affective power and mobilizing force may be explicable in terms of the psychological stresses imposed by identity-threatening physical dislocations and the ecological transformations imposed by new economic forms, demographic patterns and forms of political rule. Marx, for example, in the 1844 *Manuscripts* assigns causal primacy to estrangement from nature as the source of private property and the other consequential dimensions of estrangement. Significantly, too, in Marx, Durkheim and other theorists of industrial modernization, dislocation comes to be associated with a crisis of self-identity: estrangement from the world is also a form of self-estrangement – the anomic individual is also one who is threatened with loss of identity to the point of suicide.[12]

Related psychological mechanisms may also be at work in many local environmental campaigns: to save a local wood, flower-meadow or bog from building development or road construction. Again, as suggested by the term 'NIMBY' (Not In My Back Yard) such campaigns are amenable to sociological analysis in terms of constellations of specific social and economic interests, professional skills, access to planning bodies and available systems of symbolic meaning, but their capacity to mobilize sentiments, strike affective roots in local populations and motivate action has a psychological dimension which also requires explanation. Landscape features, woodland paths, established patterns of urban settlement, even factories, pits and slag heaps constitute the texture of the lived biographies of those who pass their lives among them. They carry reminders of past moments of pleasure or fear, come to represent whole ways of living, working and enjoying to communities of people. They are, in short, significant among the means by which we come to understand who and what we are. A threat to them can be felt as a threat to our own continuous and stable sense of identity.

Such environmental campaigns, if this line of analysis is broadly right, are not only peculiarly powerful in the psychological mechanisms they bring into play, but (despite the often dismissive response to them on the part of the left) are also very difficult to reduce to the conception of individual interest presupposed in the liberal-individualist moral discourse. This is for two reasons. First, the fight to preserve a feature of one's environment from destruction is not (or not solely) a form of instrumental action, in which some external object is protected because it is contributory to one's interests (the value of one's property, the quality of the view from the back window, or whatever), but rather, because it is included in one's sense of self and so is inseparable from one's personal well-being. This line of argument extends an already well-established critique of self-interest theories of motivation and moral perspectives which argues a fusion of interests between persons united by social bonds of many kinds. In the version I am proposing, non-human and non-living beings and features of the environment can be sufficiently biographically and symbolically invested for individuals to feel their loss as a threat to selfhood. If this argument can be sustained, then it gives a new and richer sense and content to the idea of environmental rights, as grounded in the human requirement for a physically situated sense of self.

Second, this line of argument presents difficulties for the liberal-individualist view in that the mode of entry of environmental features into the sense of self is, as we have seen, indispensably culturally mediated. The physical feature is significant and valued in virtue of patterns of meaning and cultural values which individuals are able to deploy and apply only in virtue of their social belonging. The integrity of local cultures and communities is therefore indissolubly bound up with the identification of individuals with their environments. Valued features are thus collective goods not just in that their enjoyment is shared by many individuals, but also in that the very capacity to value them and identify with them is enabled by communally sustained cultural forms.

So, where does this extended discussion of the part played by the non-human environment in human well-being take us? Human/animal continuity points to embodiment and habitat as features of moral relevance. Basic interests in bodily development, sustenance, health and reproduction, and in the ecological conditions of these, can be recognized as shared features of human and animal life. Many species of animal are also like humans in that they engage in need-meeting activity upon their environments in socially co-operative ways. Habitats are for them, as for us, not simply sources of means of bodily sustenance, but also conditions and contexts for the living of a social life characteristic of the species. But the pervasiveness and centrality of cultural forms of mediation of social activity in the human case is distinctive, and has, as we have seen, morally significant consequences. However, the open-ended variability and diversity which cultural learning, transmission and invention bequeath to human/environment interrelations in no sense undermine the case for recognizing a category of 'environmental rights': though no single set of jointly sufficient environmental conditions for human well-being can be identified as uniquely necessary, all humans do require some such set for their well-being.

But this pervasive cultural mediation of human social activity has two further consequences which tell against the liberal paradigm of the individual person. The first is that culture not only enables a limitless (but still bounded) range of possible social practices in relation to the material environment, but it also imposes upon humans a dependance upon culturally sustained normative regulation as a condition of their meeting even their most basic organic needs. Cultural belonging, and the preservation of the integrity of cultural forms is, then, a necessary condition of individual human well-being. To the extent that cultural forms themselves require a range of non-human, environmental features and relations to be routinely available as objects, conditions and media of co-ordinated human activity, then we can infer that individual human well-being is further dependent upon the availability of those ecological conditions.

The second consideration is that the individual's sense of personal identity as the continuing author of her or his autonomous activity is inseparable from her or his sense of self as physically embodied and located in a spatially extended and temporally persistent environment, whose features and relationships are made sense of and valued in terms provided by the symbolic forms available in the local culture. This, I submit, is not susceptible to analysis in terms of some set of external, instrumental conditions of identity and its preservation, but is constitutive of it. This is to imply, among other things, that a threat to the culture, including the non-human living beings, physical objects and relations which are symbolically and practically incorporated within it (but not, of course, without residue), will be, and will be experienced as, a threat to the personal integrity of the individuals who live the life rendered possible by that particular eco-socio-technological form. So we can go beyond the claim that any adequate concept of the basic interests of individuals must include reference to their requirements as social beings (and as such requiring a range of possibilities for social communication and participation) and as living organisms (and so as bearers of organic needs and vulnerabilities as well as habitat-requirements). Human individuals (at least) have basic interests in virtue of their embeddedness in socio-cultural and ecological webs of interdependence, and in virtue of their embodiment. These interests are marginalized to the point of exclusion in the main streams of liberal-individualist moral and political thought.

But the argument above takes us a critical step beyond this re-constitution of the notion of individual basic interests, to a recognition of environmental and socio-cultural relations as in part constitutive of the self. We cannot wholly conceptualize what a person is in abstraction from their social belonging and spatio-temporal location and physical setting. This puts very tight constraints on the construction of the concept of 'basic interests'. These features of the physical and social world which enter into and constitute our sense of self are not dispensable features which we may or may not choose to value or assign significance to. They are features which are basic in the sense that only in virtue of their presence can we hold on to a sense of ourselves as choosers, valuers and assigners of significance at all.

Of course, it is important not to draw these constraints too tightly. I am not claiming either that personal identity is wholly constituted in and through socio-cultural and physical relations and symbolic investments, or that individual well-being is generally favoured by ecological conservation and cultural conservatism. In its social-relational aspect this is, indeed, the direction taken by one of the leading philosophers of the so-called 'new' right, Roger Scruton.[13] There are two primary reasons why the arguments above do not lead in this direction. The first is that to speak of individuals having requirements or interests as social beings and as embodied, living beings is not to credit all existing socio-cultural and economic forms as unproblematically or sustainably meeting those requirements. To the extent that they do not, and, indeed, to the extent that they by their fundamental dynamic systematically destroy them, as in the case of industrial capitalism, a moral case can be offered for the injunction to change those forms.

But the identity-constituting dimension of social relations and spatial locations is not so readily dealt with. In some contexts it does, indeed, form a deep psychological source of resistance to proposals for radical change. In other contexts, disaffection from existing social and economic forms is itself rooted in the obstacles they place in the way of the formation of stable and satisfactory forms of identity: the humiliations and exclusions suffered by ethnic, religious or sexual minorities in oppressive and intolerant cultures, or the physical displacements and disorientations suffered by indigenous peoples in the face of large-scale 'development' projects. There are numerous currently well-publicized examples which bear this out. The Chipko ('tree-hugging') movement in the Himalayas from Kashmir to Annachal Pradesh is simultaneously a struggle to preserve the forests, and a way of life dependent upon them, from commercial logging and a struggle by women for more power in their local communities.[14] The Penan people of Sarawak have also waged an effective struggle by building defensive blockades against the vehicles of loggers who are destroying local rain-forests at a rate which would lead, at the present rate, to virtually complete exhaustion of the forests by the turn of the present century.[15] Still more well-known are the struggles of indigenous peoples in the Amazonian region of South America against logging, ranching and hydro-electric schemes.[16] Especially in the latter case, indigenous peoples have developed unprecedented forms of political co-ordination and shown great skill in attracting favourable global media publicity. The extent to which prevailing social and environmental relations and practices both sustain and undermine personal identities is an important, but insufficiently recognized condition for the success of such popular mobilizations.

A second reason why these arguments about identity do not take us in a (conservative) universally 'preservative' direction is that personal identity is only partially and provisionally constituted by its socio-cultural and physical setting. We are able to carry with us, in the form of symbolic capacities and representations, the identity-sustaining features of our social-relational and physically located past into new social and physical environments. This is an ability we have. It is a remarkable one, a testimony to our life-long capacity for cultural learning and adaptation. However, to note it as an 'ability' is not to concede that its achievement is a matter of routine, or that it is an ability which can be exercised independently of conditions or without limit of scope. Moving home is, for example, rightly recognized as a major life-trauma (next only to bereavement or major illness). The person who has moved home is still (just about) recognizable as 'the same person', but the reordering of the personality which is required is often considerable. If a physical move coincides with the requirement to adapt to a new social and cultural setting, then the demands on identity will be still more powerful. Similar considerations apply to those who live through rapid environmental and socio-cultural transformations within a locality, and sometimes demands are made which exceed the adaptive powers of the personality itself: a 'crisis of identity' ensues.

These commonplaces of our experience are marshalled here as a reminder that though we may, for some intellectual purposes, think of individuals 'in abstraction' from their 'embeddedness', and though we must, for some political purposes, acknowledge that the best interests of individuals are often served by the transformation of social and ecological relations, the 'concrete' individual is always partly formed by the social and ecological relations of the past, features which persist even under new relations.

Back to the Human/Animal Opposition?

Now, it may be asked, if these arguments about the distinctively culturally mediated and identity-constitutive features of the human relation to their environmental conditions of life do, indeed, persuade us of the case for a category of 'environmental rights', have we not, in the process, rejected that very premiss from which we began? Have I not, in making significant concessions to my imagined 'humanist' opponent of human/animal continuism, succeeded in restoring human/animal dualism? If my argument tends to show the pertinence of a category of environmental rights for humans, perhaps it does so at the expense of such considerations with respect to non-human animals?

It was never my purpose to deny difference, indeed, morally very significant difference, between humans and other animal species. The thesis of human/animal continuism does not require this. On the contrary, it suggests a comparative elaboration of both similarities and differences between species. The value of the comparison with non-human animals was to bring into sharp focus those requirements which humans and many non-humans share as 'living natural beings': their embodiment brings with it requirements to meet organic needs by way of interaction with an environment capable of sustaining them, and a vulnerability to a range of potential harms which we have yet to consider. Many animals are also like humans in that their need-meeting activities are socially ordered and in that the living of a characteristic social life is also in itself a component as well as a condition of well-being. But where humans appear to be distinctive, as we have seen, is in the culturally mediated character of their social life and need-meeting interaction with their environments. This has important consequences for any view of rights as grounded in basic interests, or needs. A class of 'identity needs' is to be understood as inseparable from sustained relations between persons and significant features of their social and spatial setting.

All species have environmental needs, or 'habitat requirements', and this includes humans, too. However, depending on the characteristic mode(s) of life of the species concerned, our conception of what such needs amount to has to be differentiated. In the human case, what is required is an acknowledgement of the interweaving of ecological and socio-cultural relations both as necessary conditions for well-being and as 'moments', or components, in the constitution of identity, where identity is itself central to well-being. There are, in this, echoes of numerous earlier writers. This comes close to the notion, advanced by Marx in the early *Manuscripts*, that the properly human relation to nature is one which reunites, or synthesizes, the organic need-meeting with the aesthetic and the spiritual. The notion of distinctively human 'identity needs' is also present in much individual psychology, most famously in the work of A.H. Maslow.[17]

The 'distinctively human' character of this class of needs does not, to my mind, tell against the naturalism of the approach I have adopted here. On the contrary, it demonstrates that such an approach can both acknowledge and illuminate human specificity. Identity needs of the sort I have suggested can be understood as emergent features of a specifically human mode of satisfying a broad set of requirements which are shared with many non-human species. However, the distinctively human character of identity needs is not self-evident. Many mammalian species, and perhaps birds, display a social and psychological complexity in their interaction with their environments which suggests that to them, as well, habitats are more than simply 'life-support systems'. The young of many species devote much of their lives to 'play', in which there is no direct connection between activity and the meeting of any organic need; some animals, especially primates, display responses to unfamiliar objects that are hard to describe in terms other than curiosity, and so on. Somewhat more challenging for anyone who would deny such interpretations are the very marked pathological symptoms which animals display when they are kept in forms of confinement which meet their organic requirements but obstruct fulfilment of psychological needs.

Rights and Responsibilities: Human and Animal

So far I have deliberately deferred discussion of the allocation of responsibility for the meeting of morally valid claims of individuals. Now it is time to address this matter directly. On the rights view adopted by Regan, a right only exists where some individual can be assigned moral responsibility for meeting the morally valid claim of the putative right-holder. In the case of putative animal rights, the 'responsible individuals' are those (human) moral agents with whom the animal interacts. On the 'thin', negative conceptualization of rights used by Regan this is, indeed, relatively unproblematic. The bearers of responsibilities to animals are enjoined to treat them with respect, to refrain from harming them, and so on. Generally, these are responsibilities which are met by refraining from action, rather than moral requirements to act, although Regan does think that recognizing an animal's rights entails being prepared to intervene on its behalf if its rights are being abused by some other moral agent. It is, I think, fair to say that the general tendency of the animal rights approach – and certainly Regan's version of it – is to advocate a practical dissociation between humans and animals. Each of the animal-incorporating human social practices which I've discussed involves some human intervention in lives of animals, some restriction, however benevolently intended, upon their preference autonomy. This tendency in the approach has been noted by others. Keith Tester, for example, uses it to suggest that animal rights can be interpreted anthropologically as a contemporary 'taboo' on relations with animals.[18]

We have already seen that this conception of rights and responsibilities comes up against serious difficulties once we explore the implications of the social and ecological embeddedness of individuals as bearers of putative rights: the conditions of acquisition and exercise of the abilities protected as 'rights' cannot, in general, be taken as unproblematically given, but themselves require action to ensure their sustained provision. Substantive rights are claims which entail responsibilities of a positive kind: to provide enabling resources, or to directly meet need. Regan does not address the issues which arise at this point, partly because this negative view of rights abstracts from social-relational conditions of well-being for animals, and partly (but relatedly) because he considers only what he calls 'basic' as distinct from 'acquired' rights and responsibilities.

Several of the arguments I have deployed so far tend to suggest that if non-human animals can be said to have rights, or to be objects of direct responsibilities on the part of humans at all, then this is frequently because of the social relations in which they stand to humans. Stock-animals which have been rendered dependent upon humans by a long historical process of selective breeding, enclosure and eco-regulation, for example, cannot be well served by being 'liberated' into the wild. The same is true of many pet animals, such as dogs and cats whose evolutionary history has been bound up with human habitations. But if humans do, so to speak, 'inherit' responsibilities of a positive kind to animals humanly rendered dependent, then it is not easy to see how such acquired responsibilities should be allocated or shared. In many cases the institution of private property in practice does the allocation. We hold pet-owners responsible for meeting the needs of their pets, and for ensuring that they do not harm humans or other owned animals.

A fully consistent rights view would have to reject the institution of private property in non-human subjects-of-a-life, however, and so would not accept the legitimacy of this solution. Moreover, as we have seen, contemporary societies increasingly institutionalize animal-incorporating social practices (such as animal husbandry) in ways which obstruct any simple allocation of causal powers, and so of moral responsibilities, to specific human agents.

The options before us in the face of considerations like these are either to admit that there simply are insufficient grounds for conceptualizing human responsibilities to animals as anything more than restraints (*de facto*, Regan's position) or to find some other way of morally justifying an allocation of responsibilities among or to the community of human moral agents. The obvious parallel here would be with the twentieth-century radicalization of the human rights discourse through which collective responsibility for the welfare of dependent or disadvantaged humans is accepted by national or (by delegation) local state authority. This shift, as we have seen, has been characterized as an extension of citizenship rights beyond the legal and political spheres to the social and economic. Such regulation of social treatment of animals as has been achieved is, indeed, based on this model, state agencies bearing a responsibility on behalf of the community to enforce legislation (often with the aid of voluntary associations of various kinds).

I have already made remarks of a broadly sociological kind about the limits to the practical efficacy of such an apparatus under prevailing inequalities of socio-economic and political power, but these comments are of a strictly contingent kind: they do not detract from the moral case that might be made in favour of the introduction of some institutionalization of 'pooled' or collective responsibility for animal welfare. My interest here, however, is not in the questions either of practical efficacy or of the moral case for collective responsibility, but rather of how to conceptualize the moral status of those to whom such responsibilities are held. Are their claims properly regarded as rights, and, if so, as citizenship rights?

These, of course, are difficult questions in the philosophy of welfare, and I do not wish to be side-tracked too far in that direction.[19] Among the strongest arguments for conceptualizing human welfare-claimants as bearers of rights are, first, that the claimant is involved in no sacrifice in dignity or self-respect and, second, that claims can be readily universalized, so avoiding stigmatization and the intrusions of means-testing. Neither of these considerations applies to non-human animals. Partly this is because these are harms to the well-being of humans which are associated with their conception of self in relation to a culturally established status-order, with its associated moral valuation. Though non-human animals do, I have argued, participate in human social practices, they do not figure in their own right in status-orders (though, of course, they may confer status on the humans with whom they are associated). Further, these considerations do not apply to animals since, though they may be objects of welfare responsibilities on the part of human moral agents or their institutional representatives, they never make claims on their own behalf.

But there is a more philosophically interesting consideration here. It arises when we consider the implications of thinking of welfare rights as citizenship rights, and it takes us back to Marx's denunciation of the bourgeois discourse of rights for its separation of the rights of 'man' from those of citizen. There are, I think, two persuasive arguments in favour of regarding welfare rights as rights of citizenship. The first is that doing so symbolically asserts a communal responsibility for the well-being of individuals as a consequence of social belonging. It is probably this symbolic aspect of welfare as a citizenship right which accounts, more than any materially redistributive effect, for the massive power for social integration possessed by modern welfare states. The second argument in favour of thinking of welfare rights as rights of citizenship is that only if welfare requirements are met are individuals capable of full social participation. In other words, linking welfare with citizenship serves to emphasize that those rights most commonly associated with a narrower political view of citizenship – the rights of freedom of information, of thought, expression and association, and the franchise – can only be fully enjoyed by individuals whose needs for education, food, shelter, leisure, personal autonomy and so on have been met.

In a limited but still significant way, these extensions of the concept of citizenship begin to answer Marx's critique of early modern 'bourgeois' rights. They begin to overcome the segregation of the rights (and needs) of 'man', as a 'natural' being, and those of the citizen. But they do so without the extension of political citizenship to other areas of social life which Marx envisaged. Massive concentrations of social, economic and political power continue to decisively affect the conditions of life and death of millions of 'citizens' who have no individual or collective rights to participate in their direction.

From the standpoint adopted by the early Marx the achievements of welfare-state liberal capitalism are a partial answer to the critique of bourgeois rights but still fall far short of full, all-round human emancipation. There are, of course, what I have called 'epistemic conservative' arguments[20] which tend to show that the form of popular-democratic communal direction of social and economic life which Marx envisaged is unachievable at the level of the scale, technical sophistication and complexity now reached in contemporary society. I remain unconvinced by these arguments, but this is not the place to engage with them. For my purposes here, Marx's moral thesis is worthy of endorsement, as a kind of regulative ideal. The idea of popular-democratic control retains its value as a social norm, an alternative vision to both welfare-state capitalism and state-bureaucratic socialism.

However, to travel this far with Marx is not necessarily to endorse the whole of his critique of the divorce of 'man' and citizen, or of the separation of the private from the public sphere. Again, the human/animal comparison is a useful starting point for our investigations. Just as the main arguments for conceptualizing the objects of welfare responsibilities as right-holders apply to humans but not to non-human animals, similarly the case for welfare rights as citizenship rights can make no sense if applied to non-human animals. *Animal Farm* notwithstanding, animals cannot be citizens. This is not, of course, to say that communities of human moral agents do not have moral responsibilities for the welfare of non-human animals. Indeed, a good deal of the above argumentation seems to me to go a long way towards showing that they do. The point, rather, is to suggest that where non-human animals are the objects of the welfare responsibilities of others, there are no correlative citizenship rights. Where human communities are responsible for the welfare of non-human animals it is not because those animals are entitled to care as citizens, but because they are needy beings whose ability to meet their own needs autonomously has been undermined by past actions of human agents (individually or collectively).

This line of argument, if it can be made to work, shows promise of yielding two morally and politically significant outcomes. The first of these is that the case for communal welfare responsibilities towards non-human animals can be developed into a non-citizenship case for human welfare rights. This case is a broadly socio-ecological one. To the extent that individual humans come to rely upon state benefits in welfare states, they do so in the main because of the effects of prevailing socio-economic relations and their dynamic. Modern capitalism is premissed on a long-run socially conflictual historical process through which populations of humans are systematically excluded from access to means of independently meeting their needs. The enclosure of common land and abolition of rights of common; the subsequent class monopolization of sources of raw materials, manufacturing plant and technically advanced means of production; and the state centralization of legitimate violence were the key conquests in this process. The larger part of the population was coerced into wage-labour, and so into economic dependency, and into meeting subsistence needs by exchange on the market rather than through independent individual or co-operative activity. This historical process whereby a new socio-economic form emerged and was consolidated, producing as it did so a dependent and subordinate human population, was intertwined with the formation of a subordinate and dependent population of non-human animals. On this perspective, the state responsibility for the welfare of socially and economically dependent humans can be seen as a partial compensation for, and implicit acknowledgement, of the moral implications of that dependence as the outcome of a coercive historical process in which the capitalist state was itself a significant actor.

The second significant outcome of the 'non-citizenship' case for communal welfare responsibilities towards non-human animals is more directly aimed at Marx's rejection of the dualism of man and citizen. The point is this: if there is a case for communal responsibility for the welfare of animals, even in the absence of a strong case for attributing welfare rights, and in the absence even of any sense that could be made of their having citizenship rights, then clearly what those responsibilities enable or provide is something to be valued on its own terms. It is true that, in the human case, food, shelter, leisure, free association, thought and expression, and so on are necessary conditions for the exercise of citizenship rights (in the narrow sense of political rights). It is also the case that to make explicit this connection is, and remains, an important argument for welfare rights. However, in the case of non-human animals, it is also clear that meeting this range – or some comparable range, depending on the species – of requirements is constitutive of well-being in itself, without the further link with citizenship. The principle of human/animal continuity suggests that if this is so with non-human animals we should also consider whether, and what extent, it is true for humans.

As we have seen, the early Marx tended to equate the private sphere with the domain of 'natural' man, and to see its protection as an intellectual denial of, and ideological obstacle, to the full flowering of human social being. He part-acknowledged, but also scorned, the puny, retrogressive and limited character of the rights of 'natural man'. I shall return in my final chapter to this question of the extent to which a notion of human emancipation such as Marx advocated can dispense with the needs and pleasures of the private sphere. But, to anticipate a little, Marx himself speaks of the future society as one in which the free development of all is a condition of the free development of each. It is difficult to understand what this free development of each might mean if it does not include, albeit in a form and with a universality not so far encountered, such general human enjoyments as eating and drinking, thinking, exploring, discovering, arguing, conversing and indulging in one another's company. There is no doubt in my mind that Marx intended it to include these activities. Why, therefore, should we not regard these activities as valuable in themselves, and worthy of protection wherever they can be enjoyed in the interstices of our still-bourgeois civilization? Perhaps, indeed, we should doubly value them as prefigurations of what life might be like in some future emancipated condition? To put my point somewhat more crudely: Marx's contempt for the 'rights of man' derives from an over-socialized and over-politicized view of human nature, one which conflicts with the naturalistic tenor of much of the rest of his thought, and which I have tried to elaborate in this text.

But there is another point. Short of the full human emancipation which Marx foresaw, we remain in the grip of powerful and uncontrolled social, economic and political forces which Marx took the lead in critically exploring. Even if Marx were right to say that protection of bodily integrity, freedom from arbitrary arrest, freedom of religious worship and so on are only required because we live in such a society, the fact remains that we do, indeed, still live in such a society. As living natural beings we share the neediness and vulnerability of other animal species, with respect both to the forces of external nature and to those of human social domination: pending our full emancipation, we should value and seek to extend whatever protections we can find.

7

The Limits of Liberal Rights II: Sources of Harm and Limits of Emancipation

Animal Harm and the Individualist Paradigm

The early modern discourse of rights affected to protect certain basic interests of individuals against possible incursions from two sources: other individuals and the public power. Typically, the latter is also conceptualized as an individual person, or a close analogue to one, capable of intentional actions, moral deliberation and responsibility. In chapter 4 I reviewed some well-established criticisms of this individualist view of the harms to which individuals are liable – there are at least three major sources of harm to their 'basic' interests which are irreducible to the intentional acts of other individuals or public authorities. These are: large institutions with a complex division of labour and a highly attenuated relationship between individual agency and institutional action; the location of individuals within wider social structures and practices whose effects upon them are unintended and often unforeseen by anyone; and, finally, so-called 'natural disasters'. The tendency of the liberal-individualist tradition to conceptualize matters of moral right and responsibility in terms of intended transactions between individuals has the effect of marginalizing or even fully excluding from moral discourse the implications of such sources of harm to individuals. To the extent that differences between individuals which might have an important bearing on their opportunities for full enjoyment of life – congenital differences in physical ability, health, intelligence, and so on – can be treated as beyond human control, as matters of 'luck' or 'chance', they cannot reasonably be regarded as injustices, or as matters of right or abuse of right.

But, as we have seen, a great range of sources of harm or benefit falls between these two conceptual poles: intentional action of other individuals, at one extreme, and 'pure' happenstance, at the other. Indeed, a good case could be made that no harm or benefit to which a human individual is subject can be a matter of pure happenstance – congenital differences of intelligence and physical ability, for example, there may well be, but how these impact on the opportunity of individuals for a full enjoyment of life will depend on the kind of society they enter, and where they are positioned within it. So soon as this is admitted, then the pertinence of the moral discourse of rights and justice must also be admitted.

This way of thinking is not, of course, uncontroversial. A good deal of political argument turns upon the question of to what extent and in what respects commonly acknowledged sources of human suffering and deprivation are alterable by individual or collective action. For Malthus, at least in the first version of his argument on population, the unavoidability of poverty followed directly from a natural fact of human biology and ecology: our tendency to reproduce at rates which outstrip our capacity to increase the supply of means of subsistence. No tinkering with social and economic institutions could offset this consequence, no matter how much we might regret it. In similar vein our contemporary neo-liberal advocates of the 'free market' view the market as a quasi-natural causal order whose outcomes admittedly differentially affect the life chances of individuals but in ways which, as unintended and unavoidable consequences, do not come up for moral appraisal as 'just' or 'unjust'. To say 'you can't buck the market' is to say that markets bring us up against material facts of life which no amount of social engineering can evade. These arguments cannot be straightforwardly rebutted *a priori*, but in each case turn on substantive social scientific claims. I'll begin to address some of these questions in the last part of this chapter when I come to consider the plausibility of a notion of emancipation as transcendence of the very conditions of the discourse of rights. For now, however, my main concern is to show that some such representation of social institutions, social practices, and forms of society/nature interaction as unalterable quasi-natural orders is necessary if the liberal-individualist view of rights is to be sustained. Once one acknowledges sources of basic harms to individuals which are irreducible to individual intentional agency, yet which are alterable and even removable by institutional reorganization, then the sphere within which talk of rights and justice is appropriate is immensely widened.

But how does all of this affect the case for animal rights? The concept of rights which Regan takes from Feinberg [1] is firmly within the individualist tradition, as we have seen. Individuals who have moral dealings with animals are required to treat them with respect, to refrain from harming them and to come to their aid when they are harmed by others. But what if the harms that befall animals are not directly assignable to the intentional acts of individual moral agents? There are, I think, some illuminating parallels with such sources of harm to human individuals. Here, again, a case can be made for recognizing some sources of harm as outside the competence of moral agents, individually or collectively, and therefore as beyond the reach of moral deliberation and action. The relation between predator and prey among wild animals would be a case in point: would the rights perspective enjoin (human) moral agents to intervene on behalf of the zebra about to be eaten by a lion? Notwithstanding widespread cheap jibes against animal liberationists, the answer is clearly, no. The source of harm to the zebra is no action of a moral agent, and the zebra has no morally valid claim to respectful treatment from the lion.

The problem for the rights perspective is not that it purports to offer protection too widely, but, rather, that it is too restrictive in the purchase it gives to moral concern. I have already considered at some length the different forms of institutionalization of animal husbandry practices – ranging from traditional pastoralism to late-capitalist 'factory' farming. The latter are forms of institutionalization which indisputably inflict systematic harms upon animals confined within them, yet which do so in ways which cannot in any direct way be assigned to individual human agency: if such animals are to be viewed as having rights, in Regan's sense, then to whom do we assign the moral responsibility to respect them? No-one involved in the process is cruel to the animals: indeed given the operation of the practice as a whole, each individual participant can reasonably claim to be contributing to the welfare of the animals – the supplier of nutrients, the electrician, the veterinarian, and so on can all act with a good conscience about their individual contribution so long as the ethical legitimacy of the practice as a whole is not called into question. We have already seen that the rights view is likely to be limited in its practical efficacy in relation to a range of treatments of animals which is widely acknowledged to be morally unacceptable. It is now, I hope, clearer that this is not merely a contingent matter, but flows from limitations in the very concept of rights employed by Regan. The individualism of this concept's view of the sources of harm to which individuals are liable tends to exclude from moral consideration effects of alterable institutional practices which cause massive harm to humans and animals alike.

We may also find some analogue to the other two categories of sources of harm to which human individuals are liable: the unintended effects of location in social structures or practices, and the consequences of 'natural disasters'. In 'factory' farming we have an instance of an established social practice which involves systematic harms of basic kinds to (non-human) animals. While these harms are not direct consequences of the intentionality of any assignable human individual, their relation to human intentionality is not merely coincidental. The overall purpose, or point of the practice – economically efficient, profitable production of meat – has among the acknowledged conditions of its achievement the treatment of animals in ways which many find morally offensive. But other human social practices affect non-human animals in ways which are unacknowledged, and frequently unintended and unforeseen: these 'affectings' may be adverse or, sometimes, beneficial.

As we have already noted, one peculiarity of human ecology is our propensity, far greater than that of any other species, to alter our environments in ways which enhance their 'carrying capacity' for populations of our species: agricultural innovation is the paradigm of this. Human eco-regulatory practices tend to simplify biotopes in favour of useful crops or stock animals. Species which could otherwise sustain populations in areas subject to human pastoralism, forestry, agriculture, and so on are therefore excluded by these human activities. Sometimes, as in the case of agricultural 'pests', destruction of these populations is intentional, and included within the meaning of eco-regulation. In other cases it is an unintended, unacknowledged and even unwanted consequence of eco-regulation. When, for example, hedgerows are rooted out in pursuit of a more efficient use of land and agricultural machinery, important habitats for plant species, and small mammals, nesting sites for birds, and so on are also destroyed. This is not part of the purpose or point of intensive agriculture, but an often unwanted causal consequence of it. The situation is closely analogous to the category of unintended harms to humans which includes health hazards associated with certain occupations, with unemployment or with poverty.

Finally, there are more diffuse ecological consequences of human industrial processes and patterns of consumption which also indirectly affect the fate of non-human populations by way of habitat degradation. The case of acid-rain is well documented in its effects on forest eco-systems, but similar arguments could be developed in relation to likely long-term effects on non-human animal populations of ozone depletion, global warming, various kinds of waste disposal, and so on. There are analogies between these examples of unintended but socially produced harms to animal populations and the effects of many so-called 'natural' disasters on human populations. As I argued above (chapter 3, pp. 67–8) the reach of human ecological effects is now global, a fact which calls into question the very concept of 'wild' animal populations.

Many of the habitat changes which affect these non-human animal populations are more or less mediated consequences of human social practices of interaction with nature. If we accept the arguments of Regan and others that non-human animals are proper direct objects of moral concern, then it is difficult to see why the harms caused to non-human animals by the unintended consequences of our social practices should not figure as *prima facie* reasons for altering them. Rachel Carson's title *Silent Spring* (Harmondsworth 1965) evokes the cost to human sensibilities of the destructiveness of modern intensive agriculture, while Regan's argument for 'direct duties' to non-human animals enjoins moral concern on behalf of the animals themselves. Here, again, however, the conceptual limitations of the liberal-individualist concept of rights which Regan employs obstruct the realization of his own moral project. The harms caused to non-human animals (and plants) by the unintended effects on their conditions of life of specific modes of human social and economic organization and practice cannot be assimilated to the required model of individual persons failing to treat the non-human animals with which they interact with due respect. Where that model is appropriate, I have conceded, the liberal-individualist view of rights may have much to offer. The point, however, is that for large classes of case where avoidable harms are done to great masses of our fellow humans and animals the model is inappropriate, and the vocabulary of rights as Regan deploys it fails to gain purchase.

Beyond Rights and Justice?

It is now time to return to the questions posed in the concluding part of chapter 4. I have tried to deploy a combination of socio-economic and conceptual arguments against liberal-individualist conceptions of rights, as they apply both to humans and to non-human animals. But the dialogue so far has also yielded some powerful considerations which tell against any hasty dismissal of the concept of rights as such. We have, for example, noted that where non-human animals are dependent on humans for their well-being, the epistemic limits on cross-species intersubjectivity constitute an untranscendable source of likely harm even where human intentions are benevolent.

I have argued that liberal-individualist views of rights offer protections to both humans and non-human animals which they cannot in fact deliver under prevailing conditions of highly concentrated property in productive resources, social and economic inequality, and market-generated relations of mutual antagonism and estrangement. I have also argued that what they promise also presupposes a limited and distorted vision of human well-being and its causal conditions. The links between the liberal-individualist concept of rights and a specific historical form of human civilization are, I think, sufficiently demonstrable for us to endorse the first Marxian claim I distinguished in the last part of chapter 4 (pp. 136, 138): liberal-individualist conceptions of right are necessitated by, and function as, legitimations of liberal-democratic capitalist regimes. An important part of their legitimating function is carried out by their occluding from the moral view sources of harm to individuals which are not reducible to individual human agency or to acts of the public power, and by their conception of individual well-being which abstracts the latter from its social-relational, developmental and ecological components and causal conditions. Comparison between the modes of life of humans and non-human animals with respect to these conditions and components of well-being yielded health and bodily integrity, environmental embeddedness, and cultural identity as central aspects of human or non-human animal (in the case of the first three) well-being which escaped protection in the promise or in the practice (or both) of the liberal-individualist discourse of rights.

But the second and third Marxian claims remain to be addressed. To what extent are the threats to well-being from which the 'bourgeois' discourse of rights hopes to protect the individual specific to bourgeois society? And is a society which eliminates those threats, and so renders superfluous (1) the 'bourgeois' discourse of rights, or (2) any discourse of rights whatsoever, a real historical possibility? Our first question may be addressed at more than one level of particularity. Clearly, the right to freedom from arbitrary arrest is one which is required only in societies with a centralized state form, specialized bodies of men charged with the maintenance of order, and so on. Many specific rights, then, are in an obvious way conceptually tied to a specific range of socio-political forms. But the deeper question, here, which Steven Lukes[2] so effectively exposes, concerns the fundamental presuppositions of social ontology underlying the liberal-individualist view of rights – that humans are vulnerable beings, seeking satisfaction of desires under conditions of relative scarcity, lacking in complete benevolence towards one another, differing in their value-commitments, and lacking complete knowledge of the consequences of their actions for one another.

Now it seems to me that Lukes's discussion is insufficiently sensitive to the difference between a form of social life in which mutual competitiveness and estrangement is institutionally fostered and normatively approved, in which limitless desires are likewise stimulated and approved, and in which the opacity of economic life to its agents is endemic, and, set against this, a possible form of life organized upon the basis of mutual co-operation, voluntary restraint in the face of scarcity, and intelligible connections between the different functions of social, economic and political life. Lukes's argument is not, as I understand it, that a socialist society with broadly these features is impossible, but, rather, that even within such a society there would remain frustrations, sources of conflict and a liability to mutual harms of various kinds. I think Lukes is right about this, but I insist on the moral importance of the differences between these two kinds of possible setting for the living of a human life. Death and bereavement, for example, are sources of suffering as intense as any humans are susceptible to. Moreover, they are insurmountable features of the human predicament, not products of any particular social form. But it is important also to recognize that there is all the difference in the world between a social setting in which the normal expectation is that death occurs in ripe old age and one in which early death in child-bearing, as a result of infectious diseases or the debilitation of poverty, is a widespread experience. Significant, also, are the differences between social settings in which death and bereavement are stigmatized unspeakable private horrors and those in which a vital communal culture offers emotional support and cultural resources for facing inevitable loss.

But, with these important provisos in mind, let us address Lukes's four 'rights-necessitating' features of the human condition, with our special focus on human/animal relations. A helpful way of structuring this discussion is offered by one of Freud's famous statements of the historical pessimist position:

> We are threatened with suffering from three directions: from our own body, which is doomed to decay and dissolution and which cannot even do without pain and anxiety as warning signals; from the external world, which may rage against us with overwhelming and merciless forces of destruction; and finally from our relations with other men. The suffering which comes from this last source is perhaps more painful to us than any other. We tend to regard it as a kind of gratuitous addition, though it cannot be any less fatefully inevitable than the suffering which comes from elsewhere.[3]

Freud's statement will serve us an exemplar of the kind of conservative thought which stands as a major intellectual challenge to radical social thinking which shares Freud's commitment to both epistemological realism and a naturalistic but non-reductionist view of human nature. No 'pre-established harmony' can be supposed to prevail between our conscious desires and purposes, on the one hand, and, on the other, our bodily powers and requirements, the forces of external nature, and the requirements of social life. In the course of the development of his argument Freud adds yet another unavoidable source of suffering – the persistence in the unconscious of unacceptable wishes, of repressed desires whose direct gratification would render social life unsustainable.

From the standpoint of a social theory which envisages the possibility of a transcendence of the requirement for rights and justice, the antagonistic relation between the forces of nature and human purposes must be regarded as similarly transcendable: a reconciliation, or harmonization, of our relation to nature. There are two distinguishable aspects to this harmonization: one, foregrounded by Freud, would require the adoption of technologies and modes of life which protected human populations from the hazards of uncontrollable natural forces – typhoons, volcanoes, storms and floods; the other, a central concern of the Marxian tradition, would require a 'pacification' of the struggle to acquire material means of subsistence, the inauguration of a commonwealth of abundance.

I argued above (chapter 2, p. 31) against the early Marx's vision of a 'humanization' of nature, as only dubiously consistent with a notion of the natural world as a purpose-independent complex of causal orders. Similar considerations tell, I think, against any vision of a human nature in which we are rendered invulnerable to natural hazards of all kinds: the causal powers at work in the natural systems we inhabit far outweigh any foreseeable development of human powers of technical control or regulation. A consequence of the acknowledgement of this would be to focus on adaptive modes of life and technologies: concentrating urban development away from earthquake zones rather than attempting to control earthquakes, to give an obvious example. That adopting and sustaining such forms of adaptation would require forms of effective moral regulation of social activity at least closely analogous to the implementation of rights and justice is, I think, fairly clear.

Ecological Scarcity and the Case for Socialism[4]

The other major aspect of our antagonistic relation to nature is generally addressed under the concept of scarcity. Scarcity is rights-and-justice necessitating in at least two distinguishable ways. First, since scarcity of any desired good implies that not all individuals may use or acquire all that they desire (or need) of it, some principle of distributive justice is required to regulate allocation to diverse needy individuals. Each individual has a right to her or his just allocation. But individuals may not share a consensus about what constitutes a just allocation, and even if such a consensus does exist, there may be differences of view as to whether any actual distribution in fact conforms to it. Moreover, not all individuals may be disposed to accept their allotted share as sufficient, even while they may recognize it to be just – greed, envy and deceit may rival a commitment to justice as sources of individual motivation. Under conditions of scarcity, and independently of the adoption of just norms of distribution of scarce goods, there will be a liability to competitive and potentially conflictual relations between individuals. Such situations, in which individuals are motivated to mutual harm, are paradigmatic loci for the discourse of rights: the erection of 'boundary posts' between the territories of estranged individuals.

The Marxian tradition of socialism has been widely understood (and has widely understood itself) as resting a large part of its case for socialism on the argument that new communal relations of production would unleash forces of production held in check by historically outmoded capitalist relations, so ending for all time the condition of scarcity together with its moral and political consequences. As I shall suggest, I do not think this the only way of reading Marx on this question, but the argument is undoubtedly widely diffused, and deserves serious attention in its own right. Perhaps the most powerful challenge to this argument which has arisen in recent times derives directly from the kind of integration of ecological perspectives into social theory which I have been advocating in this book and elsewhere.

Where thinkers on the left, such as the early Rudolf Bahro,[5] have accepted the notion of global outer limits to growth, scarcity has been directly acknowledged as a trans-historical feature of the human condition. The case for socialism henceforth could not be made to rest upon generalized and potentially limitless advances in material prosperity. Indeed, an interesting inversion takes place, in which the growth-dynamic supposedly inherent to capitalism is now seen as its Achilles' heel, and socialism is advocated on the grounds of its incorporation of the means communally to set limits to and regulate the appropriation of nature. Less, not more, material consumption is a condition of survival itself, and the emancipatory value of socialism will consist in this, together with the opportunities it will afford for forms of conviviality and intrinsic satisfaction denied by the dynamics of competitive accumulation which have prevailed under capitalism.

But, sadly for the simple clarity of this line of thought, the 'limits to growth' thesis upon which it rests is subject to serious objections, both theoretical and empirical.[6] The approach I have advocated here and elsewhere conceptualizes ecological limits as effects of specific structures of articulation between human social practices and their ecological conditions, contexts and media. Limits to growth are inherent in each such socio-economic form, but cannot be specified either as physical limits in abstraction from the socially ordered processes by which they may be reached, or as social limits in abstraction from the biological, physical and chemical systems which constitute them and which they encounter. If this approach is right, then it follows that to envisage socialism as a possibly realizable form of human socio-economic life is to envisage it as likewise affording an open but bounded range of opportunities and constraints for material appropriation of nature. Material scarcities may come to play a quite new part, to impact in quite different patterns and to be experienced in new ways in this new form of civilization, but the condition of scarcity itself will not be transcended. This way of thinking differs in its political-cultural implications from Bahro's. It does not require a cultural revolution of ascetic renunciation of material well-being as a condition of eco-socialist transition, but it shares with Bahro a conviction that scarcity and its moral and political correlates will persist into any realizable socialist future.[7]

How do the conceptual resources of the Marxian and, more generally, socialist tradition square up to this outcome of the argument? There are, I think, three broad possibilities. One is to regard the socialist case against rights (and justice) as decisive and the concept of rights as incompatible with socialism. The consequence of this is that socialist moral thought has to concede its bankruptcy in the face of what a socio-ecological analysis suggests must be a necessary feature of any realizable socialist society. The second possibility is to 'bracket' the conceptual critique of the liberal-individualist discourse of rights, and to represent socialism as a socio-economic (and ecological) order in which the promise of that discourse can at last be fulfilled. The third possibility, the one I shall begin to explore here, is the most challenging one: it is to construct a conception of socialist rights (and justice) which answers to the conceptual critique of the liberal-individualist view, and which also addresses the conditions of life which might be encountered in any realizable socialist society.

So far as distributive justice is concerned (and so far my discussion has centred on material scarcity only), Marx's principle, 'from each according to ability, to each according to needs' might seem to be the obvious starting point. But Lukes has offered a reading of Marx according to which this cannot figure as a legal or moral rule at all. Part of Lukes's reason for thinking this is that Marx does explicitly make socialist abundance, and therefore the absence of conflicting claims, a condition of the emergence of the principle. But, independently of its place in Marx's own argument, can we make sense of 'to each according to need' as a principle of distributive justice where scarcity and competing claims still persist? The most serious argument Lukes offers against this possibility is that 'those abilities and needs would be infinite, that is, unlimitable in advance, and unspecifiable by any rule'.[8] This, in turn, is linked to Marx's apparent objection to all moral rules that they necessarily abstract some specific feature of individuals as morally relevant, thus treating them unequally with respect to all other concrete and specific differences.

The Concept of Need

At least on Lukes's reading, Marx must be answered on two counts if we are to regard his principle as a rule of distributive justice. First, the abstraction through which need is singled out as the morally significant feature of individuals for purposes of just allocation of material goods has to be shown to be itself justifiable. Second, it has to be shown that needs are, indeed, 'limitable in advance', and specifiable by some rule. Of course, to adequately sustain both of these claims would take me well beyond the scope of this book, but a rough-and-ready beginning can be made.

First, the account of need which I offer would be presented in terms of necessary conditions not simply for survival, but for well-being, or flourishing, as a being of a certain kind. For the category of 'living natural beings', including humans, this must include as 'needs' the satisfaction of all those conditions required for the living of the mode of life characteristic of the species. These conditions, taken together, make up what I have sometimes referred to as 'basic interests' of individual animals, whether human or non-human. For Regan and for others in what we may loosely call the rights tradition, to say that individuals have 'inherent value' is to imply that they should not (other things being equal) be harmed with respect to these basic interests, or as I will now call them, needs. Independently of whether we accept Regan's arguments that at least some non-human animals are bearers of inherent value, the force of his anti-utilitarian arguments for recognizing such a concept in the human case seem to me to be very powerful. If, indeed, this case can be made out, then the pertinence of the satisfaction of need as the basic criterion for a principle of justice follows directly.

The second obstacle to the status of 'to each according to need' as a principle of distributive justice is the substantive indefinability of need itself. Marx himself argues that with their first act of production humans transform themselves and so also their needs: need is historically formed and culturally variable. Perhaps any attempt to systematically distinguish 'need' from 'wish' or 'desire' is tendentious. I have already tried to rule out any such conflation of need with desire by defining needs in terms of conditions necessary for well-being: many desires – for example, desires for cigarettes, or other addictive drugs – may be satisfied only at a cost to well-being. Even to deny this is to concede the conceptual distinction.[9]

Since my purpose in this phase of the discussion is to explore some of the implications of an ecological perspective for our view of what a socialist mode of life might be, I'll focus for now on material scarcity, and human needs as they bear principally upon the utilization of raw materials, disposal of waste products and the destruction or modification of ecosystems. The socialist traditions of thought offer us four broad classes of sources of cultural or historical variability of (material) needs. These are, very schematically:

1. Dominance of exploitative/instrumental social relations – where these prevail, desires may be evoked in individuals by those who have an interest in their having those desires (for example, as a condition of selling otherwise unnecessary commodities to them, or binding them to otherwise unsatisfying

work relations). The intensity of such desires, their compulsive power, is the basis for including them as a category of need – their satisfaction is frequently felt to be necessary to the well-being of the individual. Socialist and other critical theorists have attempted to mark a distinction between such artificially/exploitatively evoked desires and genuine human needs by inventing terms such as 'false' or 'compensatory' needs.

2. Forms of socio-economic organization which render the satisfaction of needs which are not peculiar to any specific society conditional upon utilization of goods and resources which would not be required under other social conditions. A fairly obvious example here would be characteristic patterns of geographical separation of places of work, residential estates and shopping facilities which require members of each household to have access to and make intensive use of private means of transport. To live at an acceptable level of general need-satisfaction, possession of one or more private cars is genuinely a necessity to many people given prevailing patterns of geographical segregation of different kinds of activity, and the logistical and other obstacles to adequate public transport provision. In such circumstances, private ownership of, or unrestricted access to the motor car is a need, but not a 'human' need. I use the term 'ancillary need' to cover this sort of case. Other writers make essentially the same point by distinguishing between 'needs' and 'satisfyers'.[10]

3. In some societies, but not all, children, the elderly and the bearers of a whole range of specific patterns of ability and disability may be disqualified from, or simply be unable to participate fully and autonomously in, social life. This category of individuals is variably constituted, depending not only upon local cultural classifications, but also upon the personal-developmental achievements, social and practical skills and so on which are *de facto* required for effective and autonomous participation as 'parent', 'employee', 'citizen' and so on in the society concerned. For these groups of individuals, specific articulations of natural differences and social norms and requirements produce definite forms of dependency – of needs which cannot, under prevailing conditions, be met autonomously, but must either not be met ('survival of the fittest: weakest to the wall'), or be met through the workings of some more-or-less specialized social institution: unpaid 'domestic' labour (usually female) within families, state financed and regulated institutions (welfare sector) or voluntary associations of various kinds ('charities'). I shall speak of these as social dependency needs.

4. The concept of need with its strong connotation of 'necessity' usually implies some notion of the meeting of a minimum standard. Often, in line

with this, 'basic' needs are defined in terms of requirements for physical survival, for life itself, rather than well-being. There are, indeed, strong arguments for such a concept of need, particularly in the context of debates about global social justice in the face of ecological limits. Without wishing to deny the purchase of such notions of basic need, I have chosen to adopt a wider, more inclusive view of need in terms of the requirements for well-being. In part this choice is motivated by a recognition that minimal survival conditions for both humans and animals may be met under oppressive, confining and degrading relations and conditions. With such conditions in mind, it seems to me important to include the notion of a life worth living within the notion of life-sustaining conditions. The opportunity to live the mode of life appropriate to the species is a good first approximation to what this concept amounts to for non-human species, but in the human case clearly needs qualification and supplementation in recognition of the historical and cultural variability of human modes of life. This is where our fourth source of variability of need arises. The historicist enthusiasm of Marx's early manuscript expresses itself thus:

> The abolition of private property is therefore the complete *emancipation* of all human senses and qualities, but it is this emancipation precisely because these senses and attributes have become, subjectively and objectively, *human*. The eye has become a *human* eye, just as its *object* has become a social, *human* object – an object made by man for man. The senses have therefore become directly in their practice, *theoreticians*. They relate themselves to the thing for the sake of the thing, but the thing itself is an *objective human* relation to itself and to man, and vice versa. Need or enjoyment has consequently lost its *egotistical* nature, and nature has lost its mere utility by use becoming human use.[11]

I have already discussed the anthropocentrism of the philosophical position underlying this passage (chapter 2, pp. 31–2). My interest in this context is in its historicism: the view of the historical process as one of cumulative advance in human cognitive and sensory powers, and the associated transformation of need – the emergence of fully human needs, as against the crude, 'animal' needs of earlier phases of history. Detached from its association with a human/animal dichotomy, there is an important element of truth in Marx's argument: there is a normative component in the assessment of need. Acceptable minimum standards of life are subject to historical shifts in line with changing social productive powers and associated normative changes.

How far do these four sources of variability in needs call into question the project of establishing a substantively definable cross-cultural, trans-historical concept of human need? Such a concept of need, it will be remembered, was acknowledged as a condition of the status of 'to each according to need' as a normative principle of socialist justice. It seems that the first three sources of variation can, at least in principle, be dealt with fairly straightforwardly.

In the case of the first, there is no good reason to regard everything which is desired, no matter how intensely it may be desired, as a need at all – whether 'false' or 'compensatory'. *Prima facie*, if consumer demand entails levels of resource use and ecological impact on a global scale (or both) which are neither generalizable nor sustainable then such demands (unlike genuine needs) do not constitute valid moral claims. In the case of the second source of variation in need, a socialist moral framework has available to it two distinct levels of analysis. If, under prevailing socio-economic forms, the meeting of generalizable human needs is possible only on the basis of ancillary material resource use and ecological impact that are either unsustainable or ungeneralizable, then justice may require, not universality of provision on the prevailing social basis (the first level of analysis) but, rather, a transition to modes of social organization that enable generalizable needs to be met in less resource-profligate ways (the second level). The availability of these conceptual moves within a socialist-ecological moral framework is of great importance in offsetting a widespread hostility to green politics as a form of contemporary asceticism, as a 'neo-puritanism'. Both state socialist (where they still exist) and late capitalist forms of socio-economic organization work with massively sub-optimal ratios between, on the one hand, ecological impacts, broadly conceived, and, on the other, the provision of material supports for individual well-being. What I have called 'ancillary needs', along with built-in obsolescence and other socially generated forms of waste, and the second-order ecological costs of environmental protection and repair, resource recycling and so on, are all sources of this disparity between the ecological impact strictly required for the pursuit of any particular human enjoyment and the actual impact of such enjoyments given prevailing forms of social and economic order.

The third source of variation in needs – the various forms of socially and naturally produced human dependency – is likewise susceptible of a two-level analysis. The needs of dependent individuals do produce obligations on the part of moral communities for their needs to be met, *prima facie*, in ways which maximize opportunities for autonomy. But – and this is the second level of analysis – where dependency is itself a consequence of alterable norms or requirements of social life, autonomous need-meeting will generally best be enabled by social reforms which facilitate and enhance social participation on the part of excluded minorities (the 'disabled', elderly and others). Where possible, strategies for eliminating or reducing dependency take precedence over the simple, direct requirement to meet the needs of the dependent. Though the material resource implications of providing these different ways for the universalization within a community of the meeting of need may be widely different across different communities, this does not tell in principle against the possibility of a cross-culturally applicable concept of need.

The fourth source of variability – historically shifting and culturally differentiated normative standards of material well-being – constitutes a more intractable intellectual obstacle to need as a moral basis for a socialist standard of justice. All I have space for here are a few sketchy indicators as to how the problem might be approached. First, in current circumstances of global maldistribution, a concept of basic needs rooted in the bio-medical model of negative health (as absence of disease) would be sufficient to make the case for the justice of massive global redistribution of means of consumption, on the principle 'to each according to need'. Second, even to retain a more inclusive concept of need defined in terms of well-being, as I would prefer to do, does not necessarily concede the 'subjectivity' of all assessments of need, or the essential 'unlimitability' of human need. One consideration is that normative standards do not become established independently of forms of discussion, criticism and self-reflection which are more-or-less available in all human societies. Under contemporary conditions of economic and ecological global interdependency and given current communications technology most 'affluent' populations are aware of the extremes of privation which exist over much of the rest of the globe: excesses of waste, destructiveness and super-abundance can be recognized as injustices in the terms already available within the locally established normative orders of the more materially affluent societies. The key problem here is not the difficulty of making out the moral case, but rather, the political, military and economic obstacles in the way of creating a new and more just world order.

Another consideration derives from the insight that there is no 'straight line' correlation between increasing material abundance and well-being. The point I have in mind here is not that material scarcity may often be offset by greater moral or spiritual well-being, but that organic well-being, bodily health, may be harmed by too much material abundance as much as by too little. For large parts of the populations of the 'over-developed' world, for example, malnutrition does not mean insufficient food (I am not saying that it never means this in these societies) but, often, too much, or too much of certain kinds of food – dietary excess and imbalance. A third consideration is that variation in normative standards surrounding material needs often takes not quantitative but qualitative forms. Communicative, social and aesthetic aspects come to play an increasingly important part in what counts as a 'good meal', for example. Such cultural variability may be acknowledged and welcomed, without any threat to the idea that human nutritional needs are, within a broad range of approximation, delimitable in advance.

In the above discussion I have, of course, confined myself to offering some considerations which tell against a range of socialist (and other) arguments against the idea of a general, cross-culturally and trans-historically applicable concept of human need. A great deal of the discussion in this book, and especially in the last three chapters, can be read as a prolegomena to such a view of need appropriate to a naturalistic but non-reductionist account of human nature, and sufficiently rich to ground a socialist view of rights and justice. I have not, however, attempted in this work to formally present this view of human needs, or to argue for it from first principles. Suffice it to say here that my view of needs has much in common with and is influenced by that developed from different premises by Len Doyal and Ian Gough.[12]

It is conceded that scarcity will continue to affect all human societies, and that socialism, if it is attainable, will be no exception. It is also conceded that whatever moral case can be made for socialism, it cannot, any more, rest on the transcendence of scarcity, and so on surpassing those conditions which rendered vulnerable and competitive individuals subject to a morality of rights and justice. On the contrary, the abandonment of a horizon of unlimited growth poses the questions of needs and distributive justice with an accentuated centrality and urgency. However, a preliminary case, at least, has been made for the viability of a view of needs as grounding rights and norms of distributive justice that is richer in content than the liberal-individualist rights tradition and not obviously susceptible to the principal lines of objection to which that tradition is vulnerable. Considerations foregrounded by encounters both with ecological politics and the philosophy of animal rights are centrally at work in the production of these conclusions. But, equally, the socialist character of the moral reasoning required should be evident. More than this, it should also be clear that the realizability of a view of rights and justice grounded in environmental, social, developmental and bodily needs would presuppose something like the all-round human emancipation which Marx distinguished from more narrowly political emancipation: the bringing of all aspects of social life with a bearing on individual well-being, including our practices of interaction with external nature – under normative communal regulation. Whatever its current vicissitudes this has always been the central socialist aspiration.

Thus far, of course, I have spoken only of material aspects of human need, and of human need in abstraction from the needs of other animal species. There is, of course, a further swathe of consequences of 'post-bourgeois' ecological scarcity for the ways we are to regulate our relations with other species. In the vision offered by the animal liberationists there is a kind of parallel to the utopianism of the erstwhile socialist commonwealth of abundance: the possibility is envisaged of a human life lived without harm to our non-human animal kin. Earlier in this book I have offered arguments against the realizability of this vision. Humans cannot live without causing the deaths of other animals which they either use directly as food, or whose habitats they appropriate or modify for food production or other purposes. This is an ineradicable feature of the human predicament. It is also the predicament of other animal species, though, unlike us, they have limited powers to alter their mode of life, and no power to reflect morally upon the significance of their plight.

Socialist Morality and the Treatment of Animals

So, what considerations should govern the relations between humans and non-human animals in a post-capitalist future? Much of my answer to this question has been anticipated or rehearsed in earlier phases of my argument. It seems to me that animals already included in forms of human social life suffer abuses some of which may be addressed by the extension of the liberal-individualist view of rights beyond the species-boundary. In important respects, however, this is a problematic conceptual strategy and one of limited practical efficacy. Regan's version of the animal rights case (the version which I find most persuasive) does, I think, allow me to accept his view that non-human animals are proper objects of direct moral concern without being logically required thereby to accept either the notion of animal rights, nor yet that of equal rights. Three features of moral rights in the paradigm human case seem to me, as I have argued, to carry across the species boundary particularly badly, or not at all. These are: (1) reciprocity in mutual recognition of rights, (2) the links between (natural) rights and citizenship, and, most of all, (3) rights as autonomously made (or authorized) moral claims. These considerations seem to me to tell powerfully against Regan's preferred strategy of according (liberal-individualist) rights to non-human animals. This is compounded by a series of considerations which suggest that, at least under prevailing socio-economic patterns of animal use and abuse, the moral case for rights is liable to be practically relatively ineffective as a source of protection from actual harms.

The drift of my argument so far does, I think, yield the outlines of an alternative framework for moral thinking and practical action. Regan's case for the extension of human moral responsibility to non-human animals is accepted. So is his claim that this responsibility may properly derive from considerations of harms and benefits to animals themselves, independently of the significance or consequences of modes of treatment of animals for the humans involved. This is the position he describes (I think somewhat misleadingly) as the 'direct duty' view. The focus of my argument upon the necessity of health and bodily security and ecological and social embeddedness to well-being opens up to moral reflection the extent to which human social practices may sustain or undermine the conditions of life for non-human species. Where populations of non-human animals are cut off by human practices from the conditions under which they are able to autonomously meet their needs and so live the life of their species, the consequences are either extinction, local or global, or some form of human intervention deliberately to sustain suitable habitat by checking the offending social practice or imposing some kind of artificial, compensatory mode of need-meeting through incorporation within human social forms. Where dependency in either mode is a consequence of human activity, there is a place for a notion of acquired responsibilities on the part of humans for the animals affected. Regan's concern is almost exclusively with what he calls 'basic' or 'unacquired' rights and responsibilities.

As against many advocates of animal rights, my position also recognizes co-evolution and interdependency between humans and numerous other animal species such that the inclusion of animals within human social practices (as for example with commensalism – pet-keeping and the like) does not necessarily violate the conditions essential to their well-being, to their living a life appropriate to their species. The concern in such cases would be to ensure a proper moral regulation of those practices, rather than to seek their abolition. In other cases, such as intensive rearing of livestock, where a violation of the conditions of well-being of the animals involved is intrinsic to the practice, abolition of the practice is morally required. However, the perspective I have offered tends to show the extent to which any such acknowledgement of moral responsibility for animals would require quite deep-level transformations of human social and economic arrangements, structures of power and patterns of land occupancy and use. Such changes could not be achieved on the basis of a moral appeal on behalf of animals only, but would require broad alliances with human social groupings committed to such changes, often on other grounds.

This, in turn, suggests that arguments for and against specific changes in land use or management, proposals for 'development', should properly integrate the implications for non-human populations of habitat destruction as a consideration in its own right alongside considerations of economic benefit, employment, amenity and scientific interest. I am a long way from a clear view of how such considerations may be weighed, but that such considerations should be included, and as a matter of justice, seems to me a moral position with strong arguments behind it. One very obvious difficulty for the general view I am advocating here is the requirement, when 'cross-species' justice is at issue, to detach the concepts of justice and responsibility (as requirements upon moral agents) from the concept of correlative rights (fully applicable in my view only to moral agents). In deciding questions of land use, I suggest, human communities, or their representative institutions, have a responsibility to do justice to non-human inhabitants of the habitats which are liable to be altered by human action, but I do not claim that the individual animals liable to be affected can properly be said to have moral rights. They are, as moral patients, proper objects of moral concern, but not subjects of rights.

The socialist principle 'to each according to need' may, I have suggested, be properly read as a principle of distributive justice. In the case of communities of human moral agents, needs may be self-defined and so ground rights correlative to principles of justice and to communal responsibilities. One strength of the socialist principle of distributive justice is that there is no ontological obstacle to its extension beyond species boundaries. Though, I have argued, the case for attributing rights to non-human animals faces severe intellectual obstacles, their 'neediness' as natural beings is a feature shared with human animals. Moreover, a needs-based view of justice has the further advantage of extending the scope of cross-species moral concern beyond the narrow circle of species whose individuals satisfy Regan's subject-of-a-life criterion. Need understood in terms of conditions necessary for living well or flourishing is a concept applicable not only to all animal species, but to plant-life as well. As we saw, Regan's position entails a sharp boundary within the range of animal species, such that on one side individuals are held to have equal rights with humans, but on the other to have no moral status whatsoever. No matter how reflective our moral intuitions, this must remain a powerfully counter-intuitive position to maintain. The needs-based view of inter-species moral responsibility and justice I advocate here suffers from no comparable difficulty.

There are, of course, other difficulties, which I have all too little space to address in this text. One such difficulty is shared with the rights view. It is that an untranscendable asymmetry in human and animal constitutions makes 'paternalism' in the assessment of need and application of standards of justice across the species divide unavoidable. The only advantage which a needs-based view has over the rights view in this respect is that at least a refusal to speak of the rights of non-human animals explicitly acknowledges that this is the case: when the needs of non-human animals are taken into account, it is humans who are doing the 'taking into account' and also it is humans who assess the needs of those animals. A second source of difficulties is closely related to this. I have already (above, pp. 162–5) addressed the topic of epistemic obstacles to the assessment of well-being across species-boundaries, and combined with unavoidable human/animal asymmetries this looks to be a very serious problem indeed. If the needs of animals are undeterminable, then the status of the socialist principle as a principle of distributive justice across species-boundaries is called into question. Moreover, to introduce sociological considerations, the way is epistemically open for (human) interest-governed assessments of non-human animal needs to render practically nugatory any formal commitment to cross-species justice.

But the epistemic limits at work here do not constrain us so tightly as this suggests. First, for those animals sufficiently psychologically complex to provide grounds for the application of the concept 'preference autonomy', the correlative human moral responsibility would be, *prima facie*, to refrain from destroying those conditions under which these animals are able to autonomously meet their needs. There are no good reasons for believing that there is an epistemic limit to determining what those (habitat) conditions are in any particular case. Second, for the less psychologically complex animal species the extent to which a 'subjective' component enters into the appropriate notion of well-being is correspondingly less. For members of those species, research in behavioural ecology is a well-grounded (but, of course, fallible) source of independent checks against partial, 'anthropocentric' assessments of need.

Finally, these last considerations point in the direction of possible ways of addressing one of the most notorious sources of difficulty for any attempt to 'extend the circle' of moral concern beyond the boundaries of the human species. This is the question, already mentioned in passing, of 'weighting'. As we saw, Regan's strategy is to argue for a concept of rights and justice premissed on cross-species equality of inherent value, but to devise secondary rules which justify preferential treatment for humans under some sets of circumstances where it would be deeply counter-intuitive not to do so. The outcome of this strategy is, in the end, not far removed from the utilitarian one of a 'pre-distributive' equality between species capable of pleasure and pain which allows (contingently) for a post-distributive pattern of pleasures and pains in which animals may fare rather badly.

A needs-based strategy such as the one I advocate here faces directly comparable problems. Would cross-species justice involve giving equal weight to human and animal needs? First, we may note the presupposition in the question of absence of harmony of interests between humans and animals with respect to the satisfaction of need. Ecological considerations led us, above, to reject as utopian the notion that relative scarcity as a source of mutual antagonism among humans might be overcome. Similar considerations suggest that while specific sources of harm to non-human animals may be abolished or mitigated, there is no realizable future in which humans can live without harming or destroying their non-human kin. Ecological scarcity implies the non-transcendability of rights-and-justice necessitating features of human life. Where the relations between humans and animals come up for moral evaluation, scarcity implies the non-transcendability of justice-necessitating conditions, even though the discourse of rights is not fully applicable for other reasons.

So, short of a retraction of moral concern back within species-boundaries, these questions of the comparative weighting of human and animal needs and requirements cannot be avoided. A first approach to the problem involves recalling the distinction between justice as equality of treatment and as equivalence of treatment. Marx's tendency to confuse the two was one source of his scepticism about rights, as always the right to be unequal. But there is no need to follow Marx in this. Justice requires difference of treatment in the face of morally relevant differences. Implicit in much of the above argument has been a recognition that while humans and other animals as 'natural beings' have needs in common, there are great species-specific differences in their patterns of need and modes of satisfaction.

A comparison of humans and most species of non-human animal with respect to the concept of need exhibits human peculiarity in a number of respects. First, because of their learning abilities, their flexible powers of social co-operation, and their ability to modify their ecological conditions of life, humans are far more adaptable than other species. In this context, I mean by this claim that humans are able to survive in the face of an unusually wide range of diverse environments, including extremely bleak and inhospitable ones. On the other hand, human psychological complexity, the role of social, cultural and ecological relations and conditions in the formation of identities, and the place of internalized normative standards in the valuation of quality of life, make for a uniquely wide space in the human case between what we might call survival conditions and conditions of well-being, or flourishing. Put another way, the complexity and multi-dimensionality of need in the human case renders humans vulnerable to a range of sources and types of harm to which individuals of other species are ontologically insusceptible. To be prevented from practising her religion may reduce a human to utter misery, but can have no meaning as a harm for a horse or dog (Darwin not withstanding).

To advocate a needs-based view of justice is not necessarily to advocate a view of individuals of different species as identical in their needs. On the contrary, to treat non-human animals as though their needs were identical to those of humans would be both absurd and cruel. For many species of animals, especially categories taxonomically and phylogenetically widely separated from humans (conventionally, but ungroundedly referred to as 'lower animals') the distinction between conditions of survival and conditions of well-being, so central to the elaboration of any adequate concept of human need, is reduced to the point of disappearance. Once its basic nutritional and reproductive requirements have been met a grasshopper, a snail, or an earthworm has little in the way of further requirements for self-realization, or intellectual satisfaction. By contrast, a caged gibbon may suffer psychologically from lack of stimulation and boredom, yet suffer less than, say, an isolated chimpanzee from loss of opportunity to live a dense social life with its fellows. These forms of species-specific diversity in the structure of need, and in the extent to which conditions of well-being exceed conditions of mere survival, do seem to coalesce and overdetermine one another in the human case. Any conception of justice adequate to cross-species encounters would be required to be sensitive to such differences in the structure and scope of need, and would license appropriate differences of treatment.

The question now arises: does this licensing of differences of treatment amount to the abandonment of an egalitarian view of justice in favour of what Regan rejects as 'perfectionist' views? In view of the proposed ontological differences represented by the different taxa making up the animal 'kingdom', the distinction between a difference-respecting egalitarian principle of justice and a 'perfectionist' view (which grounds differences of entitlement in possession of different attributes, or 'excellences') becomes difficult, if not impossible, to sustain.

In the face of continuing human/animal conflicts of need, grounds can be provided on either view of justice for meeting the needs of humans where they necessarily arise at the expense of the needs of other animals. The thesis of human moral obligation to animals is required to offset any tendency to abuse the licensing of differential treatment: what may be justified as necessary to the meeting of need may not be justified for just any desire, however trivial or whimsical. This is, admittedly, a sketchy and merely preliminary gesture in the direction of a solution of some of these problems. Further development of the position in the face of critical responses will be required if we are to discover whether it is more rationally sustainable than its rivals.

Desires, Instincts and Emancipation

So far my discussion has operated under the supposition that the problem of scarcity could be dealt with solely as a relation between human needs (together with variable ways of socially ordering their satisfaction) and the external 'natural' environment and the conditions of life it supplies. But, for humans, actual ecological limits are set by the interrelation of such environmental conditions with socially organized modes of recognition/stimulation of desire, rather than need. For example, a widely used anti-capitalist argument with ecological premisses is that capitalist expansion is based on an ever-spiralling stimulation of desires for material consumption. Capitalism cannot do without this as a condition of capital accumulation, and yet our ecological 'life support' systems cannot in the long run sustain the material consumption it evokes.

We have seen, above, that socialism cannot, in the face of contemporary social ecology, any longer be advocated as the transcendence of material scarcity. However, the argument about capitalism as a motor of desires for material consumption suggests a related but different ecological argument for socialism: that the ever-growing disparity between material desires and the ecological conditions of their satisfaction, which today sustains outrageous global inequalities and threatens ecological catastrophe, can be mitigated under socialist social relations. The suggestion is that material aspirations outstrip ecological conditions either because the cultural system of late capitalism stimulates desires which otherwise would not arise, or because it excludes large sections of the population from non-material satisfactions which are consequently displaced as 'compensatory' material aspirations.

Either way, the assumption about human nature at work is one in which material aspirations, at least, are supposed to be highly susceptible to normative regulation and would, indeed, be so regulated by a legitimate socialist moral order. This question, again, takes me beyond the limitations of this text, but for now it is simply of interest to note the complementarity of this ecological argument for the normative regulation of desires with the Durkheimian critique of 'anomie' as a pathological condition of capitalist modernity.

But these are considerations which can apply only to human individuals and populations. One consequence of the naturalistic ontology of human/animal continuity which I have insisted upon throughout this text is to call into question the widely held sociological assumption of human psychological malleability. Here we are returned to my quotation from Freud. If the threat to human well-being posed by the forces of nature may not be overcome, but only mitigated in ways which are still residually rights-and-justice necessitating, what of Freud's other sources of suffering? I have already said a good deal about bodily frailty, but relatively little about Freud's third source of suffering: that arising from our relations with one another. Freud was, of course, committed to the view of mutual aggression as a primary drive, or motivation, affecting all relations between humans. Institutional forms such as private property, he conceded, may accentuate and socially focus such aggressive dispositions, but social reform could achieve only their displacement onto other objects, not their transcendence.

For Freud, Lukes's second condition for the transcendence of rights and justice, complete mutual benevolence, is unattainable for reasons having to do with the human psychic constitution. But Freud simultaneously runs an independent argument which coalesces in its conclusion with the argument from primary aggression, and complements its pessimistic cast. This is the argument for the necessity of the repression and 'mutilation' of infantile sexual impulses in the course of individual psycho-sexual development. Monogamous, heterosexual, genitally focused sexuality is not a 'natural' or 'spontaneous' outcome of developmental processes in Freud's view, but, on the contrary, is imposed on the individual by the social power vested in the patriarchal family. This, again, as Freud's phylogenetic narrative makes clear, is no sociological contingency: the authoritative confinement of the sexual instinct to exclusive non-incestuous heterosexual bonding is necessary to the sustainability of orderly social relations as such. The social is here recognized as a causal order which resists individual desires and purposes.

Though the social, for Freud, is to a degree successful in normatively moulding sexual behaviour, and even forming the normative view of the self and its appetites, the repressed and mutilated desires and drives of earlier phases of development continue to have their effects, often unacknowledged, on the conscious lives and affective relations of their bearers. Guilt at the persistence of unacceptable desires, displaced infantile fears and envies reappear as seemingly irrational hatreds and sources of aggression.

Here, then, if there is any truth in Freud's account of human individual nature, are some strong reasons for expecting any society, including any realizable socialist society, to be marked by competitive antagonisms which derive neither from material scarcity, nor from antagonism-accentuating institutions such as private property. Rights and justice would still be required to morally order such a society. The easy way out of Freud's challenge would be to fall back on a wholly social-constructionist view of human emotions and desires. The seriousness of the challenge posed by a position such as Freud's for the view I have been advocating is precisely that such a retreat would be inconsistent with any naturalistic view of the human. The human/animal comparison indispensable to the approach I have adopted predisposes us in favour of attributing to humans a complement of emotional and motivational capacities and dispositions which must be viewed as inherited and no less characteristic of the species than upright posture, speech and sociability.

Of course, there is quite a gap between a naturalistic predisposition in favour of accepting some such complement of inherited psychological capacities and dispositions, and preparedness to accept the specific account of human instincts offered in the later writings of Freud. There are, indeed, some fairly decisive objections to Freud. One good source of grounds for scepticism is in the Darwinian standpoint which Freud himself adopted. If natural selection is supposed to result in adaptation, or, especially in the human case, adaptability, and if humans arrived at their present instinctual complement as a result of natural selection, then why should their instinctual drives be so irreconcilably at odds with their need for social life, itself so evidently built into their evolved character as a species?

Freud's great strength, however, by comparison with other naturalistic traditions in thinking about human nature is his refusal to think of human instincts as fixed dispositions, expressed indifferently across diverse historical and cultural settings. There is a kind of argument, common among popularizers of animal ethology, which proceeds from the alleged universality of some basic behavioural dispositions – aggression, territoriality, male dominance, hierarchy – across a range of animal species to the 'naturalness' and hence unavoidability (without dire consequences) of certain institutions and practices in the human case.[13] These arguments are generally, but not always, politically conservative in character. In any case, they are generally vulnerable to several complementary lines of critical argument. First, the universality they proclaim can commonly be shown to be spurious or tendentious (or both). Animal species, even quite closely related species, exhibit striking species-specific differences in mode of life with respect to such proclaimed regularities as the social relations between the sexes, the distribution of care of offspring, the defence of territory, and so on. Proclaimed generalizations can often be shown to be a function of the imposition of ways of classifying animal behaviours which are ethologically ungrounded, and are 'loaded' in favour of the political moral which later gets drawn.

Second, popular ethology is generally unreflective in its subsumption of human practices and institutional forms under the behavioural taxonomies which are held to be applicable to non-human animals. The 'mapability' of animal territoriality onto the human institution of private property is a case in point. As a historically emergent and non-universal institution private property cannot be viewed as a direct expression of an inherited instinct or behavioural disposition. The strength of Freud's metapsychology – notwithstanding its demonstrable specific failings – is that it takes account of social life as a causal order which shapes and regulates the psychic life and expressions of the individual, and of culture as a medium through which individual humans give sense to the mutations and transformations of their own psychic lives. But Freud does this without abandoning his naturalistic commitment, without retreating into mind/body, nature/culture or animal/human dualisms. Central to Freud's approach is a distinction between, on the one hand, basic instincts or drives, which are few in number and more-or-less universal to human kind, and, on the other, various forms of psychically modified and culturally mediated expressions of those basic drives. This enables a broadly Freudian approach to account for inter-individual and cross-cultural differences in personality forms, developmental patterns, motivational and emotional dispositions, pathologies and so on while holding on to a definite general view of human individual nature.

Now, one notorious difficulty with this kind of explanatory strategy has to do with the epistemic problems of lack of experimental or observational access to alleged instincts or basic drives other than by way of analysis of their immensely diverse and fluid particular expressions. How do we know that there are any underlying psychological constants at all, and, even assuming there are, how do we decide between rival theories as to what they might be? How, connectedly, do we ground identifications of this or that particular character trait, act of aggression or pathological symptom as 'expressions' of this or that general underlying desire or instinct?

There are certainly no simple answers to such questions; indeed, convincing answers of any kind may be, in the nature of the case, unattainable. However, there are ways of rationally grounding such claims, and sources of pertinent evidence, even though neither are likely to be conclusive. Psychoanalytic methods of free-association and analysis of chains of signification are one such source. They can be complemented by palaeo-anthropological considerations: from what we know about the conditions and modes of social life of our hominid ancestors, what psychological equipment does it make sense to suppose they would have evolved? Freud's own phylogenetic speculations are a gesture in this direction but one, of course, by now hopelessly outdated. Another source against which both these sets of considerations might be tested is a critically employed comparative ethology, focusing upon the psychological similarities and differences of our closest primate kin. A fourth source of considerations bearing upon the possibility of human psychological constants is, of course, social anthropology. How far is it possible or plausible to identify a common repertoire of emotional possibilities and motivational dispositions underlying the admittedly very significant differences of social organization and cultural meaning which the anthropological literature reveals? I do not of course, wish to anticipate the outcome of such research. My purpose here is solely to present my reasons for thinking, first, that to attribute to humans some common pattern of basic motivations and a common emotional repertoire is not incompatible with the recognition of cultural diversity and historical change and, second, that attempts, such as Freud's, to advance a human instinct theory need not stay at the level of mere speculation.

There is a further source of evidence pertinent to such a theory, and it is one which takes us to the point of this excursus on human nature. This further source of evidence is the widely recognized category of socially-generated psychological illness and, more broadly, disabling distress. It is, of course, significant that the primary evidential support for psychoanalysis itself came from such sources. Independently of the success of his 'talking cure' and, indeed, of the particular explanatory narratives which Freud and his followers devised, these case-studies constitute a body of evidence bearing upon the limits of human psychological adaptability to the requirements imposed by occupancy of specific subject-positions in various patterns of social life. This is perhaps the strongest ground of all for thinking of the psychic life of the individual as a definite causal order, with its own intrinsic properties and mechanisms. With respect to each individual, social life offers a sequentially proffered structure of constraints and affordances through which he or she is physically and psychically formed. But with respect to each form of social life, the subject-positions it defines are successively occupied by human (and non-human animal) individuals with a definite endowment of capacities, dispositions, liabilities and requirements. If any specific pattern of social life imposes constraints on the forms of expression available to its members, it is also true that the requirement that society provide a context for the sustainable well-being of its members also sets constraints on the range of possible (sustainable) social forms.

The heuristic value of a general theory of human nature such as that provided by Freud is precisely that it allows us to explore the socially and culturally distributed patterns of psychological distress as so many symptoms of the differential pressures brought to bear by a social order on its subjects: pressures which may push individuals beyond the limits of their powers of psychological adaptation. This is, of course, a widely used and quite controversial form of critical social analysis. It presupposes a certain 'softening', or 'opening' of the hard, closed concept of instinct which Freud tended to adopt in his later writings.[14] The possibility that different positionings of individuals in relation to a social order, and that transformations of social orders might make important differences to the prospects of individuals for personal happiness, psychological integrity and social belonging has to be allowed for, as against Freud's unremitting later pessimism.

But if we do take such forms of critical social analysis seriously – and the naturalistic view of human nature I have advocated implies that we should – then there is one very politically important consequence: we should not suppose that any hypothetically desirable society we may care to invent will create the kind of person its moral order requires. It is true that the colossal state-bureaucratic regimes of Eastern Europe and the USSR which are currently disintegrating under the weight of their own unresolved contradictions could never be justly described as socialist societies. But this alone is not the sole reason why they manifestly did not create the hoped-for socialist man and woman, but, rather, produced frustrated would-be subjects of consumer capitalism, religious fundamentalists and ethnic bigots in heady mixture with libertarian idealists and heroic resistance to indefensible oppression. These phenomena are symptoms of the limits to the reach of social forms into the individual psychic space, even where totalitarian forms of cultural authority are rigorously imposed.

None of this should be taken as an argument against political struggles for fundamental institutional change, should the conditions for such change arise again. But it is an argument, if any further were needed, for the widest possible democratic participation in the shaping of institutions in line with the needs and aspirations of those who are to live within their constraints. It is also an argument for the continuing pertinence of an authoritative morality of rights and justice – albeit one enriched by socialist and ecological reflections and made realizable by an extension of communal regulation of a common social life. This is partly because we can have no good reason for thinking that the relations among humans, and between them and other species, may be fully pacified under any realizable human future, but also partly because the 'private space' will continue to stand in need of protection against the emergence or consolidation of any new oppressive public power.

Notes

1. Introduction

1. A term coined, so far as I am aware, to introduce a new environmental paradigm into sociology. See W.C. Catton and R.E. Dunlap, 'Environmental Sociology: A New Paradigm', *American Sociologist*, 13, 1978, pp. 41–9.

2. The most influential advocates of these positions have been, respectively, Peter Singer and Tom Regan. See P. Singer, *Animal Liberation*, London 1976; and T. Regan, *The Case for Animal Rights*, London 1988. See also, M. Midgley, *Animals and Why They Matter*, Harmondsworth 1983, esp. chs. 5 and 6.

3. The comment comes in a discussion of the American writer Aldo Leopold in Regan, pp. 361–2.

4. See, especially: C. Pateman, *The Sexual Contract*, Cambridge 1988; C. Gilligan, *In a Different Voice*, Cambridge, Mass. and London 1982; C.A. MacKinnon, *Toward a Feminist Theory of the State*, chs.8–13; A.J. Arnaud and E. Kingdom, eds., *Women's Rights and the Rights of Man*, Aberdeen 1990; E. Kingdom, What's *Wrong with Rights?*, Edinburgh 1991; C. Smart, *Feminism and the Power of Law*, London and New York 1989, esp. ch. 7; A. Phillips, '"So What's Wrong with the Individual?" Socialist and Feminist Debates on Equality' in P. Osborne, ed., *Socialism and the Limits of Liberalism*, London and New York 1991, pp. 139–60; and J. Hartwig, 'Should Women Think in Terms of Rights?', *Ethics*, 94, 1984.

5. S. Rose, 'Proud to be Speciesist', *New Statesman and Society*, 26 April 1991, p. 21; and J. Jenkins, 'Beast in Man', *New Statesman and Society*, 3 May 1991, p. 23.

6. S.R.L. Clark, *The Moral Status of Animals*, Oxford 1977, p. 108, quoted in J. Benson, 'Duty and the Beast', *Philosophy*, 53, 1978, p. 541.

7. This works, at any rate, for most vertebrate species. Even those which are markedly sexually dimorphic are readily recognizable 'in the field'. I am not, of course, postulating similarity of appearance as in any sense definitive of species membership.

8. P. Singer, 'All Animals are Equal', in T. Regan and P. Singer, eds., *Animal Rights and Human Obligations*, Englewood Cliffs 1976, p. 150.

9. L.P. Francis and R. Norman, 'Some Animals are More Equal than Others', *Philosophy*, 53, 1978, pp. 507–27, p. 527.

10. Ibid., p. 508.

11. Ibid., p. 520.

12. Ibid., p. 523.

13. It is one way of resolving the dispute between liberal rights and communitarian

traditions in political philosophy. See J. Bernstein, 'Right, Revolution and Community: Marx "On the Jewish Question"', in Osborne, pp. 91–119. I return to the question of the historical plausibility of this idea in chapter 2.

14. M. Midgley, *Beast and Man*, Brighton 1979, p. xiii. Midgley's work, and especially this book, have had a strong influence on the formation of the approach presented here.

15. The thesis of 'human/animal continuity' does not, therefore, endorse the thesis of a 'boundary breakdown' betwen humans and animals: 'By the late twentieth century in United States scientific culture, the boundary between human and animal is thoroughly breached. The last beach-heads of uniqueness have been polluted if not turned into amusement parks – language, tool use, social behaviour, mental events, nothing really convincingly settles the separation of human and animal. And many people no longer feel the need for such a separation; indeed many branches of feminist culture affirm the pleasure of connection of human and other living creatures' (Donna J. Haraway, *Simians, Cyborgs and Women: The Reinvention of Nature*, London 1991, pp. 151–2). This 'pleasure of connection' with other living creatures does not require us to deny human distinctness from other species, nor yet human uniqueness (so long as we recognize that each other species, too, is unique). An undefined sense of wholeness and unity of the world, what Barry Richards has called the 'Eupsychic Impulse' pervades much of the literature and culture of radical political ecology (see B. Richards, 'The Eupsychian Impulse', *Radical Philosophy,* 48, Spring 1988, esp. p. 9). Though I have not elaborated the philosophical underpinnings of my argument here, it should be clear that they are realist in orientation, with the focus on interaction between independently identifiable structures and practices.

16. This process is exceptionally well analysed in S. Horigan, *Nature and Culture in Western Discourses*, London and New York 1988, ch. 5. See E. Linden, *Apes, Men and Language,* Harmondsworth 1976; P.Q. Hirst and P. Woolley, *Social Relations and Human Attributes*, London and New York 1982, pt. I; and Midgley, *Beast and Man,* pt. 4.

17. K. Tester, *Animals and Society: The Humanity of Animal Rights,* London and New York 1991, pp. 150 ff.

18. H. Salt, *70 Years Among Savages*, London 1921.

2. Marx on Humans and Animals

1. This chapter incorporates, with some revisions, 'Humanism = Speciesism?', *Radical Philosophy*, 50, Autumn 1988, pp. 4–18, reprinted in S. Sayers and P. Osborne, eds., *Socialism, Feminism and Philosophy*, London and New York 1990, pp. 235–74. I would like to thank Jean Duncombe, Jean Grimshow, Roy Edgley, Joe McCarney, Lisa Hooper, Chris Arthur, and Oriel Sullivan for their helpful criticisms of earlier drafts and also Tim Hayward and Howard Feather for their especially detailed and challenging comments. Participants in the sociology seminar at Sussex University, the political philosophy seminar at the University of East Anglia, successive conferences on Realism and the Human Sciences, and students at the University of Essex made helpful comments on versions of this argument; many have been incorporated into this version. I am, finally, very grateful to Steve Horigan and Nick Bunnin for many stimulating discussions on this topic.

2. K. Marx and F. Engels, *Collected Works*, vol.3, London 1975, p. 276. See, for an important commentary upon and development of this idea, A. Collier, 'The

Inorganic Body and the Ambiguity of Freedom', *Radical Philosophy*, 57, Spring 1991, pp. 3–9.

3. G.A. Cohen, *Karl Marx's Theory of History: A Defence*, Oxford 1979. See especially pp. 201–7 and 322–25.

4. I say something more about Marx's 'mature' views on the relation between human emancipation and nature in 'Marxism and Natural Limits', *New Left Review*, 178, Nov/Dec. 1989, pp. 51–86, and in 'Ecology, Socialism and the Mastery of Nature: A Reply to Reiner Grundmann', *New Left Review*, 194, July/August 1992, pp. 55–74.

5. Marx and Engels, p. 275. The secondary literature on Marx's early work is, of course, immense. See, in particular, C.J. Arthur, *Dialectics of Labour*, Oxford 1986; S. Cornu, *The Origins of Marxian Thought*, Springfield, Illinois 1957; G. Markus, *Marxism and Anthropology*, Assen 1978; R. Norman and S. Sayers, *Hegel, Marx and Dialectic*, Brighton 1980; B. Ollman, *Alienation*, Cambridge 1971; and A. Wood, *Karl Marx*, London 1981. N. Geras, *Marx and Human Nature: Refutation of a Legend*, London 1983, is an important source on Marx's later view of human nature. Almost all commentaries mention in passing Marx's contrast between the human and the animal, but few give it sustained critical attention. J. Elster, *Making Sense of Marx*, Cambridge 1985; and G. Markus, *Marxism and Anthropology* are exceptions. In a very recent work, (*Society and Nature: Towards a Green Social Theory*, Hemel Hempstead 1992) Peter Dickens uses the philosophical framework of Marx's early *Manuscripts* as the basis for an environmental social theory in a way which has much in common with the approach advocated here.

6. Marx and Engels, p. 276.
7. Ibid., p. 273.
8. Ibid., pp. 301–2.
9. Ibid., p. 277.
10. Ibid., p. 276.
11. Ibid., p. 277.
12. Ibid., p. 305.
13. Ibid., p. 303.
14. Ibid., p. 297.
15. Ibid., p. 306.
16. Ibid., p. 305.
17. Ibid., p. 301.
18. Ibid.
19. Ibid., pp. 296–7.
20. Ibid., pp. 303–4.
21. Ibid., p. 276.
22. Ibid., p. 302.
23. Ibid., p. 274.
24. Ibid., p. 239.

25. A useful introduction to the debates surrounding biological determinism is A.L. Caplan, ed., *The Sociobiology Debate*, New York 1978. There are many effective critiques, among the most trenchant being the classic M. Sahlins, *The Use and Abuse of Biology*, London 1977; S. Rose, ed., *Against Biological Determinism*, London 1982; and S. Rose, L. Kamin and R.C. Lewontin, *Not In Our Genes*, Harmondsworth 1984. Feminist perspectives are given in J. Sayers, *Biological Politics: Feminist and Anti-Feminist Perspectives*, London 1981; and L. Birke, *Women, Feminism and Biology*, Brighton 1986.

26. Marx and Engels, vol.1, 1975, p. 453.

27. H.E. Gruber, *Darwin on Man*, London 1974, p. 290.

28. Marx, letter to Engels, 19 December 1860, in Marx and Engels, vol. 41, Moscow 1985, p. 232: 'Although developed in the crude English fashion, this is the book which, in the field of natural history, provides the basis for our views.'

29. Some of the most fascinating evidence of cultural transmission comes from the more than twenty-five years spent by Jane Goodall and her associates observing a wild chimpanzee colony at Gombe, in Tanzania (see J. Goodall, *In the Shadow of Man*, Glasgow 1974; and *The Chimpanzees of Gombe: Patterns of Behaviour*, Harvard 1986. Chimps are frequently observed using sticks as 'tools' to 'fish' termites from their mounds. They first strip off leaves to make the sticks suitable for the purpose, and juveniles learn the appropriate skills by observation and imitation of their seniors. See, however, S.J. Gould's interesting discussion of Goodall's interpretations (S.J. Gould, Review of J. Goodall (1986) and other texts in *New York Review of Books*, 25 June 1987, pp. 20–25).

30. Recent studies have even called into question the distinctiveness of the human capacity for language. Although earlier attempts to train captive chimpanzees and other primates to speak were not successful, R.A. and B.T. Gardner did manage to teach the chimp Washoe to use sign language to some degree. E. Linden's experiments with plastic symbols have also been adduced as evidence of an intellectual capacity for language in some primates. Of course, language can be defined so as to exclude these as genuine cases of language-learning and all such experiments have methodological weaknesses. Nevertheless, it is hard to read this literature without being convinced of a much greater continuity between humans and other primates with respect to their reasoning and symbolizing powers than has been widely assumed. See R.A. and B.T. Gardner, 'Early Signs of Language in Child and Chimpanzee', in *Science*, vol. 187, pp. 752–3, and E. Linden, *Apes, Men and Language*, Harmondsworth 1976. A good, balanced account of the debate is given in S. Walker, *Animal Thought*, London 1983, chs. 9 and 10.

31. See, for example, Midgley, *Beast and Man*, ch.2.

32. See note 29 above.

33. This is not, of course, to deny that there are connections between well-being and the fulfilment of potentials. Marx is, I think, right to argue that the opportunity to fulfil one's potential is, for humans, a need. It follows that the fulfilment of potential is a necessary constituent of well-being. But not all potentials can be actualized within the timespan of an individual human life, or within the context of any particular culture. Some potentials must simply remain unactualized. Moreover, as I have suggested above, the actualization of some human potentials would be undesirable. In other cases, the simultaneous realization of two contrasting potentials may be impossible or undesirable, even though there may be nothing problematic about either taken separately. These considerations show that the concepts of human potential and species-being are by themselves insufficient to establish a defensible view of well-being. A good society would encourage the actualization of some potentials and discourage others. Its institutional framework would include enabling conditions for the fulfilment of a diverse range of potentials amongst its citizens, but it would also set limits to this range and establish constraints on the actualization of undesirable potentials. Further ethical principles and reasoning are required to establish and defend the outlines of such a society. A theory of human nature is an essential part of the rational grounding of any view of human well-being, but it cannot be substituted for an adequate moral theory.

34. See references in note 25, above. Also, of course, these misuses pose specific issues for feminist analysis. See R.A. Sydie, *Natural Women, Cultured Men*, Milton Keynes 1987; A.M. Jaggar, *Feminist Politics and Human Nature*, Brighton 1983; C. MacCormack and M. Strathern, eds., *Nature, Culture and Gender*, Cambridge 1980, and V. Plumwood, 'Women, Humanity and Nature', in Sayers and Osborne, ch. 10.

35. I have commented elsewhere on Marx's, and, especially, Engels's later responses to Darwinism. See T. Benton, 'Natural Science and Cultural Struggles: Engels on Philosophy and the Natural Sciences', in J. Mepham and D.-H. Ruben, eds., *Issues in Marxist Philosophy*, vol. 2, Brighton 1979.

36. Marx and Engels, vol. 3, p. 302.

37. An important figure in the development of this understanding was the late T. McKeown (*The Role of Medicine*, Oxford 1984). See also the essays by L. Rogers and G. Bignami in S. Rose, ed., *Against Biological Determinism*; and L. Doyal (with I. Pennell), *Political Economy of Health*, London 1979.

38. Somewhat paradoxically, an important source for such views of need has been the work of H.A. Maslow (see Maslow, 'A Theory of Human Motivation', *Psychological Review*, London 1943, pp. 370–96; and *Motivation and Personality*, New York, Evanston and London, 2nd edn., 1970). Though he advocates a 'holistic' and antidualist view of human nature, Maslow's hierarchical classification of needs (physiological, safety, love, esteem and self-actualization) has been open to interpretations which, in effect, restore a dualism of 'lower' and 'higher' order needs. Important recent discussions of the concept of need with a direct bearing on my argument in this book are K. Soper, *On Human Needs*, Brighton 1981; and L. Doyal and I. Gough, *A Theory of Human Need*, Basingstoke 1991.

39. A very useful introduction to the literature on this is M. Redclift, *Development and the Environmental Crisis*, London 1984. See also D. Goodman and M. Redclift, *Refashioning Nature: Food, Ecology and Culture*, London and New York 1991.

40. Marx and Engels, vol.3, p. 336.

41. Ibid., p. 337.

42. See note 30, above.

43. Marx and Engels, vol.3, p. 304.

44. Ibid., p. 275.

45. Ibid., p. 276.

46. See C. Levi-Strauss, *The Raw and the Cooked*, London 1970; and M. Douglas, *Purity and Danger*, London and New York 1984.

47. See an earlier attempt: T. Benton, 'Biological Ideas and their Cultural Uses', in S.C. Brown, ed., *Objectivity and Cultural Divergence*, Cambridge 1984, pp. 111–33.

48. See papers in B.R. Wilson, ed., *Rationality*, Oxford 1970, especially S. Lukes, 'Some Problems about Rationality' (pp. 194–213), and M. Hollis 'The Limits of Irrationality' (pp. 214–220). See also M. Hollis and S. Lukes, ed., *Rationality and Relativism*, Oxford 1982, *passim*, but especially W. Newton-Smith, 'Relativism and the Possibility of Interpretation' (pp. 106–22); and R. Horton, 'Tradition and Modernity Revisited' (pp. 201–66); and Roger Trigg, *Understanding Social Science*, Oxford 1985, ch. 4.

49. This approach is exemplified in the work of M. Foucault. See especially M. Foucault, *Discipline and Punish*, Harmondsworth 1977; and *The History of Sexuality*, vol. 1, Harmondsworth 1981. A valuable critical response to Foucault is included in P. Dews, *Logics of Disintegration*, London and New York 1987, chs. 5–7 and conclusion.

NOTES TO PAGES 52–65

50. See, on limits to malleability, R. Lichtman, 'The Production of Human Nature by Means of Human Nature', and the subsequent discussion in *Capitalism, Nature, Socialism*, 4, June 1990. See also A. Collier, 'Scientific Socialism and the Question of Socialist Values', in J. Mepham and D.-H. Ruben, eds., *Issues in Marxist Philosophy*, vol. 4, Brighton 1981, esp. pp. 5–13.

51. See J.Z. Young, *An Introduction to the Study of Man*, Oxford 1971, esp. ch. 34, section 7, pp. 482 ff.

52. See references in note 25 above.

53. See R.A. Hinde, *Ethology*, Glasgow 1982, and *Individuals, Relationships and Culture*, Cambridge 1987; W.H. Thorpe, *Animal Nature and Human Nature*, London 1974. Also R.H. Hinde, 'A Biologist Looks at Anthropology', *Man*, 26, pp. 583–608.

54. A rather obvious aspect of our nature to include, one might think. Note, however, its absence from Winch's trilogy of birth, sex, and death, in P. Winch's 'Understanding a Primitive Society', in B. Wilson, ed., *Rationality*, pp. 78–111.

55. See, for example, N. Hartsock, *Money, Sex and Power*, Boston 1984 (also Hartsock's contribution to S. Harding and M. Hintikka, eds., *Discovering Reality: Feminist Perspectives on Epistemology, Metaphysics, Methodology and Philosophy of Science*, Dordrecht 1983).

56. D. Morris, *Human Zoo*, New York 1970.

57. S.J. Gould, *Ever Since Darwin*, Harmondsworth 1980, ch. 32.

3. The Social Life of Animals

1. Jim Mason, 'Brave New Farm', in P. Singer, ed., *In Defence of Animals*, Oxford and New York 1988, pp. 92–4.

2. My definition of domestication, here, is based on that given by J. Clutton-Brock in *A Natural History of Domesticated Mammals*, London and Cambridge 1987, though deliberately modified. Her original reads 'A domestic animal is one that has been bred in captivity for purposes of economic profit to a human community that maintains complete mastery over its breeding, organisation of territory and food supply' (p. 21).

3. Ibid., pp. 15–16.

4. Ibid., p. 15.

5. Ibid., pp. 110–11.

6. See N. Elias, *The History of Manners: The Civilizing Process*, vol.1, Oxford 1978, pp. 203 ff; R. Darnton, *The Great Cat Massacre and Other Episodes in French Cultural History*, Harmondsworth 1985; and the discussion of these in Tester, p. 674.

7. K. Thomas, *Man and the Natural World*, Harmondsworth 1983, pp. 109–10.

8. See, on this and related problems of human/animal comparison Haraway, esp. chs. 1 and 2.

9. Thomas, p. 110.

10. See references to Pliny on the use of 'lap-dogs' in first-century A.D. Rome (p. 44) and Francis Galton on pet-keeping among indigenous Americans (p. 15) cited in Clutton-Brock.

11. Tester, and the anthropological tradition he cites, focuses on this dimension of human/animal relations. Amazonian cultures are particularly rich in this respect. See G. Reichel-Dolmatoff, *Amazonian Cosmos: The Sexual and Religious Symbolism of the Tukano Indians*, Chicago and London 1971, esp. ch. 7. I am grateful to Richard

228

Wilson for this source.

12. Midgley, *Beast and Man*, ch. 2.

13. Mary Midgley, for example, subtitles *Beast and Man* the 'Roots of Human Nature'. I am, however, a long way from endorsing Keith Tester's systematic interpretive rule that all thinking about animals is covert thinking about humans. In Tester's view, for example, 'animal rights is not about animals, and as a fetish it is arguing that if we construct a selfhood which is divorced from animals, we will become better humans' (p. 177). See my review article on Tester's book, 'Animals and Us: Relations or Ciphers?', in *History of the Human Sciences*, vol. 5, no. 2, 1992. It is, I think, quite reasonable to suppose that the advocates of animal rights are quite genuinely concerned about animals but still to think that a lot can be learned about humans through reflection on and study of animals. Jane Goodall referred to chimpanzees as: 'those amazing creatures who can teach us so much about ourselves even whilst we become increasingly fascinated by them in their own right' (Goodall, *In The Shadow of Man*, p. 13). Interestingly, in his review of her later *The Chimpanzees of Gombe*, Stephen J. Gould takes Goodall to task precisely for not pursuing this thought sufficiently consistently. Noting her preoccupation with chimpanzee analogues of problematic human behaviours, he goes on to ask: 'What are we missing by parsing the behaviour of chimpanzees into the conventional categories recognised largely from our own behaviour? What other taxonomies might revolutionise our view – for taxonomies are theories of order? ... What does the prison of our language do to the possibilities of interpretation? What would a taxonomy based on things *not* done look like? How can we comprehend the soul of a creature whose watchword is flexibility with a language that parcels actions into discrete categories given definite names?' (Gould, p. 24). In her recent book *Humans and Other Animals*, London 1989, Barbara Noske also develops this theme.

14. Tester, p. 46.

15. See my review article, cited in note 13, above.

16. See T.J. Kalikow, 'Konrad Lorenz's Ethological Theory: Explanation and Ideology, 1938–1943', *Journal of the History of Biology*, 16, 1983, pp. 139–73.

17. See Clutton-Brock, ch. 6. As she points out (p. 192) this has very serious implications. If the current trend for less profitable domesticated breeds to die out is not stopped, some part of the genetic diversity of the original populations will be irreplaceably lost.

18. See, for example, G.M. Berardi and C.C. Geisler, eds., *The Social Consequences and Challenges of New Agricultural Technologies*, Colorado 1984. Howard Newby and Peter Utting focus their contribution on the concentration of capital in the UK agricultural, food processing and marketing sectors, and its effect on rural social structures. However, they comment in passing: 'Clearly, the growth of agribusiness raises important issues relating to social effects such as technology control, dietary change, economic sovereignty, public accountability, and the concentration of economic power in the production of a basic need, food' (p. 285). Quite a list!

19. See chapter 5, note 6.

20. Keith Thomas gives us a sophisticated and well-illustrated account of the role of animals in the shifting configurations of class in the early modern period in England (see, especially, *Man and the Natural World*, pp. 102–9, on breeds of dog in relation to class, and pp. 181–91 on the selectivity of campaigns against cruel sports). He argues that the urban middle classes were able simultaneously to assert their own moral superiority through the extension of moral concern to animals, and to regulate or

abolish those working-class sports which were liable to lead to breaches of order on grounds of their cruelty. Keith Tester links both aspects together in what he calls the 'Demand for Difference'. He shows how the early nineteenth-century agitation against cruelty to animals was linked with fear of revolution and the requirement to 'civilize' the lower orders: 'For Erskine and Pulteney, cruelty to animals made plebeians less squeamish about decapitating the monarch, whilst the urban workers should be living a life of labour; they could not be allowed to enjoy bull-baiting when they should be working to keep their families. ... Windham, a long-standing opponent of anti-cruelty legislation, said that "The bill, instead of being called A Bill for preventing cruelty to Animals, should be entitled, A Bill for harassing and oppressing certain classes among the lower orders of the people"' (Tester, p. 107).

21. This association of cruelty with pleasure may well go some way to explaining the prominence of the Protestant sects in the early modern shift of sensibilities towards animals. 'Clerics were often ahead of lay opinion and an essential role was played by Puritans, Dissenters, Quakers and Evangelicals' (Thomas, p. 180).

22. Ibid., p. 98.

23. Ibid., p. 119.

24. Ibid., pp. 188–90.

25. Ibid., pp. 302–3.

26. The following exposition of Regan's views is based mainly on his *The Case for Animal Rights*. An excellent brief statement of his position is given in his contribution (ch. 2) to P. Singer, ed., *In Defence of Animals*. I have also found his 'Introduction' to T. Regan and P. Singer, eds., *Animal Rights and Human Obligations*, Englewood Cliffs 1978, very illuminating. B.E. Rollin, *Against Rights and Human Morality*, Buffalo 1981, advocates a rights view not far removed from Regan's position.

27. Regan, p. 117.

28. Ibid., p. 81.

29. R.G. Frey, *Interests and Rights: The Case Against Animals*, Oxford 1980.

30. M.P.T. Leahy, *Against Liberation: Putting Animals in Perspective*, London 1991, see esp. ch. 2. Regan is not Leahy's only target. Other writers frequently chastized for their anthropomorphism are Konrad Lorenz, Charles Darwin, V. Hearne (*Adam's Task*, London 1987), M.S. Dawkins (*Animal Suffering*, London 1980), D.R. Griffin (*Animal Thinking*, Cambridge, Mass. 1984) and Midgley (*Animals and Why They Matter*).

31. Leahy, p. 133.

32. See, for example, ibid., pp. 52 ff.

33. The hero-worship of Wittgenstein is sometimes taken to extremes: 'Aquinas is right; and it is a credit to his genius to have put animals so neatly into a perspective consistent with Wittgenstein's analysis' (p. 154).

34. Ludwig Wittgenstein, *Philosophical Investigations*, Oxford 1963, p. 174, quoted in Leahy, p. 132.

35. Leahy, pp. 142–3.

36. See Midgley, *Animals and Why They Matter*, esp. ch. 12. A more sceptical position is provided by T. Nagel, 'What Is It Like to Be a Bat?' in *Mortal Questions*, Cambridge, Mass. 1979.

37. 'If however, as I have argued, the recognitional capacities of dumb creatures are parasitic upon the human paradigm, and to that extent attenuated, then to talk of concepts is to over-emphasise the similarities to human beings at the expense of the differences' (Leahy, p. 150).

38. See Gould and Noske, note 13 above.

39. L. Wittgenstein, *Zettel* (eds. G.E.M. Anscombe and G.H. Von Wright), Oxford 1967, paragraphs 518–20, p. 91, quoted in Leahy, p. 131.

40. Leahy, p. 194.

41. Ibid., p. 195.

42. See Regan, *The Case for Animal Rights*, esp. pp. 271 ff.; J. Feinberg, in D. Lyons, ed., *Rights*, Belmont 1979; and J. Feinberg, *Rights, Justice and the Bounds of Liberty*, Princeton 1980.

43. Leahy appears to accept some version of 'perfectionism', based on both his evolutionary 'scale' and also on differences in natural feelings of compassion and so on between less or more distantly related individuals. The latter does take him to the point of acknowledging racial difference as a basis for discriminatory treatment: see Leahy, p. 172.

44. Regan, *The Case for Rights*, pp. 243 ff.

45. There is, of course, an extensive empirical literature on this. See, for example, J. Gregory, *Sex, Race and the Law*, London 1988; A.E. Morris and S.M. Nolt, *Working Women and the Law*, London and New York 1991; and A. Coyle and J. Skinner, eds., *Women and Work*, Basingstoke 1988, esp. 'Introduction' by A. Coyle.

4. The Radical Case against Rights

1. S. Lukes, *Marxism and Morality*, Oxford 1985.

2. J. Rawls, *A Theory of Justice*, Oxford 1972. Interestingly, Brian Barry (in *Theories of Justice*, vol. 1, California 1989, pp. 203–8) uses the question of the moral status of animals as a way of showing how problematic Rawls's notion of the 'original position' is: either we have to imagine non-human animals as equal participants in drawing up the social contract, or they fall entirely outside the limits of justice.

3. M. Sandel, *Liberalism and the Limits of Justice*, Cambridge 1982.

4. Ibid., p. 150.

5. Ibid., p. 183.

6. D. Hume, *A Treatise on Human Nature*, ed. by C.A. Selby-Bigge, Oxford 1978, pp. 494–5, quoted in Sandel, p. 169.

7. A. MacIntyre, *After Virtue: A Study in Moral Theory*, London 1981, p. 65.

8. Ibid., p. 66.

9. Ibid., p. 69.

10. Ibid., p. 65.

11. Bernstein, pp. 91–119.

12. Ibid., p. 113.

13. K. Marx, 'On the Jewish Question', in Marx and Engels, vol. 3, p. 166.

14. Ibid., p. 155.

15. Ibid., p. 163.

16. Ibid., p. 164.

17. In his exemplary critical discussion of this text, Russell Keat argues against this reading. On his view it is the abstract character of civil rights which presupposes the mutually estranged relations of capitalist civil society, rather than liberal rights as such. The virtue of socialism is that it substantively realizes liberal rights, both preserving and transcending them. See R. Keat, 'Liberal Rights and Socialism', in K. Graham, ed., *Contemporary Political Philosophy*, Cambridge 1982, p. 79. Though my reading of Marx on this question differs from Keat's, I am largely in agreement with the

substantive position he advocates.

18. Marx and Engels, p. 166.

19. Ibid., p. 168.

20. This is not, of course, entirely unreasonable, in the light both of this historical experience and of the centrality accorded to property rights in the work of influential political philosophies. See R. Nozick, *Anarchy, State and Utopia*, New York 1974: 'Our main conclusions about the state are that a minimal state, limited to the narrow functions of protection against force, theft, fraud, enforcement of contracts, and so on, is justified; that any more extensive state will violate persons' rights not to be forced to do certain things, and is unjustified' (p. xi).

21. Marx and Engels, vol. 3, p. 162.

22. Ibid., pp. 163–4.

23. Keat, pp. 73–4.

24. P.Q. Hirst, 'Law, Socialism and Rights', in P. Carlen and M. Collison, eds., *Radical Issues in Criminology*, Oxford 1980, pp. 58–104.

25. E. Burke, *Reflections on the Revolution in France*, Harmondsworth 1969.

26. R. Scruton, *The Meaning of Conservatism*, Harmondsworth 1980: 'For the conservative the state is not a machine, but an organism – more, a person. Its laws are those of life and death, sickness and regeneration. It contains reason, will and friendship. Not all its citizens lie at an equal remove from it; some enjoy privileges that others may not have. For its substance is power and its form authority. There is no equal distribution of the first of these that does not dissipate the second' (p. 50).

27. See, for example, MacKinnon: 'Hierarchies among men are ordered on the basis of race and class, stratifying women as well. The state incorporates these facts of social power in and as law. Two things happen: law becomes legitimate, and social dominance becomes invisible. Liberal legalism is thus a medium for making male dominance both invisible and legitimate by adopting the male point of view in law at the same time as it enforces that view on society' (p. 237). Some feminist approaches go beyond this, in arguing that law, or 'legal discourse', is intrinsically masculine in its abstract, universalizing insensitivity to particularity and difference. More nuanced feminist critiques of legal rights are to be found in Kingdom, *What's Wrong with Rights?*, and C. Smart, *Feminism and the Power of Law*, London and New York 1989.

28. Article 17 of the *Declaration of the Rights of Man and Citizen* (1789) in W. Laquer and B. Rubin, eds., *The Human Rights Reader*, New York 1989 (and other collections).

29. See chapter 7.

30. Keat p. 72.

31. T. Campbell, *The Left and Rights: A Conceptual Analysis of the Idea of Socialist Rights*, London 1983, p. 33.

32. In Britain, the Taff Vale case of 1901 resulted in a House of Lords decision making unions liable for losses incurred by employers as a result of union action. The 1906 Trade Disputes Act reversed this, granting immunities to unions and their officials from legal liability for losses arising from trade disputes (a very useful summary of this process is to be found in J. Westergaard and H. Resler, *Class in a Capitalist Society*, Harmondsworth 1976, pp. 222 ff). Successive waves of anti-union legislation in the 1980s have, of course, largely restored the powers of employers in this, as in many other respects.

33. Rawls, p. 204.

34. Keat, p. 70.

35. Tom Campbell provides a useful classification of concepts of rights (based on W. Hohfeld's scheme): liberties (or 'privileges'), claim-rights, powers, and immunities. On this scheme, I have a 'liberty' to do x if there is no law prohibiting my doing so, and a 'claim-right' if and only if others have an obligation either to permit me to do x (what Campbell calls a 'negative' right) or to give assistance for me to do it (what Campbell calls a 'positive' right). Powers and immunities are legal capacities to affect the legal standing of oneself or others, or protections from such capacities. Hohfeld's liberty-rights ('privileges') and Campbell's 'negative' rights are both negative rights in my usage here. See Campbell, pp. 28 ff.

36. B. Simon, *Education and the Labour Movement: 1870–1920*, London 1974, p. 11.

37. B. Simon, *The Two Nations and the Educational Structure 1789–1870*, London 1974, p. 357. His quotations are from J. Kay-Shuttleworth, *Thoughts and Suggestions on Certain Social Problems*, 1873, p. 51.

38. See J.S. Mill, *The Subjection of Women*, New York 1986. The great evolutionist and social reformer A.R. Wallace went so far as to pin his hopes for the future of the species on the higher moral choices which would be made by fully emancipated women (Wallace, *Social Environment and Moral Progress*, London 1913, chs. 16 and 17).

39. T.H. Marshall, 'Citizenship and Social Class', in *Sociology at the Crossroads*, London 1963. The contradictory character of class and citizenship is more fully explored in T.H. Marshall, *The Right to Welfare and Other Essays*, London 1981. Sociological commentaries on Marshall include D. Lockwood, 'For T.H. Marshall', *Sociology*, 8, 1970, pp. 363–7; A.H. Halsey, 'T.H. Marshall: Past and Present, 1893-1981', *Sociology*, 18, 1984, pp. 1–8; and B.S. Turner, 'Outline of a Theory of Citizenship', *Sociology*, 24, 1990, pp. 189–217.

40. W. Laqueur and B. Rubin, eds., *The Human Rights Reader*, p. x.

41. Of course, it should not be supposed that the implementation of 'negative rights' is cost-free. Jeremy Waldron makes the point well: 'In liberal theory, governments are not thought to be instituted merely to *respect* people's rights ..., but for their better enforcement and protection. Someone's religious liberty is not fully secure unless the government makes a positive effort to protect him from interfering bigots of another persuasion. ... So it is not true to say that the traditional liberal rights require from governments nothing more than omissions whereas modern socio-economic rights involve costs. All rights – even rights to liberty – are costly to uphold' ('Nonsense Upon Stilts? – a Reply', in J. Waldron, ed., *Nonsense Upon Stilts*, London and New York 1987, p. 157).

42. For example, Adam Ferguson: 'It should seem, therefore, to be the happiness of man, to make his social dispositions the ruling spring of his occupations: to state himself as the member of a community, for whose general good his heart may glow with an ardent zeal, to the suppression of those personal cares which are the foundations of painful anxieties, fear, jealousy and envy' (*An Essay on the History of Civil Society*, Edinburgh (1767), 1966 ed., p.54). See also T. Benton, 'Adam Ferguson and the Enterprise Culture', in P. Hulme and L. Jordanova, eds., *The Enlightenment and Its Shadows*, London 1990.

43. See, for example, S. Andreski, ed., *The Essential Comte*, London 1974, ch. 1.

44. See M. Cranston, 'Human Rights, Real and Supposed', in D.D. Raphael, ed., *Political Theory and the Rights of Man*, London 1967, p. 50. In replying to this line of objection, J. Waldron makes use of Ronald Dworkin's distinction between 'concept'

and 'conception'. The forms of words used in the *Universal Declaration* and other such statements may specify some particular conception of a potentially universal concept. The right to holidays with pay, for example, is admittedly applicable only in a society with a certain range of employment relations, but 'the use of that form of words should not blind us to the possibility that nevertheless some universal human interest, one that transcends wages and the forty-hour week, may be involved' (Waldron, p. 180).

45. See M. Barrett, *Women's Oppression Today*, London and New York, 2nd edn., 1988, ch. 6; M. Barrett and M. McIntosh, *The Anti-social Family*, London 1982; and L. Davidoff, 'Beyond the Public and Private: Thoughts on Feminist History in the 1990s', in *Passato e Presente*, Autumn 1992.

46. Bernstein, for example, appears to come close to this view: 'Nonetheless one might object to what has been said here that it inverts the very point of our having rights; namely, to protect us from illegitimate interference by society. The problem with this objection is simply that it is very difficult to conceive of significant choices or of actions that would not either be deemed to be 'full participation in the life of society as a whole' or ruled out as seeking personal advantage against the good of the other members of the community' (p. 115).

47. Celia Wells, 'The Decline and Rise of English Murder: Corporate Crime and Individual Responsibility', *Criminal Law Review*, 1988, pp. 788–801, pp. 795–6. I would like to acknowledge the help of my colleague Sheldon Leader in guiding me to and through the literature on corporate liability.

48. S. Field and N. Jörg, 'Corporate Liability and Manslaughter: Should We Be Going Dutch?', in *Criminal Law Review*, 1991, pp. 156–171, p. 159. As advocates of this individualist view, they cite H.L.A. Hart, *Punishment and Responsibility*, Oxford 1968, p. 228, and A. Vincent, 'Can Groups be Persons?', *Review of Metaphysics*, 42, 1989, p. 678. See also F. Pearce, 'Corporate Crime: A Review Essay', *Critical Social Policy*, 19, 1987, pp. 116–25.

49. Field and Jörg, p. 158.

50. Ibid., pp. 169–70. See also D. Bergman, 'Whither Corporate Manslaughter?', *New Law Journal*, October 1991, p. 1381.

51. Field and Jörg, p. 159. Other attempts to devise constructions of corporate liability which are designed to address these problems, include: S. Box, *Power, Crime and Mystification*, London 1983; and B. Fisse and J. Braithwaite, 'Accountability and the Control of Corporate Crime', in M. Findley and R. Hogg, eds., *Understanding Crime and Criminal Justice*, Sydney 1988.

52. On these problems of regulation and enforcement see, for example: A. Saunders, 'Class Bias in Prosecutions', *Howard Journal*, 24, 1985, p. 176; N. Cunningham, 'Negotiated Non-compliance: A Case of Regulating Failure', *Law and Policy*, 9, 1987, p. 69; W.G. Carsons, 'White-collar Crime and Enforcement of Factory Legislation', *British Journal of Criminology*, 10, 1970, p. 383; L. Everest, *Behind the Poison Cloud: Union Carbide's Bhopal Massacre*, New York 1986.

53. Wells, p. 791.

54. R. Sennett and J. Cobb, *The Hidden Injuries of Class*, Cambridge 1977.

55. F. Pearce and S. Tombs, 'Bhopal, Union Carbide and the Hubris of the Capitalist Technocracy', *Social Justice*, vol. 16 no. 2, 1989, pp. 116–145, p. 133.

56. C. Perrow, *Normal Accidents*, New York 1984.

57. Pearce and Tombs, p. 131.

58. See World Health Organisation, *Targets for Health for All*, Copenhagen 1988. For the situation in the UK, see P. Townsend and N. Davidson, *Inequalities in Health:*

The Black Report, Harmondsworth 1982; and M. Whitehead, *The Health Divide: Inequalities in Health in the 1990s*, London 1987.

59. See Whitehead, p. 79.

60. O. O'Neill, *Faces of Hunger*, London 1986, p. 17.

61. See C.B. MacPherson's classic *The Political Theory of Possessive Individualism*, Oxford 1962. See also N. Abercrombie, S. Hill and B.S. Turner, *Sovereign Individuals of Capitalism*, London 1986.

62. See Lukes, *Marxism and Morality*, pp. 56-7.

63. Ibid., p. 34.

64. Ibid., p. 35.

5. Beyond the Sociological Critique

1. In a Leicestershire County Council debate on fox-hunting, a Labour motion was opposed by Liberal Democrat Mr David Bill, on the grounds that 'The Hunts had planted much of the wild animal habitat in the county. Abolishing hunting would be a move towards a prairie landscape' *(Horse and Hound,* 6 February 1992, p. 28). Significantly, the argument failed to call into question the economic system which restricts our options in the countryside to a choice between fox-hunting and a 'prairie' landscape!

2. On movements against vivisection, see: N.A. Rupke, ed., *Vivisection in Historical Perspective*, London and New York 1990; C. Lansbury, *The Old Brown Dog: Women, Workers and Vivisection in Edwardian England*, Wisconsin 1985; and R. Ryder, *Animal Revolution: Changing Attitudes Towards Speciesism*, Oxford 1989.

3. M.E. Cooper, *An Introduction to Animal Law*, London 1987. See also L. Birke, 'Better Homes for Laboratory Animals', *New Scientist*, 3 December 1988, pp. 5-4. In a recently defeated amendment to the Swiss Constitution, animal experimentation would have been forbidden except where an experiment could be shown to have 'decisive significance for the preservation of human or animal life or the relief of considerable suffering' (I. Rodger, 'Swiss Vote Yes to Animal Testing', *Financial Times*, 18 December 1992).

4. S. Rose, 'Proud to be Speciesist', p. 21.

5. Rob Stepney, 'Body before Conscience', *Guardian*, 11 October 1991, p. 34.

6. See, for example, the survey given by R.D. Ryder in 'Speciesism in the Laboratory', in P. Singer, ed., *In Defence of Animals*, pp. 77-88. See also D. Sperlinger, ed., *Animals in Research*, Chichester 1981; B. Rollin, *The Unheeded Cry: Animal Consciousness, Animal Pain, and Science*, Oxford 1989; and M.A. Fox, *The Case for Animal Experimentation*, Berkeley 1986. On the specific point at issue, the way in which the social-relational context in which regulation is supposed to operate may obstruct the realization of the purpose of legislation, see J. Hampson, 'The Secret World of Animal Experiments', *New Scientist*, 11 April 1992, pp. 24-7.

7. Lynda Birke, 'Science, Feminism and Animal Natures, II', in *Women's Studies International Forum*, vol. 14 (5) 1991, pp. 456-7. See also L. Birke, 'They're Worse than Animals', in L. Birke and T. Silvertown, eds., *More than the Parts: Biology and Politics*, London 1984; Z.T. Halpin, 'Scientific Objectivity and the Concept of the "Other"', in *Women's Studies International Forum*, vol. 12, 1989, pp. 284-94; and N. Tuana, ed., *Feminism and Science*, Bloomington 1989.

8. For further explanation of this concept, see T. Benton, 'Marxism and Natural Limits', *New Left Review*, 178, Nov/Dec. 1989, esp. pp. 63 ff. See also 'The

Malthusian Challenge: Ecology, Natural Limits and Human Emancipation', in Osborne, pp. 241–70; and 'Ecology, Socialism and the Mastery of Nature: A Reply to Reiner Grundmann', *New Left Review*, 194, July/August 1992, pp. 55–74.

9. K.M. Walsh, *The Survival of Hill Farming in the Lake District National Park*, unpublished Ph.D. Thesis, University of Essex, 1991, esp. ch. 7.

10. See M. Redclift, *Sustainable Development: Exploring the Contradictions*, London 1987; D.E. Goodman, B. Sorj, and J. Wilkinson, *From Farming to Biotechnology: A Theory of Agro-Industrial Development*, Oxford 1987: and D. Goodman and M. Redclift, *Refashioning Nature: Food, Ecology and Culture*, London and New York 1991.

11. M. Aglietta, *A Theory of Capitalist Regulation*, London 1979.

12. Goodman and Redclift, pp. 87–8.

13. Ibid., p. 88.

14. Ibid., pp. 100–101.

15. See H. Newby and P. Utting, 'Agribusiness in the United Kingdom: Social and Political Implications', in G.M. Berardi and C.C. Geisler, eds., *The Social Consequences and Challenges of New Agricultural Technologies*, Bowlder and London 1984, pp. 265–89.

16. Goodman and Redclift, p. 92.

17. The general tendency amongst writers on the new intensive agricultural regimes is either to focus on the socio-economic relations among human actors (e.g. Newby and Utting) or to write about the treatment of animals in abstraction from the human socio-economic structure (e.g. J. Mason, 'Brave New Farm?', in Singer, *In Defence of Animals*). The point I am making here is that these should be analysed as interrelated aspects of a single process.

18. It should be clear that I am not here attempting to provide a history, or periodization, of these processes of change, but, rather, some broad analytical-theoretical differentiations which would, I hope, illuminate any such historical enquiry. In fact, the historical processes of emergence and consolidation of the 'factory' farm have, as would be expected on the Goodman/Redclift analysis, been uneven and discontinuous, with respect to both different aspects of the labour process and different sectors of livestock production. Their concept of 'appropriation' characterizes this very well. Economic, social-relational and political conditions combine together with specific biological constraints (which vary from species to species) and biotechnological 'solutions' to enable reorganizations to occur in some areas but not in others. Jim Mason's account of the development of intensive production, first in egg and chicken-meat production, and then with pigs, veal-calves and other species reflects this unevenness, though it is relatively under-theorized with respect to the economic and political aspects of the historical shift he describes (see Mason).

19. I have attempted to develop ways of conceptualizing human social activity in relation to nature which differentiate them according to the different ways in which human intentionality articulates with external conditions, contexts and media, and with the causal mechanisms activated thereby. I have criticized accounts which give a central place to 'productive-transformative' intentional structures as against those involved in primary-appropriation, eco-regulation and much domestic labour (see Benton, 'Marxism and Natural Limits').

20. The implications of the new biotechnologies are, of course, currently a major topic of public concern, and critical research which spans the biology/social science

divide is urgently needed. See Goodman and Redclift, chs. 5 and 6; and P. Wheale and R. McNally, *Genetic Engineering: Catastrophe or Utopia?*, Hemel Hempstead and New York 1988.

21. Mason, p. 90.

22. J. Erlichman, 'The Meat Factory', *Guardian*, 5 October 1991, p. 4.

23. This is made explicit in some of Regan's work, for example, in his contribution to Singer, ed.: 'People must change their beliefs before they change their habits. Enough people, especially those elected to public office, must believe in change – must want it – before we have laws that protect the rights of animals' (p. 14).

24. Quite independently of this general argument, it is also clear that the modern 'agri-food system' implicates virtually all food production in animal abuse, in ways which make the option of vegetarianism increasingly difficult to sustain. See, for example, J. Erlichman, 'Vegetarians Face Dairy Dilemma', *Guardian*, 18 October 1991, p. 5.

25. H. Newby, *Green and Pleasant Land?: Social Change in Rural England*, 2nd. edn., Hounslow 1985, pp. 113–4.

26. M. Tracy, *Governments and Agriculture in Western Europe: 1880–1988*, 3rd edn., Hemel Hempstead 1989, pp. 360–1. Of course, it needs to be recognized that not all farmers would see restrictive legislation, so long as it was generally enforced, as against their interests. Reporting on a statement by five eminent veterinarians in the *Veterinary Record*, James Erlichman wrote: 'They warned that the public mood about animal welfare was changing, and that vets would do themselves no good if they defended factory farming. ... They did not, however, blame farmers, or at least those who hate what they must do. "Many farmers now acknowledge that they were compelled to develop systems of extreme confinement in response to the need to produce food as cheaply as possible in the absence of effective legislation to protect the welfare of the animals", they said. "Such farmers are now leading the call for legislation that will protect not only the animals but also their own pride in stockmanship"' ('Cruel Cost of Cheap Pork and Poultry', *Guardian*, 14 October 1991, p. 4).

27. These distinctions can be reformulated as types of responsibility, or duty, sidestepping the issue of rights in the case of non-human animals.

6. The Limits of Liberal Rights I

1. See A. Assiter, *Althusser and Feminism*, London and Winchester 1990, ch. 3.

2. Carol Smart, *Feminism and the Rule of Law*, London and New York 1990, p. 147.

3. For example, Kingdom, *What's Wrong with Rights?*, esp. p. 84. See also MacKinnon, esp. chs. 7–10; Haraway, esp. chs. 1–3; M.G. Fried, ed., *From Abortion to Reproductive Freedom*, Boston 1990; and C. Gilligan, *In a Different Voice*, Cambridge, Mass. 1982, esp. ch. 5.

4. Clutton-Brock, pp. 36–41.

5. Ibid., pp. 55–6.

6. This tells against a tendency, common within 'green' political circles, to idealize non- or pre-industrial societies as ecological utopias. Tim Ingold's argument develops the point well ('In Search of the Noble Savage', *Horizon*, BBC 2, 27 January 1992).

7. See J. Habermas, *Legitimation Crisis*, London 1976, esp. pp. 4 and 14–16.

8. See W.H. Matthews, 'The Concept of Outer Limits', in W.H. Matthews, ed.,

Outer Limits and Human Needs, Uppsala 1976; and Benton, 'Marxism and Natural Limits', pp. 51–86.

9. I do not, of course, intend to leave the impression that such peoples are merely helpless or passive victims of such processes. On the contrary, as I shall argue shortly, we have many examples of environmental threats of this kind providing occasions for innovative and often successful forms of political mobilization and resistance. See R. Moody, ed., *The Indigenous Voice: Visions and Realities*, London and Copenhagen 1988.

10. See, for example, C. Merchant, *The Death of Nature: Women, Ecology, and the Scientific Revolution*, London 1982.

11. See, on this, ch. 4 of Doyal and Gough. The approach to the concept of human need developed by Len Doyal and Ian Gough, first in their 'A Theory of Human Need', *Critical Social Policy*, 4, 1, no. 10, 1984, then in 'Human Need and Strategies for Social Change', in P. Ekins, ed., *The Living Economy*, London and New York 1986, and subsequently in *A Theory of Human Need* is of very great importance. Though their method of arguing differs in several respects from my own, their conclusions are very similar, and I am greatly indebted to their work.

12. Durkheim, of course, had an exclusively social, and not environmental aetiology, though his arguments, especially in book 1 of *Suicide*, are most questionable. In effect, he moves from a statistical demonstration of the non-sufficiency of (some) environmental factors to a conclusion as to their non-necessity. E. Durkheim, *Suicide*, London 1952.

13. See Scruton: 'And once it is clear that a major and perhaps central part of those concepts and perceptions is inherited, then custom, tradition and common culture become ruling conceptions in politics. If these provide the common man with a sense of the value of his acts, then his self-identity and his allegiance to public forms are ultimately one and the same' (p. 38).

14. See, for example, S. Jain, 'Standing up for Trees: Women's Role in the Chipko Movement', in S. Sontheimer, ed., *Women and the Environment: A Reader*, London 1991.

15. 'The Last Blockade', *World in Action*, ITV, 12 January 1992. See also M. Colchester, *Pirates, Squatters and Poachers: The Political Ecology of Dispossession of Native Peoples of Sarawak*, London and Selangor 1988.

16. See S. Hecht and A. Cockburn, *The Fate of the Forest: Developers, Destroyers and Defenders of the Amazon*, New York 1990; and Chico Mendes, *The Fight for the Forest: Chico Mendes in His Own Words*, London 1989. See also the review essay 'Amazon Thoughts' by M. Goldman, in *Capitalism, Nature, Socialism*, vol. 3 (1), March 1992, pp. 125–132.

17. See, for example, A.H. Maslow, *Motivation and Personality*, New York, Evanston and London, 2nd edn., 1970, esp. ch. 4.

18. See Tester and also the review by T. Benton in *History of The Human Sciences*, vol. 5, no. 2, 1992.

19. This is not, of course, to suggest that these issues do not deserve fuller treatment in their own right. Much important philosophical work is now being done on the relations between needs, rights and citizenship. See, for example, R. Plant, H. Lesser and P. Taylor-Gooby, *Political Philosophy and Social Welfare*, London, Boston and Henley 1980. The work of Peter Townsend and his co-workers has also been of immense value in defining need in relation to the conditions of full social participation: 'The possession by individuals and families of relatively low resources does not automatically mean they are in poverty, but only if they are thereby unable to have the types of diets, participate in the activities and have the living conditions and amenities which are customary in that

society' (P. Townsend, ed., *The Concept of Poverty*, London 1970, p. 42).
20. See Benton, 'Marxism and Natural Limits', pp. 56 ff.

7. The Limits of Liberal Rights II

1. See Regan, ch. 8, and also p. 413, and Feinberg.
2. Lukes, esp. pp. 61–70.
3. From 'Civilization and its Discontents', in S. Freud, *Civilization, Society and Religion*, Harmondsworth 1985, p. 264.
4. A major recent philosophical inquiry into the questions at issue here is K. Lee, *Social Philosophy and Ecological Scarcity*, London 1989. Lee takes the principle 'to each according to need' as defining a socialist approach to distributive justice, and also shares with my approach the advocacy of a close relation between needs and rights. Tim Hayward ('Ecosocialism – Utopian and Scientific', *Radical Philosophy*, 56, Autumn 1990, pp. 2–14) offers a detailed but sympathetic critique of Lee's approach to the concepts of rights and justice which is broadly endorsed in my argument here. See also the very valuable discussion of related themes in R. Norman, 'Socialism, Feminism and Equality', in Osborne.
5. For example, R. Bahro, *Socialism and Survival*, London 1982.
6. See F. Sandbach, 'The Rise and Fall of the Limits to Growth Debate', *Social Studies of Science*, vol. 8, 1978, pp. 495–520; F. Sandbach, *Environment, Ideology and Policy*, Oxford 1980; and H.S.D. Cole et al., *Thinking about the Future: A Critique of the Limits to Growth*, London 1973. J. Simon, *The Ultimate Resource*, Oxford 1981, presents an extreme 'technological optimist' alternative to the 'limits' perspective.
7. The question of whether coping with ecological scarcity requires a 'new asceticism' is an important, but very complex one. See, especially, M. Ryle, *Ecology and Socialism*, London 1988, ch. 4; K. Soper, *Troubled Pleasures*, London and New York 1990, pt. 1 'Towards a New Hedonism'; and K. Soper, 'Greening Prometheus', in Osborne.
8. Lukes, p. 57.
9. See chs. 1–3 of Doyal and Gough.
10. J. Seabrook, 'Needs and Commodities', in Ekins, pp. 56–69.
11. Marx and Engels, vol. 3, p. 300.
12. See note 11 to ch. 6 for references.
13. A particularly sensitive attempt to link ethology with the human social sciences that avoids the criticisms listed here is R.A. Hinde, *Individuals, Relationships and Culture*, Cambridge 1987.
14. In pioneering a naturalistic approach to thinking about human nature which has much in common with that attempted here, Mary Midgley makes just this distinction: 'Closed instincts are behaviour patterns fixed genetically in every detail, like the bee's honey dance, some birdsong, and the nest-building pattern of weaver birds. ... Open instincts on the other hand are programmes with a gap. Parts of the behaviour pattern are innately determined, but others are left to be filled in by experience' (Midgely, *Beast and Man*, pp. 52–3). On the broader questions posed in this part of the present chapter concerning the bearing of psychoanalysis on social thought, see I. Craib, *Psychoanalysis and Social Theory: The Limits of Sociology*, Hemel Hempstead 1989. A very useful 'map' of the immense and diverse literature on the specific topic of human aggression is Gerda Siann, *Accounting for Aggression*, London 1985.

Index

Name Index

Main entries are in italics

Abercrombie, N. 235
Aglietta, Michel 154, 236
Althusser, Louis 137
Aquinas, Thomas 230
Aristotle 85
Arnaud, A. 223
Arthur, C. J. 225
Andreski, S. 233
Anscombe, G.E.M. 231
Assiter, A. 237

Bahro, Rudolf 202–3, 239
Barrett, Michèle 234
Barry, Brian 231
Benson, J. 223
Bentham, Jeremy 83, 112
Benton, T. 227, 235, 236, 238, 239
Berardi, G.M. 229, 236
Bergman, D. 234
Bernstein, Jay 105–6, 224, 231, 234
Bignami, G. 227
Birke, Lynda 151–2, 225, 236
Box, S. 234
Braithwaite, J. 234
Brown, S.C. 227
Burke, Edmund 112, 232

Caplan, A.L. 225
Campbell, Tom 115, 232, 233
Carlen, P. 232
Carson, Rachel 198
Carsons, W.G. 234

Catton, W.C. 223
Clutton-Brock, J. 61, 173, 228, 229, 237
Cockburn, Alexander 238
Cohen, G.A. 24, 225
Colchester, M. 238
Cole, H.S.D. 239
Collier, Andrew 224, 228
Collison, M. 232
Cooper, M.E. 235
Cornu, S. 225
Coyle, A. 231
Craib, Ian 239
Cranston, M. 233
Cunningham, N. 234

Darnton, Robert 228
Darwin, Charles 34, 35, 43, 45, 214, 217, 227, 230
Davidoff, Leonore 234
Davidson, N. 234
Dawkins, M.S. 230
Descartes, René 33, 34
Dews, Peter 227
Dickens, Peter 225
Doyal, Len 209, 227
Doyal, Leslie 227, 238
Dunlap, R.E. 223
Durkheim, Emile 182, 216, 238
Dworkin, Ronald 233

Ekins, P. 238

Subject Index

LaVergne, TN USA
31 July 2010
191600LV00001B/11/A